D1035336

Mythical Inspirations for Organizational Realities

Other titles in the trilogy

ORGANIZATIONAL OLYMPIANS: Heroes and Heroines of Organizational Myths

ORGANIZATIONAL EPICS AND SAGAS: Tales of Organizations

Also by Monika Kostera

CRITICAL MANAGEMENT RESEARCH IN EASTERN EUROPE: Managing the Transition (*edited with Mihaela Kelemen*)

Mythical Inspirations for Organizational Realities

Edited by

Monika Kostera

palgrave
macmillan

First published 2008 by
PALGRAVE MACMILLAN
Houndmills, Basingstoke, Hampshire RG21 6XS and
175 Fifth Avenue, New York, N.Y. 10010
Companies and representatives throughout the world

PALGRAVE MACMILLAN is the global academic imprint of the
Palgrave Macmillan division of St. Martin's Press, LLC and
of Palgrave Macmillan Ltd. Macmillan® is a registered trademark
in the United States, United Kingdom and other countries. Palgrave
is a registered trademark in the European Union and other countries.

ISBN-13: 978–0–230–51573–4
ISBN-10: 0–230–51573–8

This book is printed on paper suitable for recycling and made
from fully managed and sustained forest sources. Logging, pulping
and manufacturing processes are expected to conform to the
environmental regulations of the country of origin.

A catalogue record for this book is available from the British Library.

A catalog record for this book is available from the Library of Congress.

10   9   8   7   6   5   4   3   2   1
17   16   15   14   13   12   11   10   09   08

Printed and bound in Great Britain by
CPI Antony Rowe, Chippenham and Eastbourne

Contents

List of Tables

List of Figures

Acknowledgements

I am very fortunate to be surrounded by friends and colleagues who have in many ways contributed to the appearance of this book. Our many conversations provided me with ideas and counter-ideas, as well as awoke my curiosity to the point where I felt I wanted to collect texts on the topic of myths and archetypes and decided to send out a call for contributions. While, for lack of space, many of them will remain unnamed, I wish to direct special thanks to the few to whom I owe special gratitude.

First and foremost, I wish to thank all the authors who responded to my call for contributions and wrote the chapters that make up this book. It was a real joy to work with you all.

I would also like to thank the friends and colleagues whose texts and conversations with me have provided me with inspiration and ideas in my thinking and writing about myths and archetypes. They are many, but let me use this opportunity to express my profound gratitude to Zygmunt Bauman, Martin Bowles, Tobiasz Cwynar, Yiannis Gabriel, Mary Jo Hatch, Heather Höpfl, Henrietta Nilson, Stanisław Obirek, Przemek Piątkowski, Patrik Persson, and Diane and Tony Watson.

Kasia Korzeniecka, Joakim Larnö, Szymon Rogiński and Peter Tillström created artwork that inspired me and that I use a lot in my writings and as illustrations to my lectures and talks about organizational myths and archetypes. Some of the work is included in the current text. Thank you very much!

Jan-Erik Malte Andersson, Klara Nilson and Patrik Persson composed music, touching the topics of the current volumes, that I listened to during the writing and that gave me much joy. I regret that music cannot be attached to the final publication – it would indeed add a lot to the message. Nonetheless, it reverberates throughout the composition of these volumes, as it does in my mind when I think of mythologies.

I would also like to thank Keith Povey and his colleagues for their excellent work in the editing process, as well as Virginia Thorp and Emily Bown at Palgrave Macmillan for their kind help and support.

My deepest thanks go to my husband Jerzy Kociatkiewicz for all the greatly inspiring talks, for the help with the language editing, and for being there.

MONIKA KOSTERA

Notes on the Contributors

Frederic Bill is a Researcher and Senior Lecturer at the School of Management and Economics, Växjö University, Sweden. His research deals with entrepreneurship and business development and he has a PhD in Business Administration.

David M. Boje is Endowed Bank of America Professor in Business Administration in the Management Department at New Mexico State University, USA. His main research is the interplay of story, strategy and complexifying. He has published articles in *Administrative Science Quarterly, Management Science, Management Communication Quarterly, Organization Studies, Leadership Quarterly,* and other journals. He is President of *Standing Conference for Management & Organization Inquiry,* editor of *Tamara Journal* and associated editor for *Qualitative Research in Organization & Management* (QROM). He serves on 13 other editorial boards.

Peter Case is Professor of Organization Studies, Bristol Business School, University of the West of England, UK. He serves as chairperson of the *Standing Conference on Organizational Symbolism* and is a member of the editorial boards of *Leadership, Culture and Organization,* and the *Leadership and Organizational Development Journal.* He has held visiting scholarships at Helsinki School of Economics and the Royal Institute of Technology of Stockholm. Peter is interested in the social and organizational impact of information and communication technologies. Recent publications include *The Speed of Organization* and *John Adair: The Fundamentals of Leadership.*

Magnus Forslund is Assistant Professor at School of Management and Economics, Växjö University, Sweden. Areas of particular interest include entrepreneurship, sports management and organizational change.

Lena Fritzén is Associate Professor in Pedagogy at Växjö University, Sweden. Her main interest is democratic processes in pedagogical practice. She problematizes – from a democratic perspective – learning, teaching and management conditions in various complex organizations such as the school- and health-care systems.

Notes on the Contributors   xiii

Heather Höpfl is Professor of Management at the University of Essex, UK. She has been interested in stories since she was a small child. Her grandfather was a great teller of tales and spinner of yarns. Her early childhood was punctuated by his return from exotic voyages with strange souvenirs and even stranger sagas. She has published on rhetoric, poetics and narratives and is fascinated by myths and legends. She is currently undertaking research with Southwest Airlines and will shortly bring back travellers' tales from her trip.

Anders Hytter has a PhD in Business Administration, and is a Researcher and Senior Lecturer at the School of Management and Economics, Växjö University, Sweden. His research is within the field of leadership and organization. Areas of particular interest are leadership and effectiveness; leadership and gender; cross-cultural management; leadership, work environment and health; human resource management.

Krzysztof Klincewicz is Lecturer at the School of Management, University of Warsaw, Poland. He is chartered marketer of the Chartered Institute of Marketing, experienced in business development in the IT industry. Dr Klincewicz has authored many academic articles and three books: *Knowledge Management: Development, Diffusion and Rejection*; *Strategic Alliances in the High-Tech Industry*; and *Management Fashions: Turning Bestselling Ideas into Objects and Institutions*.

Monika Kostera is Professor in Management at Växjö University, Sweden, and Warsaw University, Poland. She has published several books in Polish and in English, most recently *The Quest for the Self-Actualizing Organization*, and articles in *Organization, Organization Studies, Scandinavian Journal of Management* and other journals. Her current research interests include organizational archetypes, organizational ethnography, and narrative methods.

Pierre Guillet de Monthoux holds a Chair of General Management at Stockholm University, Sweden. His interests hover around the art-culture–management nexus on which he has published articles and books like *The Art Firm* 2004 and *Aesthetic Leadership*, coedited with C. Gustalsson and S. E. Sjöstrand 2007. He currently runs a nomadic European university arranging travelling workshops (see *www.nurope.eu*).

Anna Linda Musacchio Adorisio is currently visiting at New Mexico State University, USA, working on a research fellowship awarded by the

Swiss National Science Foundation. She will soon present the result of her research on *Storytelling and the Experience of Decision Making in a Banking Institution* during her PhD dissertation defence at the Università della Svizzera Italiana. She has presented her work in both European and US academic conferences. Her research interests are narrative and storytelling using a phenomenologist, post-structuralist approach.

Henrietta Nilson has many years of experience running and managing businesses. Since completing her Master's degree in Finance she has worked as a business developer and consultant for different organizations and companies. She has also found an outlet for her entrepreneurial talents in her spare time, by singing and acting in plays, musicals and operettas.

Peter Pelzer has studied economics and philosophy. He is working as an independent consultant for banks and as Visiting Reader at the University for Humanistics, Utrecht, The Netherlands. He is very much interested in understanding the processes he experiences during his projects beyond the textbook knowledge of organization and management theory.

Przemysław Piątkowski graduated from Warsaw University School of Management and is currently writing a doctoral thesis, an ethnography of the Catholic prelature of Opus Dei, at the University of Essex, UK. He teaches business strategy, but considers himself an organizational anthropologist with a particular bias towards religious organizations.

Christina Schwabenland has over twenty years' experience in voluntary sector management in the UK, in local, regional and national organizations. She completed a PhD at the University of East London into stories about the founding of voluntary organizations in the UK and in India. She is now teaching and researching at London Metropolitan University, UK, and has authored a book, *Stories, Visions and Values in Voluntary Organizations*.

Jo A. Tyler is Assistant Professor at Pennsylvania State University, a storyteller and consultant. She incorporates storytelling into her practice as an educator and focuses on it as a central thread in her research. The stories she tells draw on personal experiences of knowing and not knowing, gain and loss, work and play.

Introduction to the Trilogy: Mythologies of Organizational Everyday Life

Monika Kostera

Myths about organizations and about organizational actors are powerful stories that touch something profound in the reader or listener. They can help us see and understand many important phenomena that are invisible to the rational instrumental mind. This is not universally acknowledged, perhaps due to a large extent to the dominance of that instrumental mind for the past decades and centuries. Furthermore, myths stem from the sacred realm of experience and many people consider business and work organizations as emphatically profane – for an exploration of the distinction between sacred and profane see Eliade (1961) and Armstrong (2005/2006). However, there are times where these two realms meet, for example in ethnographic stories of organizations, where the actors draw on the realm of shared spiritual experience when referring to values and important events. Myths provide a language for these accounts, as well as ideas which people relate to when dealing with the most vital questions.

Myths are, however, not just a language that organizational actors sometimes invoke, but a frame of reference that can be discerned underneath many rationalistically minded organizations. Myths help people to see the whole not just as a sum of parts, and they socialize them and guide them throughout their lives (Bowles, 1989). This function was traditionally served by cults and religions, nowadays it is often left to work organizations: 'With the decline of the role of the Church, work organizations have become increasingly influential in their impact on peoples' thinking and behavior' (Bowles, 1989, p. 411).

Traditionally, myths describe creation, supernatural beings, heroic quests and adventures including the conquering of magical beasts (Campbell, 1949/1993). Nowadays:

> Management and Organization myths can be seen to follow the traditional myths described above. Organizations, by virtue of their competitive position in the marketplace, sometimes create images of quest and trial, struggling, like the hero, for survival against life-destroying forces. (Bowles, 1989, p. 413)

Why organizations strive to fulfil this role, and how they sometimes succeed, will be the topic of the present three volumes.

The trilogy is not a collection of texts assembled *ex post*, as a result of a conference or seminar, but rather it consists of essays requested by the editor from various scholars on a specific theme: the way they see and use myth in their research of, and reflection on, organization.

Myths and human beings

For many people 'myth' brings to mind either something not true, a false belief or erroneous idea – or else, a tale of the religious domain (albeit other than one's own religion). In the first meaning, we often encounter derogative uses of the term in the popular media, in everyday talk, as well as in academic contexts (Bowles, 1989). If we hear of a narrative labelled 'the myth of success' we may suspect that the story is not very trustworthy or rational. In the second meaning, as sacred tale, it is encountered in academia (especially among anthropologists and ethnographers), as well as in day-to-day conversations, when we speak of origin myths or mythical heroes, usually thinking of exotic or glamorous tales from times or parts of the world where the magic is still alive. Rarely is myth spoken of as part-and-parcel of our everyday life, witnessed here and now. This is exactly how it is seen in the present trilogy. Here myths are

> telling us ... of matters fundamental to ourselves, enduring essential principles about which it would be good for us to know; about which, in fact, it will be necessary for us to know if our conscious minds are to be kept in touch with our own most secret, motivating depths. In short, these holy tales and their images are messages to the conscious mind from quarters of the spirit unknown to normal daylight consciousness, and if read as referring to events in the field of space and time – whether of the future, present, or past – they will have been misread and their force deflected, some secondary thing outside

then taking to itself the reference of the symbol, some sanctified stick, stone, or animal, person, event, city, or social group. (Campbell, 1972/1988, p. 24)[1]

The question whether a myth is true or not is irrelevant (Armstrong, 2005/2006; Campbell, 2004). Myths merge outer and inner reality – the outer world provides images and the inner realm brings insights and awareness (Campbell, 1988). Myth is the fusion of these two and thus is 'true' from the point of view of human experience and consciousness and 'untrue' from the point of view of empirical history, all at the same time.[2]

According to Martin Bowles (1993, p. 414), 'Myths express in ways that we are not able to articulate, our feelings, thoughts, consciousness, or sense of our own behavior.' It is a form of art, transforming the human psyche and the soul, not by means of persuasion but through experience (Armstrong, 2005/2006). It inspires people to see life as a poem, consisting not of words but experiences (Campbell with Moyers, 1988).

Myths have accompanied humans from prehistoric times, providing guidance as how to live a more fulfilling life – humans are myth-creating beings (Armstrong, 2005/2006). Mythology elicits and supports a sense of awe before the mystery of being; provides a set of ideas that enable humans to answer the most vital questions; socializes the individual; and guides him or her towards maturation (Campbell, 1976 as quoted in Bowles, 1989). Martin Bowles (1993) also emphasizes the role of myth in social life, one beyond the 'ego psychology', enabling understanding insights offered by the collective unconscious.

Myth enables the re-enacting of the ancient sacred past, making a personal and experiential connection to the mythical ancestors and 'the beginning' itself (Eliade, 1961). It carries the experience throughout time and provides participation for the current generation in something that happened long ago, disconnecting it from its actual historical occurrence (Armstrong, 2005/2006). 'Time is what shuts you out from eternity. Eternity is now. It is the transcendent dimension of the now to which myth refers' (Campbell, 2004, p. xxii).

Myth fulfills four key roles (Campbell, 2004): namely it strives to 'reconcile consciousness to the preconditions of its own existence' (p. 3); elicit awe in the face of cosmos; 'validate and maintain a certain sociological system' (p. 8) with its norms and values; and guide the human being through the various stages of his or her life. The second and third functions, according to Campbell, nowadays have been taken over by secular orders. However, in the remaining two, myth is still irreplaceable. Yet in modern times humans have expelled myth from many areas of life, replacing it with science and rationality (Armstrong, 2005/2006; Campbell, 2004). And so, the place of traditional myth and religion has been taken over by modern myths such as film and rock music and by popular heroes such as Princess Diana or Elvis Presley (Armstrong, 2005/2006), or modern supernatural beings like The Invisible Hand of the Market (Kostera, 1995a). Martin Bowles (1997) presents management as a modern myth. According to Bowles, the values central to the myth of management are competition, the imperative of growth and function rationality. The myth is quite limited in its ability to guide individuals toward maturation and give answers to life's important questions, which traditionally are the key roles of myth (Campbell, 2004). It fails to respond to the needs of the participants and thus turns out to be inadequate as contemporary myth. It is, rather, 'an attempt to fill in the "in-between" left by declining myth, expressed in Nietzsche's comment, "God is dead", and a new mythic path' (Campbell, 2004 p. 782). And yet, it, 'amounts to a religious fundamentalism in the way it has largely monopolized the goals and informed the understandings and mindset of (late) twentieth century societies' (p. 785).

Even though myth as such is intimately connected with human fate and history, it does not mean that it is always good and leads to a genuinely more fulfilling life for its creators and supporters. There are constructive and destructive myths, myths that connect and myths that demonize the Other, myths promoting empathy and myths that generate fear and egotism (Armstrong, 2005/2006). The use of myths does not guarantee a better society or business, neither a more humane culture, nor better communication. In fact, it does not guarantee anything at all.

Organizational mythmaking

Myths are, then, rather an ambiguous organizational feature. However, being attentive to the mythical side of organizations can bring many good insights. They can be sought for directly in ethnographic material collected in organizations but they will not necessarily surface in the pure form. Contemporary life is to a high degree demythologized, and myths have often survived in culture in other narratives and art forms that reflect and try to fulfil the functions of myth, even though they, in many important respects, remain different from it (Eliade, 1963/1998). Some of their functions are being fulfilled by fairy tales (Bettelheim, 1976), psychological accounts of the human mind (Hillman, 1980; Miller, 1974), contemporary films, such as *Star Wars*, and books, such as *Lord of the Rings* (Trzciński, 2006), and tales of contemporary sociological phenomena (Gabriel, 2004a). This may be due to the fact that myth is vitally important, as a guide to how to live one's life (Campbell, 1972/1988) – or that, in fact, the myths never died but live on as a part of the human psyche (Hillman, 1980) and/ or human culture (Armstrong, 2005/2006). Ernst Cassirer (1946) pointed out that engaging with myth leads storytellers and artists into mythological consciousness, which lies at the core of humanity and offers an alternative way of being in the world. Myth is, according to Cassirer, fundamental to language and storytelling, which are the main fabric of culture. Adopting this view on the role of myth as the foundation for the creation of culture, it is natural to see myth as potentially relevant for all kinds of culture, including the cultures of business and organizations.

The literature taking up mythical themes in connection to management and organization is not abundant but there are several high-quality, interesting texts dedicated to organizational mythmaking. I will now briefly introduce three of them that have made the strongest initial impression on the way I think of organizational mythmaking.

The first book on mythical themes and their relevance for organizing that I read was *Work, Death, and Life Itself* by Burkard Sievers (1994). The book depicts the meaning of work in the context of life and death. It criticizes mainstream and popular approaches to leadership, participation and motivation, and reveals the aspects of organizational life not envisaged in mainstream texts. Among the metaphors the text adopts to shed new light upon phenomena of organizational everyday life are the Greek myths of participation and immortality. The boundary between immortality and mortality in Greek mythology is imprecise and blurred. Hades is inhabited by the souls of dead people, but also by gods and goddesses. Gods are immortal, but they sometimes destroy and annihilate each other:

> What has become obvious in applying Greek mythology and its struggle with immortality as a metaphor for participation in contemporary work enterprises is the wide similarity of psycho-social processes operating to establish and sustain a limited access to immortality. (Sievers, 1994, p. 130)

The organization is often mythologized as immortal; leaders are deified and reified, while workers are reified. All participants are, thus, devoid of their mortality. In conclusion, the book proposes a *management of wisdom* – a way of using and framing managerial knowledge that avoids reification, a view of humans and relationships in organizations that acknowledges human dignity.

The second book I would like to briefly introduce here that takes up mythical themes is a study of popular management texts as a medium for the creation and dissemination of myths by Staffan Furusten (1992; see also Furusten, 1995). The book explores how popular management books, such as *In Search of Excellence* (Peters and Waterman, 1982), *Thriving on Chaos* (Peters, 1989), *Iacocca: An Autobiography* (Iacocca, 1984), and other bestsellers, serve as the guardians of the myth of leadership. The myth gives 'the manager healing and omnipotent abilities' (p. 71) and 'this myth is important as an inconsistent norm, never possible to realize practically, but when people talk about the manager in such terms, this norm will be satisfied mentally and then individuals to a certain extent are enabled to satisfy their searching for security and meaning in life' (pp. 71–2). The popular management books are tracts about virtues and ideals, their role in society is similar to that of antique mythological biographies of heroes and demigods, or legends of saints. Staffan Furusten's study of managerial discourse (1995) concerns the creation and diffusion of popular management knowledge. The author explores the diffusion of popular management books of the 1980s in Sweden and analyses the ideas that they represent. This discourse 'propagates institutionalized myths, beliefs, institutions, and ideologies in the modern Western world' (p. 161). The myths disseminated by the books are then not only lived in organizational practice, but they serve as powerful sets of symbols to control reality. The texts are not unlike medieval Crusaders, advocating 'assent to a faith in North-American managerialism' (p. 168). I have commented in a similar way upon the role of Western management consultants in post-communist Poland (Kostera, 1995).

The third book that I think of as having contributed in a major way to my desire to collect accounts on how organization scholars view and use myth is Yiannis Gabriel's edited book *Myths, Stories and Organizations* (2004a), a collection of texts exploring the relevance of myths, legends, stories and fables for contemporary social and organizational settings. The chapters of Gabriel's book show that ancient stories are alive in the contemporary world and can be re-told and re-interpreted in ways that throw new light on how organizations work and what motivates people that populate them:

> Stories travel and stories stay. Stories cross boundaries and frontiers, settle in different places, and then migrate to or colonize other places. They resurface in different spaces and different times, preserving their ability to entertain, to enlighten, and to bewitch. (Gabriel, 2004b, p. 1)

With the narrative turn, there is a renewed interest in how they can help our understanding of social life, including the life in and of organizations. The chapters in Gabriel's book depart from a traditional tale to explore some aspect of organization, such as knowledge, crime, friendship and power. As Gabriel points out, engaging with stories means to engage with oneself, with the storyteller and with the outer world, touching the unknown and opening up new fields for exploration.

The three books have proven to me the relevance and importance of mythical thinking in organizational contexts and have made me want to see how different contemporary researchers view myths in their fieldwork as well as theorizing on matters related to organizing and organizations. Sievers' and Gabriel's books made me wonder about the relationship between mythology and social and organizational roles, as well as the role of organizations as such, that can be observed in the field or etymologically and philosophically interpreted. Organizational myth is a spontaneously emerging consciousness that bears many consequences on the individual and the collective domain. I wanted to find out how it is conceived by other scholars. Furusten's book caused me to think about the practical and often conscious uses of myth in managerial contexts and what purposes they serve. Myth can be a sort of a 'managerial tool', or a 'tool to manage' one's social and organizational role. I became interested in why and how do people use myth this way. In order to learn more, I decided to ask other researchers and sent out a call for contributions that resulted in the present collection of essays.

The three volumes present mythical thinking and consciousness in organizations, the use of myths in organizational storytelling, as well as different mythical characters present in the contemporary cultural context of organizing. The composition of this trilogy is based on the main themes and synergies of all the chapters. It is organized along three major themes/volumes that emerged from the collected material:

- *Organizational Olympians: Heroes and Heroines of Organizational Myths*, containing texts about individual characters and roles;
- *Organizational Epics and Sagas: Tales of Organizations*, dealing with stories of organizations and their mythical features; and
- *Mythical Inspirations for Organizational Realities*, taking up the role of myth and mythmaking in organizations and organizational discourse.

Notes

1. The way myth is seen in these volumes is thus different from definitions concentrating on the semiotic dimension, such as Roland Barthes' (1957/1973), that sees myth as a type of speech, a semiological system – the dominant ideology of its time serving to naturalize the social order in the interests of the bourgeoisie.
2. In Joseph Campbell's words, 'mythology is not a lie, mythology is poetry, it is metaphorical. It has been well said that mythology is the penultimate truth – penultimate because the ultimate cannot be put into words. It is beyond words, beyond images, beyond that bounding rim of the Buddhist Wheel of Becoming. Mythology pitches the mind beyond that rim, to what can be known but not told. So this is the penultimate truth' (Campbell with Moyers, 1988, p. 163).

Introduction to *Mythological Inspirations for Organizational Realities*

Monika Kostera

Myth, metaphor and inspiration

Ernst Cassirer (1946) describes myth as a mode of communication, developing alongside profane language in prehistoric times. Myth is not concerned about material reality or what actually happened in the outside world. What it refers to, instead, is an internal, spiritual reality – an experience of the divine that is beyond language. Therefore myth is a language of symbols and metaphors:

> [N]o matter how widely the contents of myth and language may differ, yet the same form of mental conception is operative in both. It is the form which one may denote as *metaphorical thinking*; the nature and meaning of metaphor is what we must start with if we want to find, on the one hand, the unity of the verbal and the mythical worlds and, on the other, their differences. (Cassirer, 1946, p. 84)

Metaphor is a one of the classical tropes, a comparison based on unusual usage of words in a new way by which they acquire a new significance (Burke, 1945). Metaphors describe and reveal things and ideas in a new light, they transfer – *metapherein* in Greek – meaning between contexts.

George Lakoff's and Mark Johnson's (1980/1983) *Metaphors We Live By* suggests that our normal way of speaking is highly metaphorical and contains cultural values. Far from being just the domain of poets and rhetoricians:

> metaphor is pervasive in everyday life, not just in language but in thought and action. Our ordinary conceptual system, in terms of which we both think and act, is fundamentally metaphorical in nature. (Lakoff and Johnson, (1980/1983), p. 3)

We 'fall in love', we 'fight against inflation', we 'take our time' – doing none of these things literally, and by describing them in this way, we say a lot about the culture we inhabit. Love is something that makes us fall, time can be taken, etc.

Metaphors are also used by researchers to describe reality:

> Scientific knowledge is shaped by the way researchers attempt to concretize the ground assumptions that underwrite their work. Images of a social phenomenon, usually expressed in terms of a favoured metaphor, provide a means of structuring scientific inquiry, guiding attention in distinctive ways. The image favours a particular epistemological stance in suggesting that certain kinds of insight, understanding and explanation may be more appropriate than the others. Different ground assumptions and the images through which they are grasped and developed thus give rise to different grounds for knowledge about the social world. (Morgan, 1983/1987, p. 21)

By means of metaphor, organization theory is able to conceptualize organizations, study objects that are elusive, complex, indefinite and paradoxical (Morgan, 1986). Some may prefer numbers to describe them. Numbers are metaphorical in regard to organizations: they cannot be reconstructed out of the numbers, but they may be described through them. Some like words from different vocabularies, such as technical, psychological, political, and so on (*ibid.*).

Barbara Czarniawska-Joerges (1988) shows the potential of metaphors to shape and inspire processes of organizing. Metaphors compare something that is less known with something that is familiar to us and help to create and 'domesticate' reality. In that role, they very often are used by management consultants who recognize their creative power and who, in fact, have made them their primary tool in their line of work with organizational change. The consultants interviewed by Czarniawska-Joerges described themselves as people who make money by coining powerful metaphors. The book portrays them as merchants of meaning; professionals whose job it is to create and sell symbolical products.

Metaphors in management may be copied from books (popular and academic publications), from art, films, old legends, myths. Sometimes the consultants create them themselves, on the spot, and they promote them with the intention of selling them as profitably as they can, for example in popular management books bringing into fashion new terms, 'buzzwords', ideas: total quality, excellence in management, re-engineering, and so on, and so on. Metaphors teach, present, frame identities and roles, help to understand old ideas in new ways, motivate and mobilize – they make people believe that things they regarded as impossible may be possible after all, they help to conceive of entirely new things. And, perhaps most importantly of all, they inspire.

Inspiration in management was until recently regarded as something at best second rated, less important, as in the saying that genius (or success) is 1 per cent inspiration, and 99 per cent perspiration. We do not hear very often of theories and discourses seriously taking up managerial inspiration – even such unfashionable notions as managerial intuition are more likely to be explored and discussed. There are exceptions, for example Sanjoy Mukherjee (2007) considers the ways in which inspiration can be helpful for entrepreneurship, Christine Galea (2006) presents an interview with sales executive Stephen Covey who claims that people need to be inspired rather than motivated, or Graham Cooke (2005) who discusses how leaders engage people's ideas, energy and inspiration. I believe that inspiration is, in fact, crucial to management, and very important to organizing insofar as we aim at something new, not just re-enacting the same old routines and treading in well-known areas. We need it and we yearn for it, just as much as poets and artists. However, management theorists and practitioners do not have their own traditional Muse, so perhaps we should consider sharing one with some of the other creative groups.

The Muses were Greek goddesses who managed the arts and sciences. They were believed to inspire artists, and in particular poets, philosophers and musicians. They were the daughters of Zeus and Mnemosyne, the goddess of memory. In the oldest tales, there is only one muse, later they become three (Melete, Mneme and Aoede). The most recent version lists nine of them: Calliope (poetry), Clio (history), Erato (erotic poetry), Euterpe (lyric song), Melpomene (tragedy), Polyhymnia (sacred song), Terpsichore (dance), Thalia (comedy and pastoral poetry), and Urania (astronomy). The Muses dwelt close to Helicon, in Boeotia. They also enjoyed taking part in prophesizing and foretelling the future, for example they were quite active at Delphi, the location of the famous oracle. Apollo, the sun god, was their leader and friend. The Muses were invoked by poets (for example Homer did that quite frequently) and worshipped by the people (for example Pythagoras advised the people of Criton to build a shrine for the Muses in order to encourage learning).[1]

Table I.1   Structure of Part I of this volume

Tale	Organizational inspiration	Authors
Medusa	Reflection	Heather Höpfl
Heavy metal	Postmodern management	Magnus Forslund
Imagination	Organizational change	Henrietta Nilson
	Diversity	Jo A. Tyler
Inferno	Sacred and profane	Przemyslaw Piatkowski
All About Eve	Alliances	Krzysztof Klincewicz
Ideal	Subversion	Christina Schwabenland
Magic	Risk management	Peter Pelzer and Peter Case
Edda	HRM	Frederic Bill and Anders Hytter

Structure of Part I

Many of the uses of mythology are allegories or metaphors – similar to the uses of myth that Ovid made in his Metamorphoses – the theme lies in focus rather than the hero, heroine or set of qualities. The mythical tales presented in the chapters serve as metaphors of an organizational issue that can take inspiration from, or be better understood through, the myth. For example, the tale of Medusa seeks to portray reflection and its consequences, the tale of Thor, the god of thunder and heavy metal music, points out the characteristics of postmodern management, etc. Sometimes the myth is adopted to show the organizational reality and the organizational reality to show myth, as in Frederic Bill's tale of the Edda and an HRM technique, throwing light on both in a blaze of insight that is due to the short circuiting between them. Table I.1 presents the different issues touched upon in this part, and the names of the authors who write about each of them.

Heather Höpfl's chapter discusses reflection and its epistemological implications through the myth of Medusa, the terrifying gorgon, whose image had the ability to turn the onlooker to stone. Medusa was killed by Perseus who held up a mirror to her. She was petrified by her own reflection. The tale of Medusa represents the organizational obsession with reason and with the degradation of embodiment. The ambivalence of Medusa helps to reveal how delusory is the striving for control over reflection and discourse, and how harmful is the preoccupation with heroism in organizations. Magnus Forslund plays with ideas of postmodern management which he links to heavy metal music as an archetypical frame of inspiration and interpretation. Heavy metal is about empowering, provoking, emotions, spirituality and irony – and all these qualities can be quite useful for creative managers. The mythical metaphor underpinning both realms can be found in the sagas of Norse gods, especially Thor, the god of thunder. Henrietta Nilson and Jo A. Tyler are both primarily interested in the domain of imagination. The first author discusses the potential for creative change and how it can be helped by mythical thinking. She has asked several of her friends to write short fictive stories about what it would be like to have the powers of a superhero in organizational settings. She and two of her artist friends interpreted the stories, creating their own fictional accounts. Imagination can help to explore these domains for organizational life that cannot easily be represented by the mainstream discourses focusing on results and behaviours. Jo Tyler's chapter focuses on powerful characters in children's books. The books of Dr Seuss contain a multitude of rich and complex archetypes that can be a source of inspiration for organizational actors. They also present a much needed aspect of organization: the respect for and the joy of diversity of roles and characters. Przemyslaw Piatkowski uses the metaphor Dante's Inferno to portray organizational distinctions between the sacred and the profane. Two characters of damned souls: Fra Alberigo and Branca d'Oria, represent organizational roles in the Inferno, as described by Dante, but also in contemporary organized settings. In Krzysztof Klincewicz's chapter the mythical character of the trickster re-emerging in the movie *All About Eve* serves to explore various shadow aspects of organizational alliances. Deceit is a common organizational behaviour – as well as part of management strategies used, for example, in the forming of interorganizational alliances. The metaphor of the trickster helps to understand the moral side of management in a way that the mainstream discourse almost entirely misses. Christina Schwabenland considers the potential of the ideal for subversion in organizations. She adopts mythical metaphors to throw new light on various aspects of the founding of voluntary organizations. These founding stories tend to become mythical themselves, and using a mythical frame to interpret them helps to see a potential for change and liberation. Peter Pelzer and Peter Case take up the role of magic in contemporary thinking of risk management. Figures are supposed to represent the disenchanted world, but in actuality they can be seen as belonging to the magical domain of numerology and can be used as a powerful mythical metaphor to portray and interpret many phenomena in the field of risk management. It also empowers actors to act in the face of uncertainty. Frederic Bill and Anders Hytter investigate how the mythical characters of the Edda can throw new light on some HRM practices – and vice versa. IDI is a sociometric tool used to measure personality traits considered to be important in organized settings. The main behavioural styles derived from this tool reveal interesting consequences for organizational communication when linked to mythical characters. Modern HRM can be used as a metaphor for mythical tales and sagas can be a metaphor for today's HRM practices, adding depth and human relevance to the discourse in the process.

Structure of Part II

The second Part of the book contains more theoretical, concluding chapters. The chapters take up three aspects of myth: its role, its use and its origin (archetype), and relate these to various aspects of organization, from complexity, through leadership to modes of organizing available to human actors at a given time. Table I.2 presents the topics and the authors.

Two aspects of the role of myth in organizations: complexity and truth, are discussed, respectively, in David Boje's and Linda Musacchio Adorisio's chapter, and in Pierre Guillet de Monthoux's text. The former is based in an ethnographic account of Wells Fargo Bank, itself a mythical organization of the American West. The chapter uses the ethnographic material to show how myth is created from more ephemeral emergent stories. The chapter shows the relevance of theories of myth-making for the understanding of organizational complexity.

Pierre Guillet de Monthoux's chapter is an ironic reflection on the role and usefulness of myth in the form of a fictional dialogue. Myth and metaphor can be seen as fostering cynicism and acrimony, as much as they are celebrated by organization theorists. Lena Fritzén considers the use of myth in organizations for developing the professional competence of leadership. Learning is about developing new ideas and perspectives, not only acquiring new techniques and abilities. Myth helps to find new

Table I.2　Structure of Part II of this volume

Aspect of myth	Aspect of organization	Author
Role of myth	Complexity	David Boje and Linda Musacchio Adorisio
	Truth	Pierre Guillet de Monthoux
Use of myth in organizations	Professional competence of leadership	Lena Fritzén
Archetypes	Collective unconscious	Monika Kostera

viewpoints that are based in people's tacit knowledge and experience. Finally, I conclude the book and the entire trilogy with a reflection on the role of myths in organizations which I link to archetypes of the collective unconscious.

Note

1. The term *museum* is derived from the Greek *mousaion,* which signified a temple of the Muses. It is traditionally a place where people cultivate knowledge and wisdom.

1
Reflections of Medusa

Heather Höpfl

Encountering the Gorgon

It is early in November 2006, and I am in Trento in northern Italy as the guest of Professor Antonio Strati. I am here to spend six weeks at the university working with his Masters course and contributing to the doctoral programme. We have an apartment belonging to the university near the river and a short walk from the Palazzo Albere which houses the Museum of Modern Art. On this particular evening we are going to visit an exhibition of the work of Franz von Stuck. It is clear from the outset that Antonio is very much on home territory in the museum. The staff know him and he wanders around the gallery with his usual charm and bonhomie. He has exhibited here and he very kindly gives me a catalogue of his exhibition of photographs. It is Silvia's birthday in the next few days and Antonio has bought her a new digital camera which he gives her as an early present so that she can take some photographs of the exhibition and of us (see Figure 1.3, p. 24). The head of the museum introduces the exhibition. There is a crowd of perhaps 150 people there, one or two extremely well behaved children and ourselves. Harro with a working knowledge of Italian listens sagely while I try to grasp one or two things from my long past study of Latin: more useful for reading than listening. The introduction goes on for 35 minutes and the audience is rapt. There is no polite coughing to indicate that the speaker has spoken beyond patience. This audience is genuinely interested in the explanation which is offered, the history of the works, a short biography, the way the exhibition is organized. Then, after all this: to the exhibition itself. We go up the grand staircase of the old palazzo and through the elegant rooms. The work is dramatic and commanding but none more so than the blue and black painting of Perseus turning

Figure 1.1 Prof. Antonio Strati at Palazzo Albere

Phineus to stone by holding up the head of Medusa and I turn the corner to where it occupies an entire wall with the shock of encountering the familiar in an unexpected place. I have known Franz von Stuck's Medusa for a long time. Paul Coates' (1991) book, *The Gorgon's Gaze: German Cinema, Expressionism, and the Image of Horror* has been on my desk for a long-time with the von Stuck Medusa on its cover. In fact, more than this, I have brought this book with me to Italy because Monika Kostera has asked for contributions to her forthcoming book on organizations and mythology and I have decided to contribute a chapter on Medusa. So here I am in the Palazzo Albere. I turn a corner and look into the face of the Medusa and I am petrified. Well, of course, I mean only that I am rooted to the spot by this extraordinary intersection of intentions. Even when I came to the exhibition I did not make the connection with von Stuck's painting. Here is the shock of recognition. I have been pondering the Medusa very much of late and thinking about the act of reflection. Now I stand before her and I am annihilated by recognition.

This chapter is about Medusa but more precisely it is about how the myth of Medusa throws light on the notions of reflection and blindness. When Perseus holds up his shield to Medusa, she is slain by her own reflection.

Reflections

In the preface to his fascinating insight into German cinema and images of horror, Paul Coates observes that 'if one defeats the Medusa by directing a mirror against her, one simultaneously becomes blind to one's own monstrous status as the murderer of an alterity – usually feminine – demonized by one's own projections' (Coates, 1991, pp. x–xi) (see also Docherty, 1996). This idea of the annihilation of alterity is a powerful one and one which will be explored in this chapter. First, however, it is necessary to give attention to the myth of the Medusa and to examine its implications and currency.

The famous painting of Medusa by Caravaggio, now in the Uffizi, Florence, was painted sometime after 1590, and depicts the image of Medusa with which we have become familiar. She is the terrifying monster of antiquity: too terrible to be looked upon. Her hair is a writhing mass of snakes. Her terror mirrors our own. Yet, this is the image of Medusa transformed. Medusa is one of the three gorgons. She is the mortal one. The daughter of the Titans, Phorcys and Ceto, Medusa was renowned for her beauty and for her luxurious abundance of hair. She and her sisters, Stheno and Euryale, served as priestesses in the Temple of Athena. However, Poseidon was overcome by passion for Medusa and either raped or took her freely in the temple. This act of desecration was punished by Athena who transformed the beautiful Medusa into the monster of myth and legend. Her hair became a mass of snakes, her body covered in scales. She became so terrifying that those who looked upon her were turned to stone (Lemprière, 1788/1963). It is Perseus who slays Medusa. Defending himself with his shield, he does not look upon her but only on her reflection. He holds up the shining surface and she is slain. She is slain by reflection. But, even in death, the head still has the power to destroy. Medusa herself is sometimes identified with the Libyan serpent-goddess of wisdom and the name Medusa is said to derive from the Sanskrit *medha*, Greek *metis*, and Egyptian *met* or *maat* all words meaning wisdom (see Dourley, 1990).

The myth of Medusa has held an appeal since antiquity and the fact that a quick search of Amazon books produces over 500 titles of books with Medusa, Gorgon or Perseus in the title perhaps confirms the longevity of these ancient stories. Why this should be the case appears to be related to the ambiguity of the imagery. As Brunel (1996) points out, the Medusa is both a mirror and a mask with all the wealth of associations which go with each. However, there is more at work here than a simple ambivalence. The Medusa is the personification of such alluring beauty that she causes Poseidon to desecrate the temple of Athena and, at the same time, Medusa is so terrifying and violent that she causes men to fall down and die at the mere sight of her. Clearly, there is a primitive terror at work here. The imagery is so rich that it is impossible in such

Figure 1.2   Ancient artifact, Medusa talisman 1–2 century AD; Trento, Castello del Buonconsiglio

a short chapter to do justice to all the interpretative possibilities. Consequently, this chapter focuses on two very specific aspects of the story. First, as identified above, the notion of annihilation by reflection – the blindness which is caused by the annihilation of alterity, and by implication, the nature of fascination (see Brunel, 1996)[1] both of which are qualities of the mask and the mirror.

Specularization

The Latin word for mirror is speculum and usually refers to polished metal which can be looked at (from *specio*). This is a term which is well known in contemporary uses in a variety of forms. From the surgical instrument, the speculum, used for gynaecological examination to the everyday use of words such as speculator, spectator and spectacular the mirror provides a fascinating focus for discussion. To speculate is to observe, to reflect upon, to contemplate, to theorize. Following Lacoue-Labarthe (1989, p. 209), it is argued here that the process of

specularization is founded on a model of the tragic in which the spectator can only speculate. That is to say, Lacoue-Labarthe (1989) argues that
in the face of the tragic one can only 'attempt to circumscribe it theo-
retically, to put it on stage and theatricalize it in order to try to catch it
in the trap of (in)sight [(*sa*)*voir*]' (1989, p. 117). This observation applies
both to the subject matter of the chapter, as theorization – that is to
say, my speculations on the myth of the Medusa, and to the myth of
Medusa itself, as theatricalization, and operates in the 'trap of (in) sight'
where theorization reveals that the 'only remedy against representation,
infinitely precarious, dangerous, and unstable (is) representation itself'
(Lacoue-Labarthe, 1989, p. 117). Although this idea sounds rather complicated, it deals with the object viewed in the line of sight and the
object viewed via specularization, that is to say in this context, as the
object of speculation. Lacoue-Labarthes is saying that when the object is
elevated to the status of subject of speculation, it is mortified by insight.
In relating this back to the story of the Medusa, the point is that the
myth holds that to gaze upon the Medusa is to face the terrible consequence of being turned to stone. The observer is petrified by the sight of
the monster. Lacoue-Labarthe's analysis suggests a different possibility.
He argues that the object of the speculation is mortified by that speculation: annihilated by reflection. Metaphorically, Medusa is slain by
speculation.

What this means, despite the tortuous language, is that theorization
kills. The subject, here Medusa, is destroyed *because* Perseus does not look
at her. He kills her via reflection. She is not killed by a frontal onslaught
which would require a confrontation with her monstrosity but via the
elevation of her monstrosity into a mere mirage (from the French *mirer*
meaning to be reflected, to look at oneself in a mirror). Perseus is able
to slay the Medusa by reducing her to mere reflection and this reflection
enables him to kill her in the flesh. The implications of this are vast. In
truth, the audacious Perseus is like the theorist who in the process of
creating a vast mirage of meaning kills the very subject s/he wishes to
present – with all its complexities, distortions and ugliness – with the
weapon of an elegant formulation, a reductionist model, a theoretical
illusion. All life is drained from the subject and yet, like Perseus, the
heroic theorist picks up the trophy of his/her slaughter and parades it on
his/her shield as a symbol of conquest. When Perseus slays the Medusa,
he gives her head to Athena to put on her shield so that those under
the Aegis will be protected. This move in theoretical terms functions in
a similar way. Armed with what s/he firmly believes to be the sword of
truth, the latter-day Perseus not only deprives the subject of vitality but

then parades the death as the mark of a supreme achievement. This is part of what Lacoue-Labarthes means by *the trap of insight*. There is a danger in believing that theorization results in a necessary and desirable mortality: that the death of Medusa rids the world of ugliness, or evil. In practice, what is mortified is alterity and, as Coates observes, frequently this is a feminine alterity which, as Kristeva says (is the) 'other without a name' (Kristeva, 1982, p. 58). By a tidy ordering of experience, by reduction to simple constructions and by a profound desire to annihilate *the other*, the theorization detaches the person from the experience, Perseus is not engaging in the talking cure, he is bent on destruction. This creature of allure or revulsion who compels or repels must be destroyed and so Perseus lives on in legend as the hero who slew the Gorgon, deprived her of her mortal life and restored order.

The pharmacology (*pharmakon*) of this operates via the formula where remedy itself is mortification. In other words, the killing of the Gorgon has implications which induce a further mortality. The argument is inherently unstable, induces dizziness, fails and falls. This, in itself, is tragic to the extent that the argument, like the myth, is subject to its own annihilation, subversion and demise.

Speculations on mortality

In his book, *The Truth in Painting*, Derrida (1987) has traced Kant's *Critique of Judgement* (1790) in order to pose questions about what art is, about how it can be apprehended and about how it can be evaluated. He concludes that every discourse on art presupposes a discourse on the frame: presupposes a distinction between what is intrinsic to the work of art and what is extrinsic. By identifying a frame which separates what is inside and what is outside, according to Derrida, Kant, by implication, defines not only the frame but also the framing of the frame. This is the *parergon* and over a third of *The Truth in Painting* is given over to the examination of this term. Parergon is usually defined as a by-work, a complementary or parallel work, but which as used here might be understood to be a by-*product*. The parergon, therefore, is concerned with all that is associated with the work of art but not a part of it – just like the frame of a painting. The parergon is associated with the work but secondary to it. At the same time, its significance vacillates since it marks the boundary of the work, identifies the point of difference and draws attention to the limit of the work itself. Although secondary, the frame can cancel, erase the art, be ludicrous, inappropriate, lavish, ornate, minimal. Whatever. The point is that the frame stands in relation to the work. My point here is that, just as theorization holds the theorist in the *trap of insight*, so the frame distorts and sometimes cancels what it circumscribes. It is likewise a trap. In this context, I am mirroring [speculating] on how the frame functions in the Medusa story as the construction of the reflection which kills. The living body of the monstrous Gorgon is only put to the sword via the elaborate construction of her image which permits her destruction. Like surveyed masses reduced to simple statistics and measures of tolerance, she is destroyed in the flesh because she is first rendered illusion.

This notion of the parergon has far reaching implications for the nature of the frame since it marks the point of undecidability between inside and outside, being both insignificant and secondary and, at the same time, liminal and defining. It defines and yet in defining cancels. If, therefore, art is the act of putting together, joining and fitting, and if management is, indeed, concerned with art, then an understanding of the parergon has serious implications for the study of management. This is because the frame, the parergon, restricts, limits and characterizes what it contains. It annihilates by reflection. What it constructs around the thing in itself is at variance with the idea that thing can live independently of the frame. Rembrandt's study of the anatomy class shows a group of students framing the dead body which they will begin to dissect in order to understanding the living. Yet the frame distorts the meaning of what it contains and may usurp that meaning to become the very definition of what it contains. In the anatomy class, the study of the dead defines the functions of the living. Of course, this is a rather distorted example but I hope it serves to pose some questions about the relationship between reflection and annihilation. Here, even in the construction of the argument is the inescapable dynamic of power: the power to define and capture. The myth of Perseus is offered without question as a tale of heroic quest. It is his mission to slay the Medusa and he is clearly the hero of the tale. Yet the Medusa represents what cannot be killed off by mere will. The fact that her severed head wields power after her death indicates an appreciation of the idea that evil is neither reducible nor so readily destructible. Like the Glenn Close character in Adrian Lyne's 1987 film *Fatal Attraction*, the Medusa is indestructible.

Blind

In 1990 Derrida was invited to curate an exhibition of drawings and paintings for the Louvre. The exhibition, *Les Mémoires d'Aveugles* (Memories of the Blind) sought to explore the boundary between his writing and works of art where the images themselves were constructed as parergonal to his writings. This was a challenge to the conventional relationship between art and text where text is normally parergonal to the image (see Höpfl, 2006). *Mémoires d'Aveugle* deals with blindness, memory and self-portraiture. The subtitle for the exhibition was 'The Self-Portrait and Other Ruins'. In the text of the exhibition, Derrida proposes what he calls the *'abocular hypothesis'*. This notion *frames* the work, and Derrida gives attention to this concept in *Mémoires's* introductory and concluding sections. The term itself, ab-ocular, carries with it the duality of meaning of from, *out of* the eye and, at the same time, *from*, separated from the eye. However, there is a further meaning at work here since the modern French term aveugle (blind) can be traced directly to the Latin ab-oculis: something *from* the eye, that is, the eye is less than *and* also *nothing* from the eye, nothing can be seen. Derrida is talking about his own blindness: metaphorical and literal. In fact, for two weeks Derrida suffered from an eye affliction which left him unable to close his left eye. In short, Derrida is arguing that the artist is blind, the object of attention always invisible. It can only be invoked by memory. The artist is blind to the present. He is also saying that drawing/art, like language, requires the play of absence and presence and that this too is invisible.

There are interesting implications to be carried forward from these ideas. When Derrida's argument regarding the blindness of the artist is carried over to the analysis of speculation developed earlier, it is possible to compare the work of the theorist to that of Derrida's artist. However, this is not simply a matter of comparing the theorist to the artist, or saying that speculation and recollection work with a similar dynamic. Rather, it is to point to the same blindness. Neither can see their subject matter at the time they come to address it. Both share an ab-ocular vision. When Perseus kills the Medusa, he kills her by working through her reflection, her representation. The construction of the image is what permits the execution in the flesh. He has to be blind to Medusa or he would be petrified. It is tempting to detail the ways in which the image of Medusa represents a seductive evil. Medusa is the appeal of a beautiful solution with great powers of fascination and attraction which transforms itself into a nightmare of terror and unimaginable horror: a terror so great that men cannot look upon it. They can only speculate. Life it seems is full of a naïve belief in beautiful solutions which increase revenues, improve quality, change structures, massacre the innocent. Unless they are regarded fully, and I mean this in the literal sense of the term *regard*, that is *to look upon, gaze, observe*, the evil of such constructions is not seen, a blind eye is turned to the subject, the true power of the horror is annihilated. Moreover, like the artist, the theorist relies on a

Figure 1.3 Seen through a lens: Sylvia Gherardi and Harro Höpfl, von Stuck exhibition, Trento

blindness which is not acknowledged, which is found in the blinding play of absence and presence. S/he, as artist/as theorist, cannot see what memory makes her/him blind to and this blindness becomes the frame for an art of a theory: without '(in)sight [(sa)voir]' (Lacoue-Labarthe, 1989, p. 117). If Medusa is Metis, then wisdom is slain as the price of the destruction of alterity.

Blinded by reflection

When Perseus hold up the mirror to the Medusa, when he holds up his shining shield, she is slain by her own reflection, blinded by reflection, cannot see. The mirror as the speculum which induces speculation, forces back on the perpetrator and victim the images which appear in the reflection. When Perseus holds up a mirror to the Gorgon and her condition he confronts her with his 'reality' and she is paralyzed by the reflection. Not surprising that by the sixteenth century the slaying of Medusa was held up as a motif of the conquest of the senses by reason. What Medusa reflects back to Perseus is his own construction, a monstrous power, and what she reflects back to herself is mortification. If, in more general terms, this blindness permits the person who must gaze into the speculum to be converted to the logos, then they will be able to demonstrate their conversion to order, to the power of the frame and will have, by that submission, demonstrated control over hysteria and, by implication, over the hystera (womb). The order of the framing will prevail over the disorder of the content. Sanity as the logic and order of what is clean, clear, classified, well structured becomes synonymous with the absence of ambivalence. The frame blinds as a 'misleading pretext' (Hoad, 1986, p. 43) by its trajectory and closure. It jealously guards its blinding: *la jalousie*. To be blind is to be caught 'in the trap of (in)sight [(sa)voir]' (Lacoue-Labarthe, 1989, p. 117). Seen in this way, the therapeutic quest of the organization is concerned with framing but the consequences of this are the paralyzing effects of blindness, a loss of sight, of sa-voir. The problem is, of course, that it is impossible to know how to begin to *reflect* on these issues (see Irigaray, 1985).

An organization fit for heroes

In privileging constructions over physicality, the organization comes to reproduce itself in theoretical articulations – as paradigms and matrices – and to understand itself in metaphysical terms as the product of its own reproduction. Within this logic, the organization seeks to reassure itself of its power over monstrosity, over women and disorder. In this context, Perseus is the hero of the organization. The organizations want to create a heroic notion of progression, a confident and bold representation of the future – and this is inevitably a masculine construction. The feminine is required to remain silent or to present itself according to its representation as viewed through the male gaze: to produce itself in a way which ensures its own annihilation.

As part of an obsession with slaying monsters, organizations have become fanatical about metrics and monitoring. Elsewhere, I have examined the etymology and significance of the matrix as an organ and instrument of reproduction (Höpfl, 2000a; 2000b; 2002) and argued that embodied reproduction is replaced by the reproduction of text. The matrix is regulated so that its cells show location and defining characteristics on the basis of power relations. This power derives from the ability to define, to authorize and regulate the site of production. Understood in this way, the matrix defines what the organization regards as 'good' and, therefore, worthy of reproduction. If the slaying of Medusa represents the triumph of reason over the senses, it also represents the mortification of the flesh. Reason triumphs as death might triumph over life.

In the relentless pursuit of future states, organizations as purposive entities seek to construct for themselves the empty emblems of the object of the quest: high quality standards, improved performance, an ethical position, dignity at work, care for staff and so forth. In part, this is because the purposiveness of organizations is without end – indeed *can* never end – and, therefore, the notion of any real completion is antithetical to the idea of trajectory. Strategy produces more strategy; rhetoric gives birth to more rhetoric; and text to more text and so on. The construction of the organization in abstract organizational categories is intended to console in the absence of the hope of restoration. In effect, the organization has *no sense*!

Under the aegis of mortality

Moreover, the vicarious and representational has more seductive power than the physical and disordered other. These emblems function to register the loss as representation. For this reason alone, the emblem of loss is melancholic and pervades the organization with melancholy. It cannot offer consolation because ironically it can only recall that there is a loss. Perseus slays Medusa, puts us all under the aegis of death. This may appear like protection but the loss is a powerful one like the loss of the ability to distinguish between good and evil. The argument presented here is concerned with the heroic quest of the organization and its implications (cf. Jung and von Franz, 1988). The pursuit of the heroic leaves us blind to the power of monstrosity and evil and thereby makes their power greater. These are not simply annihilated by reflection. Theoretical constructions do not compensate for wickedness and frequently do little or nothing to improve conditions in the organization or the world in general for that matter. The paradox at the root of this argument is one of power. The positions discussed in this chapter cannot easily be reconciled because they pose the physical against the metaphysical and in doing so implicitly challenge the organization's construction of itself.

In seeking to construct themselves both as sublime manifestations of male desire and as unattainable ideals, organizations lay themselves open to inevitable failure. The therapeutic project of *saving* the organization via the rule of logic, via insistent authority, and via psychology, is a process of mortification. Moreover, it is founded on a masculine sublime fabricated to reflect the male ego, narcissistic and inevitably melancholic. The feminine has no place, no reflection, no role in this construction other than to the extent that, in an entirely selective way, it serves as an object within the construction. In this construction, the feminine is hysterical and has to be kept out because, by posing a threat to its mere representational form (to *mimesis*), it threatens order. Only if the feminine is prepared to submit itself to the symbol of the masculine construction (the erection) can it even enter into reflection. However, even then it must show a *proper* reflection *appropriate* to its status as a *property* of that construction. When the feminine lacks *propriety* it is reduced to nothing. It is a phallocentric psychology which credits itself with initiative, achievement and purpose and which defends its position by either relegation or cancellation. Clearly, part of this defense rests on power over the control of reflection, theorization and discourse, and on the control of categories and their meanings.

Medusa is ambivalence. She is both seduction and a talisman against seduction (see Baudrillard, 1990). The remedy against delusion lies in looking her full in the face. If organizations are to be more congenial places to work, they must give up their naïve obsession with heroism. Forget Perseus, embrace Medusa.

Note

1. http://www.english.uiuc.edu/MAPS/poets/a_f/bogan/medusamyth.htm (accessed 22 April 2007).

2
Heavy Metal Managing

Magnus Forslund

Introduction

... for It is a human number ...

At the age of seven, I was given my first record: *Strung Up* by The Sweet. Shortly thereafter I was given *Give Us a Wink* and *Off the Record* also by Sweet. Some say that Sweet were not heavy metal. For me however, these albums were and still are heavy and they were the starting point for my journey in the world of heavy metal. Soon I knew more bands: Motorhead, Judas Priest, Black Sabbath, Saxon, Iron Maiden, DIO, KISS, WASP, Tank, Mötley Crüe ... My friends and I listened to, read and talked about and watched heavy metal. I did listen to other kinds of music, but it was heavy metal that was my life. I must confess that I never wore black leather trousers or spandex, and it took a long time for me to let my hair grow long (and the hair stayed long only for a couple of years). But I loved the music.

Having had its latest peak during the 1980s heavy metal is now once again becoming popular. Not only die-hard fans are returning. The Average Joe is jumping on the bandwagon, resulting in Lordi, a Finnish heavy metal band winning the Eurovision Song Contest 2006. It seems as if heavy metal is again an important source for meaning creation. This says something of today's Western society and how we approach life, organizing and managing. In this context then, I began searching for relationships between heavy metal and managing. One alternative was to look for managing in heavy metal; another was to look for heavy metal in managing. What elements of the heavy metal world of symbols, myths, legends and meanings are possible to trace in the world of managing? I chose the latter alternative, not aiming to find solutions but rather inspirations to understanding managing.

Understanding heavy metal

How to understand heavy metal? There are books by people in the industry (Christe, 2003; Hunter, 2005; Klosterman, 2001; Konow, 2002). There are biographies (Kilmeister and Garza, 2003; Lee *et al.*, 2002). There are some academic works (Walser, 1993; Weinstein, 2000). A performative way of defining heavy metal is to name a couple of prominent albums; *Paranoid* (by Black Sabbath), *British Steel* (Judas Priest), *The Number of The Beast* (Iron Maiden), *Wheels of Steel* (Saxon), *Highway to Hell* (AC/DC), *Ace of Spades* (Motorhead), and urge you to listen. If you are new to heavy metal, perhaps you would say that it is loud and noisy; that it is sometimes rather difficult to hear what the singer sings; that you do not feel comfortable listening; that the texts are childish, immoral or just nonsense; ... or that you just love it. Listening to the music is however only one aspect of heavy metal. Weinstein (2000) writes that heavy metal is a musical genre with a specific code, a set of rules, that among other things concerns the *sonic*, the *visual* and the *verbal*. Furthermore we could understand heavy metal as a discourse, a sub-culture, and/or life-style, depending on which theoretical concept we prefer (Walser, 1993) There is 'something more' to heavy metal than just music.

Power is a general theme of heavy metal. In *the sonic dimension*, it is expressed in high volume since it both symbolically and literally expresses power (and thus energy). The music can and should be felt in the body, particularly in the chest. It should overwhelm and sweep the listener away. While listening to the music and afterwards you (are supposed to) feel energized and thus more capable of doing things than before. This of course mainly holds for those who enjoy the music. Those that have not yet understood heavy metal can actually feel a kind of repulsiveness and a sense of being rejected, especially since the music wants to 'get inside' the body and mind of the listener. This 'invasion' certainly can be experienced as painful. The purpose, however, is not to hurt but to empower the listener (Weinstein, 2000).

Besides conveying images of power, the *visual dimension* usually depicts something unsettling, threatening and ominous. Sometimes it borders on the grotesque and often chaos is lurking in the background (Weinstein, 2000). This includes clothing, stage shows, album covers, logos, album and song-titles. Logos are extensively used on album covers and merchandise. In order to convey the right meanings certain typefaces, especially those that are gently rounded, are avoided since they convey softness, not power. Heavy metal album covers should have elaborate artwork. Iron Maiden in particular have been successful with the imaginative character Eddie who appears on all covers, albeit in different forms: as an individual committing crime (*Killers* album), as an android (*Somewhere in Time*), or as a vague ominous shape taking form in the clouds hovering above a city (*Brave New World*). The concert stage is another important place for visual artefacts and effects. Costumes with axes and details of skeletons, (like KISS), lightning effects, stage sets (e.g., aeroplanes, inflatable dolls, pyramids, mummies), pyrotechnic stuff (e.g., explosions) and 'props' (e.g., fake animals, meat, guillotines), together support images of power and make the whole event a memorable experience.

The aforementioned is evident in *the verbal dimension*, i.e., band names, album and song titles and lyrics. Band names typically evoke images of evil, destruction and war: Anthrax, Iron Maiden, Megadeath, Riot, Slayer, Tank, Trash, Venom and Warrior. Perhaps somewhat surprisingly, religious allusions are common: Angel witch, Kingdom come, Lamb of God, Morbid Angel. The same goes for album titles: *Angel of Retribution, Back for the Attack, Bomber, Destroyer, Fighting for the Earth, Headless Cross, Honour and Blood, Killers, Ram it Down, Restless and Wild, Sacrifice, Shout at the Devil, Unholy Terror,* ... and song titles: *Breaking the Law, Hells Bells, Killed by Death, Tormentor, War Machine*. Band names and album titles provide a context in which songs are listened to. The listener is made emotionally ready for what to expect from the songs. Song titles are then of course related to the themes already evoked. Weinstein (2000) suggests that there are two major lyrical themes: *Dionysian* and *Chaotic*. Heavy metal is not a story about normality or order. The heavy metal (wo)man is an outsider, not belonging to established society. This however is not a source of grief since the prevalent order is something that should be overthrown:

> [Heavy metal] ... stands against the pleasing illusions of normality, conjuring with the powers of the underworld and making them submit to the order of the music and nothing else ... Heavy metal's insistence on bringing chaos to awareness is a complex affirmation of power, of the power of the forces of disorder, of the power to confront those forces in the imagination, and of the power to transcend those forces in art. (Weinstein, 2000, p. 38)

Heavy metal speaks of death, rebellion, destruction, resistance, revenge and vengeance. Since heavy metal was born out of blues it is not surprising that there is a clear relation to the dark and chaotic side of life. There is however more to heavy metal than that. *Dionysian themes* are prevalent. It is as if we need rest from the battle against and with evil and lose ourselves in a pleasurable now. Partying, often with girls, is heralded as very important. *Girls, girls, girls,* the song by Mötley Crüe, is perhaps a too obvious example.

Heavy metal and managing

On one hand we have managing, a process we have a fairly common sense understanding of. We know that it sometimes is described as planning, organizing, leading and controlling, We also know that the individual doing the managing sometimes is understood as a manager, sometimes as a leader. In *this* chapter, that distinction is not important. If we imagine an individual that is responsible for an organization, what is interesting is if it is possible to trace heavy metal in the way he or she manages her/his organization? In the following I will present a number of fragments in which I am searching, tracing, and evoking images of heavy metal managing.

Managing – empowering

Heavy metal is not about a power used to suppress those that are not musicians. Instead it is a power to be spread and shared among everyone involved, musicians and listeners. Heavy metal managing deals with the demand from listeners to be empowered. If employees are not, they turn to someone else. In a somewhat strange way, I find myself thinking about McClelland (1967) and his theories of needs. He wrote about a need for power that could be interpreted as a power to control the environment and hence improve the conditions for those subordinated to the leader. Maybe too obvious are discussions of empowerment and direct participation, so common a number of years ago (Fröhlich and Pekruhl, 1996) There is a difference regarding who is to win and who is to lose. Discussions about empowerment often presuppose that managers must lose some of their power to subordinates (who then are empowered). In heavy metal managing however, *everyone* is empowered. During the last eight years, Fresh, a small company in the field of indoor climate, has been aiming for this: 'we shall create the necessary conditions for both co-workers and the company to grow in harmony with each other' (Fresh, 2007).

Following heavy metal though, it might not be so important what *words* leaders use to empower. The purpose of a heavy metal singer is not to deliver text, but sound. This means that the voice of the singer participates as an equal 'instrument', alongside drums, bass and guitar. It is the *tone* of the voice to which we respond.

Managing – rebelling and provoking

Heavy metal is about rebellion and it is important to avoid that which is established in the world outside heavy metal. Even certain typefaces are avoided since they are related to official information and used by governments (Weinstein, 2000). Hence they create meanings of neutrality, efficiency, order and the established. Rob Halford of Judas Priest forcefully sings about Breaking the Law. But, this is not about anarchy but about encouraging people to walk their own paths in order to survive. Closely related to walking our own path is the sense of being on a mission, perhaps even on a crusade, where we fight for the right to . . . rock, be an outsider, not be popular or rich, create and follow your own rules, be independent . . . This is the traditional rock'n roll myth taken a few inches further. Heavy metal opens up the possibility not only to walk away from, but to turn against, and overthrow the established. If we get furious enough we will take down the opponents, smash them to pieces, wipe them off the ground and/or extinguish them completely. No mercy.

Take IKEA, the Swedish furniture company. Very early they not only rebelled against the industry concerning how to sell furniture but also how to manage the company. It never went public. They have a mission in which enabling many people to a better life is central. They make strong efforts not to compromise with their core ideology. Usually Ingvar Kamprad (founder) even travels tourist class. And, here comes the heavy stuff. If you attack their values and their mission, very quickly you will face opponents ready to fight and ready to defend what they believe in, and eventually ready to destroy you. (No that was just a joke!)

So are successful leaders rebels? Jonas Birgersson, of Framfab, certainly tried to appear as a rebel, for example by saying that there is a new economy but also by wearing anything *but* a suit. After a while and after severe problems he however had to step down, suddenly appearing as a failure. Yes, be a rebel, but in the end it is the traditional manager that rules the game – or is it? The company is still alive (while not necessarily kicking) so in a way he has succeeded. He is also still working, now with new somewhat 'mysterious' projects in Labs2. In this way he resembles the heavy metal hero who is enormously strong and who *never surrenders*. It is almost a perfect match when Iron Maiden lets the 'We Shall Fight on the Beaches' speech of Winston Churchill from World War II introduce the live album *Live After Death*. In the speech it is emphasised that surrender is not an option. Instead we will fight, fight, and fight.

If you are going to die, you are dying with your boots on, i.e. in the middle of the fight (to rock). Just as Stig Svensson (1914–2004), former chairman of soccer club Östers IF, nearly died while watching important games. No matter how bad his heart was, he was at the arena, involved in the 'battle'. It is difficult to kill a heavy metal hero since he has a tendency to transform into a dragon or some other fantasy creature with multiple heads, just as successful leaders keep on 'popping' up their (new) heads in new settings regardless of past and current problems and threats (as Churchill promises the British Empire will do in case of defeat). As Weinstein (2000) puts it, heavy metal itself is a *beast* that refuses to die.

Perhaps we can understand the perspective from Saxon (1980) in the song *Stand up for your rights*. They sing that when you are down at the bottom, you have nothing to lose and hence you can (and must) leave your worries behind and (firmly) stand up and fight for your rights.

Maybe leaders *need* to appear as rebels in order to attract followers? Jonas Birgersson did attract many: employees, investors, media, politicians and general public. He had something different to say, and what he said sort of 'rocked'. The heavy metal hero walks another path. In this sense he resembles images of entrepreneurs (Schumpeter, 1983).

So, are successful leaders entrepreneurs? At Mercatus Engineering, a SME in Sweden, they talk about themselves as knights fighting to protect our natural resources. They want to be an example when it comes to environmental technology and working methods. They want to stand out and stand up and be counted.

Managing – feelings in motion

Following the heavy metal code, managing must be *felt* in the body. Managers must be heard and seen and their 'sound' must be able to come through (walls). This could be understood as a literally loud manager, shouting to employees. I think the image is right, if the shouting is positive and empowering. Actually this can be seen at company conferences. An Internet video clip shows Steve Balmer, a Microsoft manager, entering a big conference running and shouting loud, eventually declaring: 'I love this company!' Perhaps this is the charismatic and/or transformational leader.

From vividly espousing your love for the company there is a short leap to embracing the emotionality of organizing. Heavy metal people are not afraid of expressing emotions like anger, frustration and joy. Mostly this is done by screaming, banging heads, waving hands/fists and jumping/running around. The emotions expressed are not fine or 'delicate', but rather 'rough and raw'. There is however something neat about a bunch of 'metalheads' getting all sweaty and dirty together at concerts. Suddenly they have no problem about touching each other. Also, the feelings expressed when the singer performs stage diving and then is carried around by the fans are in a way beautiful and perhaps spiritual. Then we can feel like a powerful tribe. We are strong and we are there for each other.

Organizations embarking on team building exercises seem to aspire to the same kind of emotionality. Throwing axes, climbing trees, crossing rivers ... getting dirty and sweaty, so that in the end you are stripped down to the bone ... and re-emerge naked, true and ... This seems definitely more heavy metal than, for example disco, hip-hop or pop. In this context, a somewhat twisted note is that nowadays at least one heavy metal group seems to have abandoned these 'rough and ready' exercises and instead sits down and talks about emotions. At least this is what Metallica did in order to develop as a group (as shown in the movie *Some Kind of Monster*). Even if this might be an exception, deep down we know that metalheads are emotional inside. Just listen to all these power ballads. Guitar solos can make a man cry. But, right time, right place. Just as in the world of organizations. People and *that kind of* emotion and so on are important, certainly, but there is a time and a place for everything (in other words, not here, not now). Which, in turn alludes to the emotional management performed for instance by airline stewardesses (Fineman, 1996).

Managing – being authentic, being real

On an Internet page, Mick Wall, author of a biography on Iron Maiden states that he likes Iron Maiden since he thinks they are the real thing (Wall, 2006).

In the heavy metal world, authenticity rules and pays off. As long as Iron Maiden stays true to the (heavy metal) cause, fans are buying their records and attending their shows – regardless of quality. Ingvar Kamprad of IKEA can be 'exposed' as having made a few mistakes in his past. It does not matter as long as he is true to the cause – to make a better living for many people. Part of being authentic is being real. In the heavy metal world this means to appear as one of the lads. It is usually said that Iron Maiden has been particularly successful in this respect. Despite that members of the group are wealthier than most of their fans, they appear as Average Joes trying to make good music. Poison on the other hand did appear as non-authentic fortune seekers. Why? Difficult to say. Perhaps a mismatch between music and clothes? So, while it is important to be a rebel and to stand out as a provocative entrepreneur, you must remain one of the lads, just trying to do good business. Perhaps this is why some top managers invite journalists to their homes to show how they make cookies.

Managing – 'spiritualizing'

A somewhat contradictory dimension of the heavy metal world is that, while it is important to be authentic and real, it is also important to be 'larger than life'. Shows and gestures got bigger and bigger. World dominance the goal. Being larger than life also means that you are invincible. However, this also can be understood as an allusion to spiritual or even divine dimensions (Weinstein, 2000). It is easy to find religious symbols in heavy metal. A classic song of Black Sabbath is *Heaven and Hell*. Ronnie James Dio sings about Holy Diver (album cover showing a chained priest, drowning in – (or rising out of) – a sea). The battle between good and evil is told and retold again and again.

It has been said that heavy metal is the music of the devil. To enjoy heavy metal seems to be the same as preferring Satan. But then again, have the critics actually listened to the music?

In *Prodigal Son* (1989), Iron Maiden sings that it is a *problem* that the devil has got hold of the soul and that is driving a person mad. Thus the devil is *not* portrayed as something nice.

How was the music of Wagner interpreted? According to, for example, Finlo Rohrer (2007) all music relying on tritones, a musical interval that spans three whole tones, has been understood as the devil's music, regardless of whether it is heavy metal, Wagner or *West Side Story*. In my world however you can be very anti-Satan and pro-God and still love heavy metal.[1] What is true though, is that heavy metal most often makes use of the *narrative* of God versus Satan.[2] But, that is a completely different thing. It is exactly this unreal, fantastic saga of the battle between good and evil that makes heavy metal real and authentic. It deals with important things. No bubble gums here.

In the organizational world Biberman and Whitty (1997) suggest a new paradigm for the future of work based on spiritual guidelines and principles. Cacioppe (2000) argues that we need to move beyond established paradigms toward a more spiritual and holistic view for the twenty-first century workplace. Spitzer (2000) writes about the heart of the inspired leader and uses words like faith, ethics, commitment, trust, spirit, esprit de corps and even God. 'US leaders now see themselves as priests of a divine mission to rid the world of its demons' (Monbiot, 2003).

A difference to heavy metal seems to be who/what is imagined to be demons, and who is to be saved by whom? In the world of organizations this is traceable in the idea that organizations provide and employees seek job security. Come work with us – and you are saved (from the evils of the world). Follow our code, our rules, and everything will turn out just fine for you. Taking job training and education into account, we might even say that an employee will become a 'better person' when she/he engages in (works for) certain organizations. And for sure, when Ingvar Kamprad of IKEA gathers his people in rooms and talks to them, it could be experienced as a mass with clearly religious allusions.

Managing – not that serious

While heavy metal mainly is about serious things, about overthrowing the established powers, of winning against all odds, of fighting back ... it is also aware of the importance of not being too serious. This is not Joy Division, The Cure, New Order or any other prestigious music. You should not take things *that* seriously. Deal with problems, have a good laugh and keep on rocking and fighting. Perhaps we could trace this in ideas about what managers and employees want from work(-places). It seems to be more and more common to hear the word 'fun'. For fun, Jonas Birgersson (see above) dressed up in a shirt of the Swedish hockey team or a Helly Hansen sweater. The suit was too serious. Like ordinary people members of Iron Maiden want to have fun and play around on and off stage. Eddie, their very unreal mascot, is exactly that winking eye that makes Iron Maiden real. When Alice Cooper chops off his head during his concerts, it is likewise such an exaggeration that it becomes humorous.

The existence of humour however could indicate that something less humorous is camouflaged (Rodrigues and Collinson, 1995). Perhaps it is alienation and cynicism? Arnett (1996) argues that American heavy metal fans are 'profoundly alienated from institutions that have formed the bedrock of American society for over 200 years; from their families, from their schools, from their communities, and from political and religious institutions.' I think this is an exaggeration, but maybe there is a point in acknowledging that heavy metal emerged around the time when the Modernity era came to an end and Postmodernity began (Harvey, 1990). The world now is a spectacle in which surface rules over depth. Old, new and strange things are blended together in our endless search for new sensations. Skeletons on stage? Pretending to chop off heads? Throwing meat at the audience? Nudity? Try anything once in order to contribute to the circus. Remember though that there is nothing behind this besides looking nice and cool. No deep thoughts like The Smiths. HOWEVER, from a theoretical standpoint, it is possible to say that this is only a process of illusion, in which the real pain is hidden and forgotten. Life sucks! In the heavy metal world this is acknowledged and responded to with: so, f--k it and let's party!

Now, in the business world I would argue that we can trace this in the sometimes embarrassing high pay (and fringe benefits and bonuses) that top managers are giving each other. Of course they know that this is wrong and immoral. But, what the he--, life is too short and it sucks, so . . . I also think that we can trace this in the culture of mediocracy that depicts many organizations (Jackall, 1988). Really, why should we try to excel? Why should we put in extra hours and/or aim for highest quality – really? In the everyday work life of employees I am not at all sure that there is an answer.

God of Thunder

In 1976, the heavy metal group Kiss released the album Destroyer. It included a song entitled *God of Thunder*. It is about the 'original' God of Thunder. Raised by Odin and Jörd, Thor as told in the prose Edda, uses his superior power to protect Asgard. He is first and foremost known as the God of Thunder. He is aggressive, unruly, sulky, naïve, dangerous, playful and definitively heavy metal. Besides epitomizing all essential qualities of heavy metal, Thor also has a 'sidekick' or mascot: the Hammer.

In the song it is said that Thor was raised by demons and that he was trained to regin as *the one*. Everyone else should be prepared to kneel. But look out, the individual referred to in the text not only is a God of Thunder, but of Rock and Roll as well.

Perhaps we then have come to an end. Heavy metal managing is nothing but an attempt to become a god. When I succeed, I have the power to empower you and destroy you. I can rebel and turn my back against everyone, competitors, suppliers, legislators, and so on, because I walk my own path. I stay true to my cause, whatever it might be and do business my way. When challenged I can overthrow and kill everything established. I have the right to shout, yell and generally cause rumble wherever I go, since *my* feelings are important. Compared to other gods, I am the 'real' god, since I am not like them, weak and light-hearted, but strong, so strong. I certainly am spiritual and able to hammer what is important into the heads of other people. On and off however, I am fun and I am having fun, at least until the lights go down and the music stops. Then I am alone. But that does not matter, since all in all it is just a fairytale, a saga, a fantastic journey in and through spectacles with no other meaning than...

Notes

1. Members of Stryper are outspoken Christians. For a discussion about 'white metal', see Luhr (2005).
2. See Arnett (1996) for remarks concerning that songs often are telling stories *about*, not *glorifying* or *promoting*, Satan.

3
The Superheroes

Henrietta Nilson

What is a Warrior of light? Each and everyone who understands the miracle of life, who fights for what is right and who never gives up until reaching their goal. Warriors of light have dreams, dreams of being able to obtain their goals and win the appreciation they deserve. They would never be able to accept that people are brought low by drunkenness, loneliness or other wretchedness; to resign themselves to the unacceptable doesn't bear thinking about. They are aware of their strengths and weaknesses, do not devote themselves to wasting time on struggles they know they cannot win, but instead convince their opponents how little there is to gain by fighting. On the other hand, when they have carefully thought through their decisions they don't wait for their realization; the right decision yields a profit and a wrong one a loss, and also more knowledge and wisdom that can be used the next time. (Coelho, 2003).

So, can Warriors of light also be superheroes who use their strength to make changes, improve the present and spread their light? Can the superhero, like the Warrior of light, see the world the way a child does and make it a better place, without bitterness? Warriors of light, superheroes, and fellow humans – all can wear the same hat. Everyday life holds encounters, thoughts and dreams of a better world, a better workplace, a different way of seeing the day. I present here my own three Warriors of light, whom I have chosen to call superheroes, each of them having contributed a fictive narrative. The narratives recount the day in their lives they became superheroes, and the ways in which they wanted life to be at work. In this narrative collage (Kostera, 2006) I respond with my own narrative. The narratives have then been interpreted by two more superheroes, Joakim Larnö and Peter Tillström, who have produced works of art in their illustrations of each story.

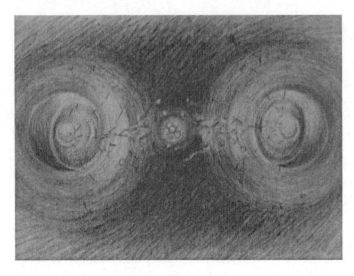

Figure 3.1   Meaningless lives by Peter Tillström

Story by Agneta Lindberg, superhero – Meaningless lives

Warriors of light often ask themselves what they are doing here. Often they find their lives meaningless. (Coelho, 2003, p. 168)

I woke up this morning and found, to my great delight, that I am a superhero, so when I get to work today, as personnel manager, I will immediately request a meeting with our CEO, known within the company as Sir. Today I have the inner strength and courage that I have lacked in all my previous meetings with Sir. I've lost count of all the times I have been forced to retreat under a barrage of sarcastic remarks, or had my head bitten off for conveying the other employees' ideas for changes and improvements.

The company I work for is completely without strategies or objectives in the matter of staff development and welfare, environmental health, and so on. You see, Sir thinks that he, and he alone, is the only one who has any say in such matters. Once, when I passed on a complaint from a member of staff, he took me to one side and spat in my ear, 'We bosses have to stick together . . .'

Now, Sir has granted me a couple of hours this morning for a briefing. Strong in my new guise of superstar, I feel none of the discomfort and dread I usually experience as I make my way to his office. The long corridor I pass along is badly lit; we really must review the lighting at work. There's certainly a lot to do, both in our working environment and within the establishment.

I knock twice on the solid oak door, 'Come in' resounds from within. Sir regards me – scrutinizes me as I sit down at the conference table, emanating self-confidence. Does he notice the change in my manner? Does he see the self-assurance and determination, qualities that I have never before shown? I must say that, unfortunately, this is the reason why every meeting on such matters has ended in crushing retreat and humiliation on my part. At every meeting, Sir's total lack of empathy and understanding for his staff has just made him get angry and, having no counter arguments, he assumes a rigid position of defence, where any exchange of information is useless – he simply does not listen. However, today I'm charged up. I take immediate command, present argument upon argument and, believe it or not, he lets me speak without interruption. From the dog-eared file that I have taken along to his office so many times before, with zero results, I pull out document after document and place them before him. Papers that we have all worked long and hard with, reflecting the staff's hopes, requests, suggestions and ideas. He is silent – unusually silent – giving the occasional comment of 'Yes, that's true' – 'That's correct'. A feeling of victory starts to well up inside me. Have I got through at last? Can we finally get started on the work that other establishments do as a matter of course? Has he really realized that it's time now? Deep down inside, he must see that it is all purely for the good of the company, for its expansion and securing its future.

A pleasant glow pervades his office. Sir has a wonderful open fireplace and the warmth from its crackling fire is removing the chill coming from the drafty windows and floor. 'Well', I conclude, 'if we agree on all these matters, I think it would be fitting that you, as CEO, be the one to share this good news with the staff tomorrow afternoon at the Christmas coffee break. It would be a great surprise, and a Christmas present they'd really appreciate!' He scrutinizes me again. 'Of course I'll tell them.' Sir is unrecognizable. Could it be that he even has a tiny bit of respect for me? We shake hands and I leave the room feeling victorious.

It seems to me that I have grown a little this morning. I return to my desk, look around, and greet everyone I see with triumph. I have won – I have got him on our side. But I won't utter a word to anyone yet – wait just a little while. I get on with the day's work. It's all so easy today – today, problems are so simple to tackle. It is afternoon and already thick darkness has descended. And yet, I think I see a light at the end of the tunnel – yes, I even woke up this morning with the feeling of being invincible. Sir and I are in agreement that the New Year would be a good time to start building teams and setting out objectives for sweeping changes at work. I look for my 'staff welfare' file – of course, I left it in Sir's office. I won't get it now. He probably needs this evening to go through all the viewpoints and suggestions for measures that need to be taken; material that I have long been amassing but that he has never before shown an interest in. Yet today, he approved the entire package – with few comments – and no objections.

No insinuations. Superhero? Me? Well, why not?

It is well into the evening and all the rooms are pitch black – next year we'll have pretty advent lights everywhere – I decide that now – and of course we have to have a Christmas tree in the entrance. One last thing before I go home – send a group mail to all our employees. I can already feel the looks of admiration when my colleagues arrive tomorrow – all the back-patting – all of them saying: 'Fantastic! Well done! You superhero!'.

'I hereby announce that Sir, will be informing you of an impending program of extensive improvements and changes for staff and workplace at the Christmas coffee break tomorrow. A decision that Sir and I, the undersigned, have taken this day.' NN – a little formal – but, whatever.

All at once I hear a familiar sound – a text message on my mobile phone. I read:

> Taking my Christmas leave now. Motoring to mountain cabin.
> Tell staff a Merry Christmas and happy New Year from me. Sir.

I race down the corridor to Sir's office. The door is ajar. The room is in darkness. Of course, he's not there. But in the dying embers of the fire I make out a few burnt fragments that were once the contents of my file. Sadly, at the end of the day, a psychopathic boss can manipulate even a superhero.

* * *

What good am I as a superhero, when everything I do is so meaningless? This fantastic superhero tries in vain to change old habits and ways and doesn't ever give up.

It could be said that the boss in the big room is modern, in so far as he is constantly moving. Just when you think that he has stopped to listen, and try to understand, a second later it is obvious that this isn't the case at all. The modern world fights a really hard battle between reality and all its ugliness, and beauty with the vision (Bauman, 1999).

Figure 3.2 Celebrating by Joakim Larnö

Story by Eva Nilsson, superhero – Celebrating

> When the warrior of light wins a battle, the warrior celebrates. (Coelho, 2003, p. 208)

I woke up this morning and found, to my great delight, that I am a superhero, so when I get to work today, I'll open lots of champagne. My co-workers and I will celebrate the fact that we have finally succeeded in designing a bed that together with the shakespur, cures all known forms of cancer.

The story began with an ordinary man named Tom Svenson. Tom had contacted us at The Bed Experts Inc. and requested a meeting. He convinced us that by using an as-yet untested method, 'miracles' could be performed. The secret lay in a potion obtained from the shakespur and 24 hours' sleep in a specially constructed bed that commenced a process of purification.

Tom told us about his old grandmother Anna, who had lived alone for many years in a cottage in the country. Using her experience and his mother's help, she would gather certain herbs that would then be dried and prepared for winter storage. Anna's favourite herb had been the 'shakespur'. The shakespur is yellow in color, consisting of clusters of flowers that produce berries after flowering. The berries are black, but the plant produces a yellowish drink, either a tea made from the leaves or a cordial made from the berries. Anna had told Tom of the herb's amazing power to reduce the size of swellings (tumours), in the people who came to see her. Furthermore, Anna said that as they drank the shakespur potion, she would gently rock them to sleep in a certain way. When her patients awoke after 24 hours' rest, Anna could declare that the tumors had either diminished in size or disappeared. Naturally, Tom was highly sceptical of Anna's story, and after having pondered over it for many years, had forgotten it.

John and Tom had been best friends ever since school. When John's little girl was afflicted by a very strange swelling in her throat a year ago, and the doctors told the parents that it was incurable cancer, Tom remembered Anna's story. Of course, Tom had to try to help the child of his best friend somehow . . . but how? Tom recalled Anna's cottage in the woods, but he was not entirely sure of its whereabouts. For a week he scoured maps and country lanes, and spoke to many old people living in the area. At last, after great pains, he succeeded in finding his way to a croft dwelling, long since burned down. He was not entirely sure what the shakespur looked like, but he knew that it was yellow and produced berries in late summer. As luck would have it, it was late summer when he began his search.

Tom was overjoyed when, growing beneath a birch tree, he found huge quantities of black shakespur berries. He fetched the woven basket that his grandmother had once given him, and started picking the somewhat dry berries. It wasn't long until the basket was full. With his feelings of expectancy rising, Tom hurried home to his kitchen. He picked over the berries, rinsed and boiled them up and then strained off the juice. And that was just the beginning . . .

According to Anna, the patient had to be rocked to sleep in a certain way. This dispersed the potion throughout the body in a special way, and commenced a purification process that eliminated the spread of the cancer, and caused the tumours to vanish. And this is where we at The Bed Experts come in. Tom wanted to simulate the rocking movement by using a specially constructed bed, and as we are the market leaders in hospital beds in Sweden, we were the obvious choice.

I tried to relate the story to the board members. They had to be informed, because the development department has to prioritize projects according to the best payoff time on investments. That is all that matters in the hard world of finance. Not surprisingly, not one of them was prepared to believe or back this cock and bull tale. How was I going to be able to help Tom? After a week of deliberation, I decided to discuss it with our heads of marketing, development and production. Everybody understood that it wasn't just about helping Tom – the survival of our company under Swedish management was also at stake. In the last two years our margins had shrunk considerably, and there was talk in the corridors of our being in the risk zone for big changes. It wasn't as hard to motivate my colleagues as I had initially thought it would be.

Now began the real work! For three months, every possible solution was outlined and calculated. We could only use evenings and weekends because obviously the project couldn't interfere with our ordinary jobs! In the meantime, Tom told us that John's daughter was getting worse. We were in a race against time.

Even today, in the light of our success, I can still hear the cries of despair in the first two months of searching, for the right components for the computer programs. Our 'prototype' bed fell apart no fewer than three times due to problems with the joints, which meant we had to start all over again with new materials and new suppliers.

We regained our courage and found new reserves of strength after visiting John's daughter and seeing how she was just getting worse and worse. Giving up never came into the equation. We have tested the bed and the incredible powers of the shakespur. After five courses of treatment, John's daughter's tumour has vanished, and the team has secured The Bed Expert's Swedish production. What's more, as the icing on the cake, today we were awarded a diploma that 'those who venture to do the impossible' are given for successful projects contributing to the preservation of mankind!

* * *

When the fight is finally over and the triumph of victory comes, the warrior celebrates. (Coelho, 2003). Helping people in times of adversity is our superhero's motive to perform great accomplishments.

Profits, moral actions and solidarity are sides of a company's daily activity that don't usually fit together. Either you support people in the establishment with no thought of reimbursement, or the desire for gain is the major driving force, and the moral standpoint has to take a back seat (Bauman, 1990).

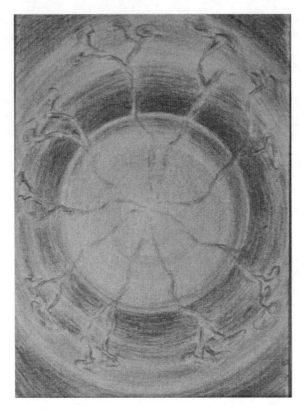

Figure 3.3   Living two lives by Peter Tillström

Story by Martin Blom, superhero – Living two lives

> Sometimes the warrior feels as if he were living two lives at once. (Coelho, 2003, p. 180)

I woke up this morning and found, to my great delight, that I am a superhero, so when I get to work today, I will arrive with that certain air that makes people sit up and take notice. Something special has happened to me, that special something that makes things happen in the way I want. Everything I've dreamed of since childhood is about to be realized, due to the extraordinary, thrilling new insight I have into what it is that makes things happen. Now, in my future dream, as I see myself arriving at work, I feel inspired to tell you what's going to take place.

The first thing I do, while I'm looking for a parking space, is look for a special one. A space with both sunlight and shade, so the beauty of the three dimensional scene enriches my eyes. The astonishing effect of nature changes my brain, as well as my perception of the present moment in encounters with my colleagues. I'm going to find that space, right enough. When I've parked I will sit for a moment, just drinking in the sun's rays streaming through the leafy trees. I will think what a wonderful day it is, another day in paradise I say to myself and smiling, I open the door. I feel wonderfully mystical. What is this amazing thing that is taking place? Am I dreaming, or is this dream real?

The first person I meet is Alfred, an elderly, smallish man with a gleam in his eye. As we say good morning to each other I notice he gives a slight nod. Next comes Emma, who also says good morning, plus a little comment – I'm tired today – haven't slept all night – I've got a lot to do today, you know, and so on. I listen to the way they speak, to their opening remarks, their voices, and way they accentuate their words. I truly believe, that last night's dream, and my thoughts on how things are realized, is here right now. I just have to be alert. One by one, people drop into the office, all with their own rituals. Some never say anything, which I also find inspiring. I wonder what is actually going on here, and how I can influence the situation so that the energy in the room is as positive as possible. All of a sudden the feeling comes again, stronger this time, and a voice from nowhere says – this is your real life, everything else is just fantasy ... make the most of the day ... live for the moment ... I am electrified, my senses ignite, and I see and hear things with such clarity, such depth, such intensity that I am practically struck dumb. I feel incredibly centred within the room, I feel calm, and yet elated. The walls in the room take on new meaning, I start to understand how Einstein felt, lost in his reveries. This is happening, and simultaneously, everything else is distinctly present. 'Have I become a superhuman, or have I always been one?' are the thoughts that occur to me. Speaking of time, it feels like I am traveling at the speed of light, and everything else is moving in slow motion. Can it be as Albert wondered, what happens if I travel at the speed of light and see myself in a mirror?

At coffee time I not only see, but hear everything going on in the room more clearly. Most of the middle-aged and over people always sit at the same places around a table. When they queue up for coffee, I know from the way they move and chat what they're going to do. There's Benny, always out of puff, who always sinks down into a chair so that the lower part of his chest is almost below his navel. He has spoken on occasion about getting into shape. 'Damn,' he says, 'think how much more we'd be able to do if we were fitter. But we're not 20 any more.' And although he laughs, he puts on a brave face. Meanwhile, something astonishing is taking place; people move differently, they change their positions, and smile a little scornfully at him, while at the same time nodding I know, I feel the same way … As I watch the drama unfold, it takes on a whole new meaning.

People are as set in their ways as programmed robots, and it's probably other people doing the programming. Where is humankind heading? And where is our planet heading if we are apparently so easily controlled? The more aware I become of what's happening in the room, the more I understand. My senses are so acute, that I even see how certain people in the room are breathing at the same time. What could I do at this moment, to give those people over there a feeling of optimism?

From morning coffee to going home, the whole day is one big thanksgiving, with all the wonderful moments that are long, yet still unbelievably quick, all the seconds that occur when you allow your senses to be clearer. Since that day I have a healthier and more open mind and I have been able to escape becoming a robot programmed by others, a robot that would still have to take the consequences of his actions. With everyone I meet I can now experience so much more, and this has led to much stronger relationships.

* * *

Time exists in the here and now. The best thing a person has is his time, the fairest division of natural resources. To devote time to someone is to give of yourself. The superhero tries to find a way to influence those around him. In every business, individuals use their own special way to communicate, which can be body language or the vocabulary they normally use. The superhero wants to change the behaviour he sees, and he also knows that transportation through time and space is possible. We can govern how the future will appear via the actions we can affect today (Normann, 2001). The hero's mental images, (Johansson *et al.*, 2007), mean he can see into the future and work out how he would like it to be. In this way, time is not something that turns like the hands of a clock, but is rather more of a linear function, where the present is part of the past, the current time and all that is to come (Normann, 2001).

Figure 3.4   Universe Conspires by Joakim Larnö

Story by Henrietta Nilson, Superhero – Universe conspires

> When somebody wants something, the whole Universe conspires in
> their favor. The warrior of light knows this. (Coelho, 2003)

I woke up this morning and found, to my great delight, that I am a
superhero, so when I get to work today my colleagues will all dive on me
to find out if the presentation is today. Great things are expected and job
satisfaction has increased immensely since I introduced the new ideas.

The Sanctuary, as I call it, the new room for thinking, has turned out
well. The writer's corner that I have set up is much used and frequented by
nearly everyone in the company. What's in there? Well, believe it or not,
there is a beautiful file containing the fictive narratives written by the
employees. They come here in their lunch hours, coffee breaks and even
when they have finished for the day. There are the most amazing narratives; you'd never believe the crazy ideas people have. I usually go there
myself when I get to work in the morning. First I have a quiet cup of coffee

and then I sit in the beautifully furnished Sanctuary, and start browsing through the file. Nicer colours on the walls, rotating work schedules, massage for the staff, are just some of the ideas that are written down.

Yes, there's the one that we started working with. Ha! It is great to see the new strengths that everyone has found, and everyone feels that they are seen now. Not just seen by their supervisors, but by the whole company. Linda is something of a girl Friday and, before the arrival of the Sanctuary, she wasn't all that happy with her situation. Ask yourself, in all honesty, what's it really like working in an office, carrying out pretty simple tasks? A place where you are hardly noticed, not even when the boss goes by. For some strange reason, there is always a wall for them to look at, instead of the person who is sitting there working. It's funny how you react, by trying to raise the tasks you're doing to a slightly higher level, mainly to make your own efforts seem more important than they really are. When you get that far, you can probably say that any small inaccuracies you may find suddenly become very big, and take up much of the time you spend at your desk. Well, that's what life was like for Linda, and it really is an overstatement to say that she was happy at work. The people there are really nice, but as for the rest of it . . .

Today it's Linda's turn to give her talk and I'm really looking forward to hearing how she's organized it. In the Sanctuary, someone came up with a great idea – a study, to be carried out in working hours!

> The study shall be carried out in the same way as papers are written at university. Each position in the company has specific areas on which you can study relevant literature. You shall also visit similar work-places and talk to people who have the same, or equivalent, positions, in order to form an impression of how you can change, improve or actually feel content with the way you work today. In this way, instead of going around throughout your career wishing for something else, you will have the chance to look at your own situation, and then see yourself in a wider perspective and compare the two. The idea is that this will produce a better workforce with people who are happier both with their jobs and their own contribution. The study will go on for ten weeks, and will later be presented to all the employees at work. Giving a presentation allows a person the chance to grow and have the opportunity to try something new. The studies will then be saved and be made available for reading in the lovely setting of the Sanctuary.

She has really excelled herself, spending weeks reading the literature concerned with her profession. It was difficult at first, but once she had got going, she sat buried in her books the whole time. Expressing herself in writing is one of her strong points, so it will be fun to read her whole study, and it's great that she can make use of her hidden talents in this way. She has paid five visits to different companies in the region, and she has really had the chance to carry out all the interviews she wanted. I believe that she has made a lot of new contacts who have also become good friends of hers.

I step up to the podium, which has the appearance of a little stage. I have butterflies in my stomach when I see all the expectant faces turned towards me. 'I'd like to welcome everyone, all the staff sitting here, and our CEO, of course, to this fantastic moment in our company. It is an honour to introduce our second study here at work, and it is a special pleasure for me to stand here and give you the contributor of essay number two. Since introducing the Sanctuary and writer's corner, we have had an incredible amount of ideas for the company. For now, we could say that the most popular idea has been these studies. The person who came up with this excellent initiative still wishes to remain anonymous. In spite of this, we would all like to thank this person, whoever you are, for great performance and a fabulous contribution. Well, as we all know, Linda is going to present her study, called "Small gestures in a large firm". I think that we are all on tenterhooks and looking forward to her findings. It will be available in the writer's corner in the Sanctuary, where you can read it for yourselves properly later on. So, without further ado, may I say: "Welcome on stage to tell us about your study entitled: Small gestures in a large firm, Lind Johnson!"'

Susanna, the personnel manager, approaches me and whispers in my ear: 'Guess what? Sven's just told me he wants to do the next study ...'

* * *

Are there possibilities for Sanctuaries at work? No, I think not. People in management ought to have open minds, see the individual and have the confidence and courage to examine their own company, as well as their own contributions to others.

In an organization full of individuals, how can one individual stand out? Every position in the organization is looking out for itself, is self-fulfilling and constantly searching for a place in the spotlight being sent out by the top boss. The virtual world of the organization is built up from the individuals' possibilities for positioning. Whether they later prove to be competent and fit to hold this status is another matter entirely. In our daily work a great deal of energy is spent on protecting our standpoints so to avoid being exposed as someone unsuitable. What this means is that every lower level position is oppressed, and is kept down by whoever is temporarily on a higher level. The flat organization is a brave attempt at change, yet positioning then occurs in other places within the organization, such as in the coffee room. Benevolence, affinity and a feeling of unity are fundamental qualities if creativity is to flourish (Kostera, 2005) but egoism and the individual's fight for his or her own good makes this impossible. We only behave like good individuals if there is something in it for us.

Maybe, there are no opportunities to implement a Sanctuary; superheroes do exist, but maybe we are living a myth if we believe that we can change the establishment. We long for a better world, but the fact that we are prepared to give a little of ourselves is maybe the thing that makes the idea of the Sanctuary, superheroes and change continue to be what it has been up till now: A myth.

4

Cats, Turtles, Grinches and Pachyderms: Mythical Inspirations for Organizational Realities in Dr Seuss

Jo A. Tyler

The literature we read as children is densely populated with archetypal characters, mythical characters that serve as inspiration for organizational realities, leaders, loners and lovers among them. While some people may have vivid memories of the Ugly Duckling, the boy with his finger in the dyke, or the various villains from the Brothers Grimm, it is the characters of Dr Seuss who remain most active in my imagination and indeed at times, seem to possess it.

Loners and lovers. Over the years, I have seen these diverse temperaments in the people I have followed, and I have exhibited them personally when I have been asked to lead. The scholarly literature teaches us that both these temperaments, loner and lover, are desirable temperaments, and that leaders are at their best when they manifest both, each in its time and place, based on situations and contingencies (Hughes *et al.*, 1998). I did not really need the theory however. I had already learned this, as a child, from Dr Seuss.

Not long ago, I was writing an article for publication when a connection to *Bartholomew and the Oobleck* (Seuss, 1949) seized my imagination so thoroughly I could not continue until I included a quote from the Magicians of Mystic Mountain Meekacave (1949, p. 18). By the time the article was finished, the quote no longer served as the minor transition I had intended. It had become the introduction. Moreover, it had re-insinuated itself in my conclusion, completing its circumscription of my ideas. The power of these characters to co-opt my writing, to wrestle with me about their positioning until they had climbed up the lines on the page, like rungs on a ladder to the very top, struck me as curious. Their energy left me musing about the influence the stories and characters of our childhood have on us as adults working in, and especially leading, organizations.

Dr Seuss's early stories, from the late 1930s to the early 1960s, were a significant part of the mythical landscape of literary post-World War II America. The whimsical characters, inventive language, simple rhythms, rhymes, and morals made Seuss stories an engaging supplement to the boring basal readers in vogue in public schools across America during this period (Hastings, 1998). At school, we would suffer through the lacklustre days of Dick, Jane, and Spot, but we would come home to Dr Seuss. His books presented us, the children of postwar America – as well our parents who read to us, and our own children, to whom we read (Inskeep, 2004) – with a wealth of archetypal characters common to the world of organizations and organizing, and to leaders in particular. The people who read these books as children in the 1950s and 1960s have grown up. They are leading our institutions – of commerce, of learning, of social service – and they have had their archetypal memories tickled not by the flat, matter-of-factness of Dick and Jane, but by the antics of the more robust characters conceived by Dr Seuss.

Much has been written about Dr Seuss as a socio-political commentator (Nel, 2002, 2005). Here, I want to depart from that level of critique, considering instead the way these characters influenced the manner in which we thought about leaders as we grew up and, as adults, inform our own leadership temperaments, be they free-agent entrepreneurs, lonely autocrats, loving, servant leaders or at some stage of development between these. Not only can we find these archetypes in our own approaches to follower-relations, we can spot them in the people around us. That is what I am going to do in this chapter. I want to show you some people I have spotted who personify four of the best-known Dr Seuss characters: the entrepreneurial Cat in the Hat, the autocratic Yertle the Turtle, the evolving Grinch and the integrated servant-elephant named Horton.

The entrepreneurial cat

The Cat in the Hat (Seuss, 1957) opens with a brother and sister home alone, bored. The Cat in the Hat comes to the door announcing his intention to play new games and do new tricks. Ignoring the hesitancy of the children and the admonishment of their pet fish, the Cat creates havoc all in the name of fun. The children are petrified, and the fish harps at them to make the Cat stop. As the mother approaches the house and the Cat realizes he is not wanted, he retreats, seeming to leave the children on their own to account to their mother for the mess. The children are scared, but the Cat suddenly reappears with the resources for a last-minute remedy, declaring, 'I always pick up all my playthings' (Seuss, 1957, p. 57). He cleans up the mess and disappears, just in the nick of time. The Cat is a classic entrepreneur. He loves the beginnings of things. The Cat loves risk. He loves to play, and at his best, he knows just when to move on. The modus operandi of this sort of leader is to see how much they can get done, how fast. They know that creativity is a messy process, and they know how to pick up their playthings so they are not caught.

As a consultant, I worked with a Cat in the Hat named Faith. Faith was the founder of a regional restaurant chain. She was an inspirational leader, charismatic and smart. She had vision and a strong sense of play. Her restaurants were places for food, but also for family and fun. A cartoon logo, quirky names for the food, and special menus for children were a hallmark. The concept was a success. She built a small board of advisors who recommended gradual growth, but for Faith the fun was embedded in novelty and in getting things going. Once a restaurant was up and running, she got an itch to start another, and another, each with its own challenging location. Faith's frazzled management team watched as each year the startup costs ate into the profits that their hard work had yielded. They would despair, but just as they reached the point of departure, Faith would take them on a retreat to thank them for their hard work and in the face of her enthusiasm and charm, they would plan for the next new restaurant. When her board recommended against the rapid growth, she dismantled her board. Finally, with the organization in a tailspin from three new openings in one year, Faith stepped aside. Like the Cat returning with his amazing clean-up machine, she appointed a new leader from inside the firm, a loyal executive with a steady hand and firm focus, who she knew could clean up her mess. He pulled the balance sheet back into the black, while Faith experimented with new ways to leverage her brand, and new ideas for different types of restaurants that could expand the family.

Like Faith, the Cat in the Hat is eager to take risks, much to the chagrin of other stakeholders. He is a high energy, inventive, confident authority figure with strong opinions about how to get things done and a tenacity that overcomes resistance. We do not ever learn from Dr Seuss what the children tell their mother about their day, but there is a second book called *The Cat in the Hat Comes Back*. It is a different version of the same tale, and in so being it gives us the clear sense that the Cat keeps moving from one house to another, trying out new games and tricks. The Cat is not interested in leading for the long term, and he cannot be bothered negotiating or with learning what it takes to manage without a mess.

Since Seuss's Cat is mostly interested in play and possibility, he does not need to learn about staying power, about sustainability. We do not see the Cat actually learning and developing because there is no clear reason to do so. He is, however, obviously bright and inventive, with the potential to learn whatever he believes will help him in his quest for fun. He is charismatic so he gets his way. He understands the power of stirring things up, and he is confident that he can clean up any mess he creates. Most importantly, the Cat gets to have fun. Entrepreneurial leaders can learn to stay connected for the long term, but it is a choice (Swiercz and Lydon, 2002).

Some children may identify with the sensible, pedantic warnings of the pet fish (Menand, 2002). In the name of balance, however, there will always be a group of children who envy the Cat's sensibilities, his creativity, and his ability to take the lead in the face of dissension.

These children will grow up to see organizations as playgrounds for play, as laboratories for experiments, and as launch pads for skydiving because they believe the message that you can do what you like, all in the name of fun, just so long as you slip out at the right moment. And they will recognize that it is easier to slip out if you slip out alone.

The autocratic turtle

In *Yertle the Turtle* (Seuss, 1950), we learn that Yertle is the king of a little pond, ruling over all that he sees. He decides that if he could see more, he could be the king of more. He orders the turtles in the pond to pile on one another so that he can, despite their complaints, climb up their backs for a better view. The view is fabulous, but when Mack, the smallest turtle at the bottom of the pile, burps, the pile tumbles. Yertle falls from his perch into the pond and becomes 'King of the Mud. That is all he can see' (Seuss, 1991, p. 179).

While the Cat in the Hat is interested in the power of ideas and the events that make them manifest, for Yertle leadership is associated with power that is more absolute: power over people that is measured in span-of-control. The interpretation of Yertle as Hitler is a common one (Nel, 2005), but for our purposes, we need only consider leaders we have actually known. They certainly abound in business organizations, which become sand boxes for accumulating power through domination and subjugation. The Yertle archetype is the quintessential 'bad manager' who wants power because of what it can bring in terms of prestige and possession. It seems that everyone has a story of a totally autocratic boss, his or her own personal Yertle. Here is the story of one I knew. I will call him Michael.

Michael rose through the ranks selling office-automation products until, by his own account; he was 'the greatest salesman ever'. So good that he was asked to train others in his techniques, Michael eventually took a job as a training director with a precision engineering firm. It was a big job in a macho organization that had a push to recruit women into management to satisfy the parent company's diversity requirements. In need of a training manager, Michael offered a job to Sally, and was congratulated by the president for 'finding some female talent'. In addition, Michael received a nice bonus, which he referred to as a bounty, for bringing a woman manager on board. Sally soon learned that she had been hired not because of her credentials, but to net Michael the bonus for hiring a woman. Michael was relentlessly dissatisfied with Sally's efforts to meet his dictatorial demands, and Michael threatened her verbally and physically behind closed doors, insisting on compliance. Ultimately, he literally exiled her to a sideline project in a remote part of the country. Stuck in the mid-west, Sally learned that Michael had been promoted, and was flaunting his larger office, the coveted company car, and a bloated staff who suffered fearfully under his arrogance. Two years later, no longer under Michael's thumb, Sally received a phone call from a colleague in Human Resources. 'Listen,' her colleague implored. Sally heard the scraping of steel file cabinet drawers and the rustling of papers. Then the colleague's voice returned. 'Did you hear that? That was me taking Michael's file out of the executive drawer and putting it in the management file two drawers down. Too bad you can't see me deleting him from the succession plan. They're making him sit in a cubicle and give back his car. How great is that?'

'Ding dong,' Sally replied, invoking a story from her childhood. 'The witch is dead.'

We can assert that Yertle is a leader insofar as he compels all the turtles from his pond, and beyond, to do his bidding. However, he does not care about those other turtles any more than Michael cared what Sally or his other employees could really offer the organization. These are leaders with an eye turned only toward what is good for themselves, and what they believe will be good is bound up with the material aspects of power, the trappings: what Yertle can see, what Michael's bonus will buy, his company car, and large staff. In their desire for a better view/office, Yertle and Michael neglect their followers, until the followers can no longer bear to serve them. Greed muffles complaints from below until a seemingly insignificant act from a seemingly insignificant worker stimulates downfall – into the mud, and into a lower drawer of the HR file cabinet. Yertle is a quintessential autocrat, a dictatorial leader whose ego and greed are eventually overcome by the power of the marginalized worker. By illustrating the social extremes of the organization – with Yertle at the top and Mack literally buried at the bottom – Seuss makes clear the notion that this sort of power is a fragile illusion, the stability of which lies not with the leader but with the followers, who ultimately make a voluntary rather than contractual choice (Kelley, 1998). While the Cat is fascinated by the result of his actions, by the changes he can affect, Yertle is only interested in one sort of outcome: personal power and prestige.

We grow up knowing that we do not want to be Yertle. We do not want to hurt Mack. In this story, however, we are not taught any alternatives. We learn nothing more about Yertle from Seuss, perhaps because there is so little to say about the King of the Mud. Yertle does not appear to learn anything from his fall (nor does Michael, who went on to become 'the best salesman ever' at another company). Yet we know that lonely autocrats can learn. We know it because Dr Seuss shows us, in another story, in the character of the lonely, jealous green Grinch.

The evolving Grinch

In *How The Grinch Stole Christmas* (Seuss, 1957), we learn that the Grinch lived on an icy peak high above Who-ville. The thing the Grinch hated most was Christmas. The thing the Whos loved most was Christmas. The Grinch decided he would steal Christmas from Who-ville. He enlists the help of his dog Max, and on Christmas Eve they pillage Christmas. They take all the trees, all the packages and all the lights – every reminder of Christmas. They pack it onto a sled, and the Grinch commands Max to drag it up the mountain. The next morning the Grinch is shocked to hear the Whos singing their Christmas song. The Grinch, who has been waiting eagerly to hear their cries of anguish at the disappearance of Christmas, goes down into the village to see what is happening. He learns that Christmas is more about a connection between people than about the presents and the trees and the trimmings. He is filled with remorse. He and Max return the property, and are welcomed into the singing circle of Whos. His previously shrunken heart grows three times its size.

This kind of transformation really happens. We tend to be sceptical of it when we see it occurring, but it occurs nonetheless. Here is the story of a Fortune 500 CEO I worked with, who transformed himself from a loner into a lover, who gathered up his bravery and like the Grinch, made amends.

In the course of 30 years, Ab had risen from selling products on the street to running the company. Playing golf one day on the local course he overheard a group talking about a leader who was bad for business, disconnected from his people, and who cared only about himself. They were talking about Ab. That was the day Ab learned that people called him the 'Ice Man'. Horrified by what he heard, he joined a country club across the state line, but could not shake the feeling the golf course was not the only course he needed to change. One day, hearing the tone of his own voice in an exchange with an employee, he resolved to change. The following day, in a succession-planning meeting there was much complaint about a struggling senior manager who had been with the firm for a long time, rising from the assembly line to Public Relations officer – the face and voice of the company. Ab listened intently as his team trashed their colleague. Everyone wanted the head of PR to be yesterday's news.

Finally, Ab spoke up. 'What's happening here is my fault. I made a mistake. I put him in that job. It was a bad decision.' All eyes were on him. Here was their CEO declaring in public that he had made a mistake. 'I didn't want to go outside. He was expedient, and I backed him into a corner where he could not really say no. He didn't want the job, and I was wrong to make him take it.' The silence in the room seemed to deepen. 'We're not going to fire him. I'm going to talk to him. I'm going to tell him that I'm sorry about the way things have turned out, and I'm going to ask him what he wants to do. When he tells me, I'm going to pay attention to the answer.' This, from the Ice Man.

Still, everyone speculated about Ab's follow through. Surely it would, like so many other things, be overcome by events. Next month at this time the guy would probably still be here, and the next month after that. Someone proposed a wager, but three days later Ab announced that a conversation had occurred and described the plan that would help the PR officer to exit with integrity. No one could believe it, but it was the first of many surprises that heralded the thawing of the Ice Man. At the end of his career, at a party in his honour, Ab expressed relief that he had been, in a manner of speaking, saved, and that he had reconnected with the operating principles of the organization he loved before it was too late.

Grinches change and people do too. The change is often triggered by a 'disorienting dilemma' (Mezirow, 1991, p. 168), a disconnect between our assumptions and our experience. Transformative learning theory suggests that we undertake a process of evaluation, of reflection, that allows us to 'build competence ... in new roles and relationships' (Mezirow, 1991, p. 169) so that we can integrate new perspectives and action into our habits. In the context of our discussion, what seems

important is not so much the change itself, but that the change is cumulative. That is, Ab and the Grinch still know how to be autocratic, how to
be task-focused when the situation requires it (Hughes *et al.*, 1998), but
that muscle is balanced with a new one: the heart. Decisions are tem-
pered by a new layer of awareness, a layer of love for the organization/the
village and the people who comprise it.

Once you've been through an experience like the Grinch's, once your
heart has grown, you get to make choices. Ab and the Grinch both get a
chance to make amends, to do the right thing. Dr Seuss ends the Grinch's
story with his newly enlarged heart. We do not know what happens to
the Grinch after that. I have always believed that in the sequel he would
move off the mountaintop, down into Who-ville. I like to think of him
becoming Who-ville's deputy-mayor. In that role he would retain all of
his shrewdness, his cleverness, and his ability to scheme, but that these
capabilities would now be tuned differently, in a way that factors in
other people, that factors in his ability to love. In this way, he would be
transformed from the loner on the icy peak into a lover surrounded by
the warmth of the village in the valley. The Grinch has to learn about
these things, and as deputy mayor, he may be clumsy at first. Ab was
not perfect. He still lost his temper on occasion, but he had reclaimed
what was right, and when he would backslide, he would make amends.
It is possible to integrate these aspects of loner and lover smoothly. Seuss
shows us a mature leader, a servant leader (Greenleaf, 1998), in the form
of Horton the Elephant.

The servant elephant

In *Horton Hatches the Egg* (Seuss, 1940), we meet Horton, a kind elephant
convinced by a lazy bird to sit on her egg so that she can have a break.
She has such a good time on vacation that she decides not to return,
leaving Horton subject to the misery of foul weather, the ridicule of
his friends, and even the taunts of circus audiences. The lonely Horton
suffers for nearly a year, but is resolute: 'I meant what I said,/ and I said
what I meant .../An elephant's faithful/One hundred percent' (Seuss,
1991, p. 110). Just as the egg begins to hatch, the lazy bird comes back,
eager to reclaim her egg. Horton is vindicated when the fledging looks
a lot like him and the circus owners return him to his home with his
elephant-bird offspring. Horton was an elephant of his word.

Once you meet Horton and you know about how he hatches the egg,
it is not a far stretch to learn that in *Horton Hears a Who* (Seuss, 1954),
Horton rescues, at his own peril, an entire tiny community of Whos,

living in a speck of dusk. In that story, Horton climbs a high mountain 'that tattered his toenails and battered his bones' (Seuss, 1996) because he knows that these are 'little folks, who have as much right to live as us bigger folks do' (Seuss, 1996). In both stories, Horton is the subject of ridicule. Still, he perseveres.

There are leaders who do balance morality and virtue with hard decisions, the needs of individuals with the needs of the business. They may not be common, but they are out there. I have met a few. Let me tell you a little about Dave.

Dave had been a seminary student before he got his MBA. He believed he could apply his values to bring about social change in organizations, change that would benefit the people and the bottom line. He rose to Senior Vice President of Human Resources in a Fortune 500 company. In a debate about how to handle a group of long-service employees who were about to be laid off, Dave suggested that they should be able to get their full retirement. The suggestion was typical of Dave, but received guffaws from other leaders at the meeting. Back in his own office, Dave worked out how to use his own budget to 'bridge' the longest serving employees so they could meet the terms of the retirement policy and receive full benefits. He did this quietly on the strength of his conviction, and it was the sort of decision he would make repeatedly throughout his tenure in that role. 'It's our job,' he was fond of saying, 'to look for the highroad. And when we find the highroad, it's our job to take it.'

When the new CEO blew into the organization, he had little time for Dave's high road. For all of the cultural changes Dave and his team had made to increase profits, but which also emphasized the human face of the organization, Dave's new boss expressed nothing but sarcasm and scorn. After an initial distancing, the middle managers and individual contributors began to see Dave as the heroic underdog. Like Horton tearing his toenails on the mountain, bearing up under the laughter and disdain of the circus crowds, Dave continued to take the high road. He continued to battle on behalf of the employees, ignoring the slights of his more senior colleagues. He had made a commitment to the employees when he joined the firm, and he stayed true to it, one hundred per cent. The high road led Dave to the very hearts of the employees. When he finally left the organization, employees remarked that there was no one left who would advocate for them so whole-heartedly.

Of all the characters discussed here, Horton (Seuss, 1940, 1954) was the first to be created by Seuss, and in him Seuss has successfully blended both the loner and lover archetypes in a complex, engaging and popular icon. Horton is huge in stature, gentle, generous, courageous and loyal.

In each of his stories, Horton bears ridicule, isolation and capture in order to rescue and protect – the essence of a strong leadership role. Both Dave and Horton take a stand, becoming nurturers even at the expense of their own egos and social status. In the end, they win out because they are fully integrated leaders. Greenleaf (1998) refers to these leaders as servant leaders, contending that the key to their strength, their very ability to serve others, and indeed the world, hinges on love (1998, p. 116). Horton and Dave are loners not because they are misanthropic or power hungry, but because they have the strength of conviction, and because of the very fact that they are lovers who put their word, and the interests of others, ahead of their personal discomfort. Discomfort is not a permanent condition, and Horton and Dave both end up with everything that matters.

Closing thoughts

It is not that one organization needs a leader who is a loner, while another needs a leader who is lover. Organizations, indeed followers, need their leaders to be both. The Cat can get things started, but the Cat cannot hatch the egg. The Cat is not likely to defend the Whos. Organizations need leaders who can take a stand for what they believe in it, even or especially when it is an unpopular stand. Organizations need leaders whose stand is informed by the love they have for their organizations, for the people and for the vision they share. Yertles must tumble, but Seuss teaches us that even Yertle could become Horton. The Grinch proves it.

Dr Seuss does more than successfully illustrate that these traits of loner and lover matter, that they can be developed and Hortonesquely integrated into an effective leadership style. He translates notions of power in ways that speak to children. He illustrates the relationship between power and greed, failure and love. He makes clear the reasons we take power, and shows us how to use it with care. He teaches us the right reasons to take it, and warns us that the high road of leadership is not always the easiest, but it is the most rewarding. He plants these ideas, these leadership traits, in the minds of young readers, tickling their archetypal memories and shaping the way they come to understand the leaders they follow, moulding the type of leaders they eventually become. We read these stories as children, so we think they are children's stories, but they leave their stamp on us. And we are all, I believe, better for it.

5
Possessed by the Organization? Dante's Inferno on Earth

Przemysław Piątkowski

Introduction

'Abandon all hope you who enter here' (*Inf.* 3:9)[1] – such is the warning that is inscribed on the gate to Hell in Dante's Divine Comedy; Saint Francis of Assisi was to say that 'now is the time of mercy, and afterwards of justice' (Bonaventure, 1968, p. 284). In Dante's poem, however, not only the souls entering Hell need to forget about God's mercy, the reader is also asked to 'abandon all hope' for understanding when reading *Inferno*. If understanding involves a 'movement of the mind from the sign to its significance' (Augustine, *De Doctrina Christiana*, quoted in Freccero, 1986, p. 100), then in Hell no such movement is supposed to be possible. It is a place of stasis, meaninglessness, of the literal. As pure infernal chaos is impossible to be poetically represented, Dante uses an ironic trick – reverses everything. Instead of lack of order a reversed order is presented – Hell becomes an organization.

This chapter focuses on two historical characters: Fra Alberigo and Branca d'Oria, Dante's contemporaries and damned souls according to his poetic vision. They occupy a small, but very significant place in Hell. Historically, Fra Alberigo was a member of the Manfredi family, the Guelph (supporters of the Papacy) lords of the city of Faenza. It is known that in 1267 he joined the military religious order of the Glorious Virgin Mary (the so-called Jovial Friars). Probably around 1284 he was involved in a family conflict over the lordship of the city during which Manfred, a close relative of his, plotted against him and insulted him in a public dispute. Alberigo pretended to have forgiven the insult. On the second of May 1285, however, he held a banquet to which Manfred and his son were invited. It was a trap. A few hidden assassins waited only for the host's signal (the words 'bring the fruit!') to attack. They killed father and son before Alberigo's eyes (Toynbee, 1968, p. 19). Branca d'Oria's story is very similar. He came from a very well-known Ghibeline house (supporters of the Empire) at Genoa. In 1275 he 'treacherously murdered his father-in-law, Michele Zanche, governor of Logodono in Sardinia, at a banquet to which he had invited him' (*ibid.*, pp. 109–10). Dante puts them almost at the lowest depths of Hell, in the frozen lake of Cocytus, among the worst kind of sinners – traitors. They suffer a very original punishment for what they had done – they had been thrown down to Hell before they actually died, their bodies had been 'snatched away' by demons and now they have no knowledge of how these bodies 'stand up in the world above' (*Inf.* 33:122–3).

The state of dissolution (or disintegration, division) in which the reader finds Fra Alberigo and Branca d'Oria is interesting for many reasons, but mainly because the whole story is 'unorthodox'. It does not seek to visualize the Church's teachings or Dante's personal religious beliefs; like most of Dante's writings it should rather be put and interpreted in a social and political context. The author of this text aims to explore and interpret the story of the encounter between Dante and Fra Alberigo in relation to organizations, the inspiration here is drawn mainly from two articles: 'Invoking Satan or the Ethics of the Employment Contract' (Ford and Harding, 2003) and 'The Organization and the Mouth of Hell' (Höpfl, 2005). This chapter is meant to be an (Dantesque hopefully) inversion of what has been already said about Hell and demons in the organizational context.

Ford and Harding conducted a study of a merger, but they focused on the 'human effects'. The article basing on this study was written 'in the form of a play' (entitled Invoking Satan), as it was difficult to portray pain 'in the coolness and remoteness of academic language' (2003, p. 1132). Heather Höpfl begins her text with 'flesh' (the experiences of organization) where 'there would normally be an abstract' and 'seeks to give attention to the imagery of hell and damnation in organizational language and theorization' (2005, p. 167). In both cases, although in very different ways, the interesting relation between the 'meta-physics of organizing' (*ibid.*, p. 173), also the metaphysics of an academic text, and the experience of the Hell on earth is explored.

Similarly, this chapter also seems to begin with 'flesh', with a story, but in Dante's *Inferno* it is impossible to say what is 'grounded in flesh' and what is an abstraction. So even though it is true that 'the reason why workers experience organizations as hell is precisely because of judgment and allocation' and, as a consequence, Hell can be seen as 'the result of an unjust allocation: of power, of influence, of income, of wealth' (*ibid.*, p. 173), the argument presented in this chapter has to go a step further. The author uses quotes from the two above mentioned articles as 'flesh', to establish the link to organization studies, but the aim of the chapter is different. It is argued here that not only the state of dissolution (in which Fra Alberigo and Branca d'Oria suffer their eternal punishment) can be observed in contemporary organizations, but also that Hell itself is an organization.

The story: *Inferno*, canto 33, verses 109–150

It is the eight of April of the Year of Our Lord 1300, the Good Friday of the jubilee year. 'Lost in a dark wood and threatened by three beasts, Dante is rescued by Virgil, who proposes a journey to the other world' (*Inf.* p. 3). Not long after the poet finds himself by the gate of Hell, walks through it, and starts his pilgrimage through the *Inferno*, the Purgatorio, up to the Paradiso. The story which this text refers to begins almost at the very bottom of Hell, in Ptolomea. Dante and his guide Virgil are walking on the surface of the frozen lake of Cocytus, strolling between heads of traitors, the worst of sinners – the rest of their bodies (souls?) are immersed in ice. It is dark, cold and very quiet when suddenly one of the heads starts talking to them:

> 'O cruel souls so wicked
> that you are given the lowest place of all,
>
> Lift the hard veils from off my face, that I
> may vent the grief my heart has soaked me with,
> one moment, till the tears freeze up again.'
> (*Inf.* 33:110–14).

He addresses them 'cruel, wicked souls' and this makes sense: since he finds himself almost at the very bottom of Hell and another two are going past him, logically they must have committed sins even worse than his. Nevertheless he has a favour to ask, he wants to weep, so he begs them to take ice off his eyes. Dante decides to take advantage of the situation and says:

> 'You'd like my help, then tell
> your name. If I don't clear your eyes, may I
> go to the bottom to this icy Hell!'

So he replied, 'I'm brother Alberigo,
the man who served the fruit in the bad garden.
Here I am paid back with interest, date for fig.'
        (*Inf.* 33:115–20).

He is Fra Alberigo, the pilgrim heard of him and his story. Responsible for killing his cousin, he is now paid back with interest for what he has done (dates were more valuable than figs; it is also an obvious allusion to the words 'bring the fruit!' that he used as a secret signal for the assassins). However, the most interesting part of the story is still to come, the pilgrim obviously cannot recall having heard of Alberigo's death, because he asks 'are you dead already then?' (*Inf.* 33:121). Alberigo answers:

'How my body stands
up in the world above, I do not know.

Such privilege has this realm of Ptolomea,
that oftentimes the soul drops down to Hell
before the Fates have cut the thread of life.

And that you may, with greater will, scrape off
the tears hardened to glass upon my face,
know that as soon as any soul betrays

As I betrayed, his body's snatched away
and taken by a demon, who controls it
until the time arrives for it to die.

The soul then falls headlong into this tank.
Perhaps his body still appears above,
the shade who chirps his winter song behind me.'
        (*Inf.* 33:122–35).

He must be really desperate, not only he responds to all the questions, he gives a lot of additional information as well; and to prove the truth of what he was saying, he points at another head nearby:

'You may well know, for you have just come down.
He is Ser Branca d'Oria; many years
have passed since he was thus encased in ice.'
        (*Inf.* 33:136–8).

Dante protests:

> 'I think you play me for a fool!
> For Branca d'Oria never died, but eats
> and drinks and sleeps and puts his woollens on.'
>   (*Inf.* 33:139–41).

He knows d'Oria very well; to his best knowledge he is still alive. So even if he has not taken seriously Alberigo's 'demon story' first, now he is presented with a proof and has to face the fact. The end of the story is by no means 'happy' in the traditional sense, but they are at the bottom of Hell after all. Alberigo reminds Dante why they had this conversation in the first place and again asks him to open his eyes, but Dante ignores him, says nothing and goes away explaining:

> 'And so I did not open them: to be
> villainous to him was a courtesy.'
>   (*Inf.* 33:149–50).

There are several reasons why this particular story is interesting. Dante Alighieri, without a doubt a genius poet, was at the same time a very original political thinker and an extraordinary person. Immersed in the vivid political life of 'pre-capitalist' Florence he pays a lot more attention to the institutional aspect of the Church, the empire and polis than most of the leading intellectuals of his time (mainly theologians). Being a loyal Ghibeline he defends the 'secular' authority of the Holy Roman Empire, or rather seeks to add theological and mystical dimension to what was then often considered as 'profane' – social and political side of life. At the same time the reality of the Church in the *Commedia* is mediated to the reader not through abstract theology, but through the pilgrim's encounters with saints (absence of any dialogue with the angels), Christ himself is seen through the love of Dante's life – Beatrice (Ryan, 1993, p. 150), and finally Hell represents Florence, his home city.

However, there seems to be only one main fundament on which the reasons mentioned above stand and it has a paradoxical nature. On the one hand

> Dante, a paragon of orthodoxy, is quite unorthodox in suggesting the damnation of the living. The Christian believes that until the final moment of earthly existence he can repent (Lonergan, 1977, p. 72).

On the other hand the whole text of the *Commedia* 'seems to demand [a quasi-biblical status] by claiming to be prophetic and divinely inspired' (Freccero, 1993, p. 183). Its inspiration was to come from Dante's authentic vision of Beatrice that was described at the end of *Vita Nuova*. This apparent contradiction asks for some explanation, as it has important consequences for interpretation. The problem that keeps being discussed by scholars is how to approach such a 'visionary' and autobiographical text. Dante himself in *Convivio* distinguished two types of allegory: 'of poets' and 'of theologians', and interprets his own works in terms of the former (Singleton, 1950, p. 78). He had never related this distinction to the *Commedia* and, as a result of various factors, for a long time the poem was subject to methods similar to biblical exegesis.

Dante's allegory

> [The] organisation, or perhaps more precisely capitalism, can perform the allocation of those who ascend into abstraction and are conformed to the metaphysics of organising and those who in every physical and mental respect are relegated to the torments and anguish of Hell. (Höpfl, 2005, p. 173)

Charles Singleton in his essay entitled 'Dante's Allegory' (1950) addressed this very problem. He challenged the dominating opinion among the Dantists of his time that 'the nature' of the literal level in the Divine Comedy is irrelevant for interpretation. The prevailing idea was that it does not matter if the *Commedia* on the literal level is based on true autobiographical experience of the author or poetic fiction, since in any case one has to 'enter into that willing suspension of disbelief required in reading of any poem' (*ibid.*, p. 80). Singleton claimed the opposite – the nature of the literal level determines the nature of the second meaning. Referring to Saint Augustine's distinction between meaning *in verbis* and *in factis*, he said that when approaching the Divine Comedy one has to answer this question and than face the consequences of his choice. If 'the literal is only a fiction devised to express a second meaning' (allegory of poets – 'this for that'; *ibid.*, p. 81), then it at all times has to have a second meaning. In other words, 'if it does not give another, true meaning, has no excuse for being' (*ibid.*, p. 81). The situation is different if the first level is literal *in factis* and not as a verbal structure, because then not all events 'yield the second meaning' (*ibid.*, p. 80). Singleton did not have a problem with making this decision: continuous efforts to treat the first level as fiction can only show 'how a poem may be forced to meanings that it cannot possibly bear as a poem' (*ibid.*, p. 81). There is an allegorical structure that comes first, before the verbal structure, and its main outline is simply: 'the journey to God of a man through three realms of the world', the 'other meanings' in the poem are 'the various reflections of man's journey to his proper end, not in the life after death, but here in this life' (*ibid.*, p. 82). 'With its first meaning as an historical meaning, the allegory of the Divine Comedy is grounded in the mystery of Incarnation' (*ibid.*, p. 84). It is theological allegory – 'this and that', with both meanings true, but on different levels, so to speak.

Many years later John Freccero proposed a different take on the problem. He agrees that to assume the 'historical' truth of Dante's prophetic vision means the end of the discussion, but at the same time points out that then one has to face another question – which parts of the Commedia are 'intrinsic to [Dante's] vision' (1993, p. 184)? In other words: since not all events 'yield the second meaning' (Singleton, 1950, p. 80), which of them do? Instead, Freccero proposes not to take Dante's vision for granted: 'a more sophisticated way of dealing with the theological claim is to consider it a literary device, an attempt to imitate Scripture rather than provide an account of a religious experience' (Freccero, 1993, p. 184). He also points to an essential flaw of Singleton's argument who, in his opinion, 'blurred the distinction between what seems real and what really happened' (*ibid.*, p. 184) by not taking into account the ambiguity of the word 'literal' seriously enough. 'Any meaning clearly intended by a human author is from a theological standpoint necessarily a literal meaning, even if conveyed by a most elaborate allegory of poets' (*ibid.*, p. 181). Therefore:

> No human author could possibly write theological allegory and still have any idea of its significance. It was precisely the point of theological allegory to take meaning out of the hands of an author and place it under the control of an exegetical tradition. (*ibid.*, p. 185)

There is no allegorical 'deep structure' that comes first and is reflected in the exegetical tradition, rather we deal with a type of, what Derrida called archiécriture (1976 in: Spiegel, 1990, p. 63), simply because the exegetical tradition reflects nothing else than yet another verbal structure. The *Commedia* resembles Holy Scriptures not because both share the same 'deep structure' – 'the journey to God of a man' (Singleton, 1950, p. 82), rather Dante tried to imitate the Bible 'by aspiring to its authority, not by copying its style' (Freccero, 1993, p. 187). The Divine Comedy should be read like regular poetry. Even if it is to be called 'the poetics of conversion' (Freccero, 1986, from the title of the book), it is still poetics – its verbal structure should only be 'judged by its coherence' (*ibid.*, p. 185), not placed against another structure.

To sum up, the encounter between Dante and Fra Alberigo at the bottom of Hell can be approached from two different, not necessarily contradictory standpoints. One can either assume that it is 'grounded in the flesh', in the history (Singleton, 1950, p. 83), or that Dante 'imitated the Bible by aspiring to its authority' (Freccero, 1993, p. 187). It may seem like a huge simplification, but it needs to be done for the purpose of this short text. As a consequence the story can be read either as a description of a state of mind (closer to the orthodox definition of Hell), or as a poetical (and political!) description of a place.

Ptolomea: 'The lowest place of all'

> Manager B reported that in his new post he had lost his sense of himself as a human being – he had to work as if he were a machine, and in the process he had become invisible. (Ford and Harding, 2003, p. 1137)

> [The] organization had become a blind, deaf and unethical monster. (*ibid.*, p. 1138)

> It is a monster that spreads disease. Manager B refers to 'anti-bodies in the system'. (*ibid.*, p. 1140)

Ford and Harding observed that 'portraying pain in the coolness and remoteness of academic language is difficult' (*ibid.*, p. 1132). As a poet Dante did not have such a problem, but paradoxically when describing the lower Hell he almost achieves something similar. His description 'omits no detail but uses no adjective' (Boitani, 1981, p. 88).

> Whereas before there had been activity, now there is stillness; before darkness predominated, now there is the sharp glow of ice; before several punishments were disgusting and nauseating, now, with the sinners immersed in ice, there is a sense of alienation caused by the hygiene that deep freezing induces. (Lonergan, 1977, p. 64).

Dante and Virgil are strolling among the traitors, 'the nearness of foot and head brings to mind a relevant verse from Genesis (3:15) referring to the crushing of Satan' (Lonergan, 1977, p. 65).

What the reader receives is not Dante's interpretation of reality (his vision); the description of Hell is meant to be literal. The problem is that 'poetry is itself imaginative representation' (Freccero, 1986, p. 95), it seems then impossible to poetically represent Hell – 'a place of stasis' (Ryan, 1993, p. 147), without falling deliberately into contradiction. Irony is inevitable. What we have in the Inferno are dead souls 'ironically represented as though they were living bodies' (Freccero, 1986, p. 101) and punishments that 'have little to do with moral theology and almost nothing with the physiology of pain' and simply 'fit' the crimes aesthetically (*ibid.*, p. 105). So since the body–soul relation is reversed and, instead of damned souls, the pilgrim encounters living bodies, then it is also 'correct to say that the punishments are sins' (*ibid.*, p. 107) in Dante's Hell and that to meet a sinner equals facing the 'reality of sin' (*Catechism of the Catholic Church*, 1995, 386–7), the real cause of the Fall of the mankind. In this case it is 'the reality of treachery', a sin that has the worst social consequences. It is a betrayal combined with denial of special loyalty (Ferrante, 1984, p. 189). It destroys trust, the very basis of social order.

Ptolomea has a unique place in Dante's Hell, using Fra Alberigo's words, it is almost 'the lowest place of all' (*Inf.* 33:110). It is one of the four areas in the frozen lake of Cocytus, the last, ninth circle of Hell. Here traitors, the worst of sinners, suffer their eternal punishment partly or fully ('like wisps of straw in glass', *Inf.* 34:12) immersed in ice. Dante's conversation with Fra Alberigo is the last encounter with a damned soul in the whole *Inferno*. The terror grew gradually up to this point and precisely here it reaches its peak (see the story told by count Ugolino, *Inf.* 33:1–78). What comes next, Canto 34 and the description of Judecca where Satan himself resides, is surprisingly no longer terrifying, it is absurd (Boitani, 1981, p. 87). T.S. Eliot found it so grotesque that he is said to have advised his students either 'to omit the last canto and return to the beginning' or 'to wait until he has read and lived for years with the last canto of the Paradiso' (Eliot, 1934 in: Freccero, 1986, p. 167).

In other words Ptolomea seems to be a place of transition between order, however infernally inverted and ironic, and absurdity. And here absurdity is nothing else than the excess of order. Satan from the last Canto 34 may be grotesque, but the way he is presented is only a natural consequence of logic that is behind the whole *Inferno*. He cannot move about, with wings beating rhythmically he is like a machine, completely deprived of personality, chews Judas and Brutus in his mouth. As a fallen angel, for Dante he is the ultimate 'ruin of beauty' (Esolen, 2003, p. xxiii). In Ptolomea logic is already suspended, and absurdity arrives precisely with the pilgrim's encounter with Fra Alberigo. This is exactly where the reader is presented with the ultimate critique of society ('the world above' *Inf.* 33:123), an apocalyptic vision of it. Hell is a city; categories of sins are connected to places, almost as if there was no distinction between the text and what it represents. '[In] such an atmosphere of congealment, of no life, of no humanity, of terrifying sin, the artistic conclusion, if not the logical or theological one, is that society is not a concourse of men, but of demons' (Lonergan, 1977, p. 72).

Dante, Fra Alberigo and Branca d'Oria in the state of dissolution

> [The] sheer intensity of the suffering that interviewees brought into the office with them surprised us and made us angry that organiza-tions can do this to their staff ... we wish to maintain this anger, to spread it among our academic colleagues, to claim its legitimacy and rationality. (Ford and Harding, 2003, p. 1132)

The traitors in Ptolomea suffer their eternal punishment in an indeed very original, unorthodox condition. They have no knowledge of how their bodies 'stand in the world above' (*Inf.* 33:123), their earthly activ-ities have been taken over by a demonic force. They are blind, they cannot weep, their grief is turned inwards and multiplies forever. Alive, but already damned, incapable of moral judgement. Their bodies 'up there' act probably as predictably as Satan at the bottom of Inferno, they mechanically 'eat and drink and sleep and put their woollens on' (*Inf.* 33:140–1). In Dante's eyes they fully deserve it. Alberigo committed a terrible sin, something which is evil 'objectively' so to speak, in accord-ance to God's law, namely a murder, but it would not be enough to put him at the very bottom of Hell – murderers are placed in the seventh circle. 'The most serious sins for Dante are those that deny the trust on which social and political relations are based' (Ferrante, 1984, p. 134).

Founded in 1261 in Bologna Knights of Our Lady were to make peace between factions, reconcile family feuds, protect the weak against their oppressors. Alberigo, as a member of this military order, was bound 'not to take up arms, save in defense of widows and orphans, and of the Catholic faith, or for the purpose of making peace between man and man' (Toynbee, 1968, p. 293). To say that his sin was an abuse of the 'proper function' and task assigned to him, an abuse of his consecrated state in the community of the Church, and that it struck the sanctity of hospitality is still not enough. He used the power coming from all these in a directly opposite purpose, an act that could only be compared to a rape. In fact, since 'each sin has political implications', in its historical and social context this one could be called 'a political rape', because it directly contributes to 'the hidden corruption that undermines society' (Ferrante, 1984, p. 137)

What it all means for the pilgrim is quite ambiguous. By meeting Alberigo he encounters the reality of treachery, he faces the sin itself. This explains the very end of the story, the poet tricks Alberigo, uses him and walks away saying 'to be villainous to him was a courtesy' (*Inf.* 33:150). In Hell, facing the sin itself, Dante acts as minister of God (Lonergan, 1977, p. 65), but so do demons(!) – the whole Hell was for Dante created by God's justice (*Inf.* 3:125). Lying to Alberigo was not the worst of the things he did to the damned souls, for example earlier he kicks 'one spirit's face' (*Inf.* 32:78)! What really goes on is, again, an act of violence against the evil itself. This can happen only in Hell, but the motivation behind it is common and natural, at least according to Dante and the Catholic orthodoxy: 'The apprehension of evil causes hatred, aversion, and fear of the impending evil; this movement ends in sadness at some present evil, or in the *anger* that resists it' (*Catechism of the Catholic Church*, 1995, s. 1765).

There is an obvious element of self-recognition in the poet's encounters with the damned – 'with Dante minister, there is also Dante sinner and pilgrim' (Lonergan, 1977, p. 66). Teodolinda Barolini in her *The Undivine Comedy: Detheologizing Dante* (1992) gives the following account of the encounter between the pilgrim and Fra Alberigo:

Frate Alberigo explains to the pilgrim that the souls of Tolomea are, uniquely, sent to hell while their bodies are still on earth, where they are possessed by devils. Dante is here troping his master fiction: instead of 'living' dead people, we now must contend with the idea of dead living people. As the outlines of the fiction becomes harder to hold onto, we succumb to it more readily, especially when the text reproduces our relation to it within itself, as occurs in the ensuing dialogue between the pilgrim and Alberigo: it seems that Branca Doria, a Genovese nobleman condemned to the ninth circle for the murder of his father-in-law, Michele Zanche...is in fact dead. The pilgrim is incredulous; Alberigo must be lying... So the pilgrim is now in the reader's position, faced with an unbelievable truth... How does Alberigo – the creature in the fiction – persuade the pilgrim to believe him? By appealing to 'reality', namely to fiction to which he belongs. His reply is one of the most remarkable intratextual moments within the *Commedia*, as the text buttresses the text, the fiction supports the credibility of the fiction ... – the pilgrim is convinced; and the poet, who has mirrored and thereby mounted a sneak attack on the reader's reluctance to believe, concludes the canto by stating as simple fact what he learned from Alberigo: in this place he found – 'trovai' – a spirit whose soul was in Cocytus, while his body was on earth. Now that the fiction has been accepted as reality, reality – in typically Dantesque inversion – can be revealed to be a fiction. (Barolini, 1992, pp. 94–5)

Barolini accurately points at the key moment in the whole *Inferno*, draws a precise line between irony and absurdity. The pilgrim, by not believing Alberigo's 'demon story', puts himself 'in the reader's position' (*ibid.*, p. 94). If we suspend her project of detheologizing Dante for a while and come back to Singleton's understanding of the structure of the *Commedia*, then maybe what the poet was trying to do was not necessarily 'a sneak attack on the reader's reluctance to believe' (Barolini, 1992, p. 95). Maybe it is an illustration of the bottom of Hell as a state of mind, a state of complete dissolution. If Dante is the pilgrim and the reader at the same time, than he reads his own life from the outside, so to speak. Unlike the Christian ideal, the person of the messiah (Christ) Jesus ('For what faith really states is precisely that with Jesus it is not possible to distinguish office and person; ... here is no "I" separate from the work; the "I" is the work', Ratzinger, 2004, p. 203), at this very moment the poet is perfectly divided.

The judgement

[For] managers the elision of their identity with the organization is such that the boundaries between manager and organization blur, so that the organization *is* the manager, the manager *is* the organization. The irony of the drama of organizations is that managers both control others and control themselves: in unleashing the worst aspects of that control upon others, they also unleash it upon themselves. (Ford and Harding, 2003, p. 1144)

There is 'a kind of death of the soul', says Saint Augustine in his *De Doctrina Christiana*, 'which consists in putting away of former habits and former ways of life, and which comes through repentance' (1873, p. 17). The pilgrim started his journey to God in the dark forest, which was supposed to symbolize Dante's suicidal thoughts. From there on he only went lower and lower into Hell, and here he is at the bottom of it. Now it is time for him either to die, or to go mad. What follows is a bit of both of course, a grotesque vision of Satan and symbolic account of spiritual death and resurrection, of conversion of the poet. He is on a pilgrimage and the aim of a pilgrimage is to clean oneself from sin, to repent, to exorcise oneself, in other words – to convert. Renouncing evil is the first step on the way; it leads to the death of the old, sinful self. In this context his acts of violence seem fully justified, but again – it is not sin/soul that he kicked or tricked, it is flesh. In this infernal 'reality' he increases the physical pain of the damned. The pilgrim/sinner and Hell/'the world above' (*Inf.* 33:123) distinctions ironically collapse once more, but they actually never worked throughout the whole *Inferno*. In the end it is also impossible to distinguish between the state of pilgrim's mind and the reality of Hell as an organization.

For Dante, Hell – the structure of the 'hidden corruption that under-mines society' (Ferrante, 1984, p. 137), or rather the reality of this hidden corruption, is an organization. Everyone, with his/her particular sins, contributes to this structural corruption and is oppressed by it at the same time, but also one is able to transcend it. According to Catholic orthodoxy this relation works all the way until death, as God's mercy is limitless, but Dante draws a line and the likes of Fra Alberigo cross it – 'the soul that commits such an act is already damned, incapable of moral judgment and it is incapable of feeling' (Ferrante, 1984, p. 192). The real-ity of this ultimate corruption is neither death nor the Augustinian evil as non-existence, but a state of complete dissolution. 'Hell – the organ-ization' created by God's justice is still able to speak through the dead and damned souls/bodies. It is 'only' a ruin of justice – 'an extraordinary inversion of the tenets of Christian theology is at work here' (Höpfl, 2005, p. 174). 'Hell – the excess of order' is silent like Satan himself. Machine-like, deprived of personality, immobile structure of corruption. This system must remain silent, but the last ones who speak in its name are like Fra Alberigo – alive but already damned.

Note

1. Dante Alighieri's *Inferno* will be referred to by the title. The cited edition is the one listed in the Bibliography.

6
Eve Harrington and All About Alliances

Krzysztof Klincewicz

Myths, archetypes and the cultural view of betrayal

Myths are interpreted as sources of virtues and sacred narratives, which reinforce values and practices in societies. They cast light on historical or pre-historical events, making sense of them and individual lives. Hatch *et al.* (2005) present myths as sources of managerial virtues, along with MacIntyre's neo-Aristotelian ethics (MacIntyre, 1984). They may, however, offer negative examples of vices and dysfunctions. Freudian references to ancient Greek mythology emphasized the dysfunctional elements, arguing that myths cannot really teach us to avoid repeating the legendary mistakes. Polytheist systems of belief were less sensible to the demarcation of right and wrong, virtues and vices, by displaying moral ambiguity. They frequently offered multiple recommendations and 'split' moralities as opposed to the Judeo-Christian or Islamic traditions. Polytheist gods were sometimes presented as tricksters, participating in internal struggles and resembling human beings with their inabilities to control emotions or to make right choices.

Modern myths are inspired by mass culture, blurring distinctions between the sacrum and the profane. It is questionable whether we could call these stories 'myths', as the name seems to be reserved for ancient, sacred narratives. Modern tales or legends give rise, however, to powerful archetypes. They set examples, which often have nothing to do with traditionally interpreted virtues. Literature since Shakespeare has displayed an unhealthy interest in negative heroes, multiplying tales of their wrongdoings. Modern books, movies and TV series deepen the moral ambiguity, as mass murderers, manipulators or 'hard' managers became new heroes of the popular culture, stimulating the needs for achievement and supporting the view that ends justify means. Regardless of ethical judgments, which will not be discussed in this chapter, these modern 'negative' myths shape our interpretations of the world and offer ready-to-use behaviour patterns or social scripts. These are then followed implicitly so that vices are promoted alongside virtues.

The present chapter focuses on betrayal and its presence in the business world, particularly in interorganizational relations. Betrayal can be interpreted as the rupture of a presumed social contract, undermining the trust of another party. The prevalent view of a traitor in Western culture is a pessimistic account of betrayal and the upcoming demise. Thus, traitors are presented as losers, whose actions are based on misguided expectations. In Dante's 'Divine Comedy', betrayers are incarcerated in the lowest level of the Inferno. Biblical Eve disobeyed God's orders and ate the forbidden fruit, bringing about the expulsion of the human race from the Garden of Eden and miserable life for herself, Adam and their offspring. Another biblical character, Delilah, helped Philistines seize her lover Samson by discovering and revealing the secret of his strength. The story of Delilah inspired the modern archetype of femme fatale, but betrayal has never been a merely feminine domain. Judas Iscariot, one of Jesus' 12 apostles, betrayed him for a bribe of 30 pieces of silver by kissing Jesus to identify him in front of arresting soldiers. Once realizing his own guilt, he unsuccessfully tried to return the bribe and finally committed suicide. Shakespeare's Lady Macbeth desired so much the throne of Scotland, that she encouraged her husband to kill the ruling king, and was able to frame innocent servants for the crime. As a queen, she gradually regretted these deeds, especially when her husband no longer resorted to her advice, and her suppressed conscience tormented her to death.

Betrayal may also be glorified as long as its premises are not self-interested, and the traitor turns into a hero. It then becomes a sacrifice for the sake of higher values, particularly in political contexts. Biblical Judith seduces the invading Assyrian general Holofernes and decapitates him after an intimate night, and thus stops the military offensive into Judea. Mythological Prometheus stole fire from Olympus and gave it to humankind, making it powerful enough to challenge gods. Odysseus devised the famous Trojan horse to secretly pass through the city walls and, thus, defeat Troy. Marcus Iunius Brutus, Caesar's assassin, was a conservative Roman senator, who resorted to the drastic measure when Caesar usurped the political power of the Roman Senate. Ancient Roman tradition that was influenced by emperors, regarded Brutus as a traitor, while Shakespeare rehabilitated him as a patriotic hero who was fighting against tyrants. Mata Hari (Margaretha Geertruida Zelle), the famous

Oriental-style dancer and courtesan, was executed by the French during World War I. She was accused of spying for enemies, while modern historians suspect that she was falsely discredited by the German secret service.

There were also cases when deceit and the instrumental treatment of others were identified as governing interpersonal relations, while being aware of these factors was glorified as a base for effective policies or religious principles. Machiavelli's 'The Prince' is concerned with cruelty and suggests that it is better to be feared than loved. Thus, subordinates and allies should not be trusted. LaVey's theology of Satanism supports Nietzschean individualism as opposed to the conformity and naiveté. It also criticizes wasting love and compassion for those who do not deserve it, and postulates revenge instead of forgiveness. Surprisingly, the rules seem to resemble the recommendations of today's management bestsellers.

The myth of Eve Harrington

The film *All About Eve*, released in 1950 and praised with six American Academy Awards, offered an original perspective on betrayal and personal success. The movie tells the story of an unknown small town girl named Eve Harrington, who gets to know a Broadway star named Margo Channing. Eve then insinuates herself into Margo's life, becoming her assistant and friend, and starts plotting sophisticated intrigues to later replace Margo in her role at the theatre and in the high society. The cynicism and the perfection of her deception made Eve a symbol of the self-interested and powerful player.

In the film, Margo Channing is the biggest Broadway star, who made her first appearance at the age of four. According to the renowned theatre critic Addison DeWitt: 'she has been a Star ever since. Margo is a great Star. A true Star. She never was or will be anything less or anything else' (Mankiewicz, 1950).[1] She has just turned 40 and is tired with theatre and fans. Furthermore, she is noticing that her young appeal and charm may soon vanish.

Eve Harrington is introduced in the movie as a 24 year-old widow who is an only child of a poor family. She had to quit school to support herself by working as a secretary in a Wisconsin brewery. When visiting San Francisco, she discovers that her husband has died, and finds comfort in watching Margo's guest performance in one of the city's theatres. That first encounter then apparently changes her life. She watches every performance of the play and follows Margo to New York, where she is noticed by Margo's friend and is formally introduced. Eve, who appears in an ugly, old-fashioned raincoat and hat, worships and compliments Margo. She then tells her own story, which makes everybody cry.

That same day, she moves into Margo's guestroom to become her 'sister, lawyer, mother, friend, psychiatrist and cop' (Mankiewicz, 1950). Being a personal assistant, however, is not her ambition. Margo eventually spots Eve trying on her costume on the stage, and her maid concludes that Eve's affection may be artificial. The maid tells Margo that 'she was studyin' you, like you were a play or a book or a set of blueprints. How you walk, talk, think, eat, sleep' (Mankiewicz, 1950). Margo becomes increasingly insecure when suspecting that Eve might want to steal her boyfriend and tries to arrange an office job for her to keep her away. But, soon it turns out that she wants to steal much more: Margo's personality.

Eve soon becomes Margo's understudy without her knowing this, and has an opportunity to participate in a rehearsal for a new play. Eve proves to be an excellent actress, but in spite of the stunning appearance: 'Eve was incredibly modest. She insisted that no credit was due her' (Mankiewicz, 1950), politely attributing all to Margo, who nevertheless realizes Eve's hidden agenda. When Margo gets stuck in the countryside, Eve supplants her on stage. She invites press representatives and receives an enthusiastic review from the renowned critic, Addison DeWitt.

With her first stage success, Eve plots to be cast in a new Broadway production and competes for the role with Margo. She tries to seduce Margo's boyfriend, Bill, yet fails. She blackmails Margo's friend, who is married to the playwright Lloyd Richards, by explaining her own actions: 'I'd do much more for a part [which was] that good' (Mankiewicz, 1950). Margo decides to give up the role and focus on private life, especially as she and Bill are getting married. Thus, Eve gets the part and becomes a new Broadway star. But, this success is not enough for her. She then seduces Lloyd Richards, and wants him to divorce his wife so that he can marry her. That way, 'the commercially most successful American playwright' and the new rising star could unify their forces.

However, Eve's plots are deciphered by Addison who has carefully followed her actions and verifies her stories. He ultimately discovers 'all about Eve'. Her real name is Gertrude Slescynski. Her parents were indeed poor, but also abandoned by the daughter. She used to work in a brewery, but had an affair with her boss and was paid to leave the town. She was never married and had never been to San Francisco. She had headed straight for New York, where she planned a sophisticated intrigue to befriend Margo and to steal almost everything from her. With this information, it becomes Addison's turn to blackmail Eve so that she has to abandon the marriage plans and enter into a cynical pact with him: 'You are an improbable person, Eve, and so am I. We have that in common. Also a contempt for humanity, an inability to love or be loved, insatiable ambition – and talent' (Mankiewicz, 1950).

Eve's dreams eventually come true in only a few months after she appears for the first time on Margo's doorstep in October. In July the following year, she becomes the youngest actress to receive the award for distinguished theatre achievements and is scheduled to go to Hollywood. After the ceremony, she finds another admirer, a young girl who calls herself Phoebe, waiting in her apartment, and telling her how much she appreciates Eve's talent and acting skills. Eve, with her pride and laziness, proposes that Phoebe start helping her. Thus, the cycle of helping, learning, deceiving and back-stabbing is likely to repeat again.

The story demonstrates how friendship can be used as a strategic resource to meet personal objectives. Dale Carnegie's *How to Win Friends and Influence People*, originally published in 1936, was one of the first popular books related to social psychology. It became a *New York Times* bestseller and offered similar advice for potential manipulators. Praising people and showing them fake interest were recommended as the best ways to gain people's friendship and trust. *All About Eve* demonstrated risky aspects of these recommendations. The excessive pride of stars made them fall as soon as they were tricked by unscrupulous imitators, who duplicitously worked their ways into the actors' lives.

The same behaviour pattern can be observed in the business realm. There are two players, one of low profile with limited resources and the other who is famous and experienced. The low profile player becomes acquainted with the admired partner, learns from her and uses her resources, while gradually taking over control of them, and developing his or her own skills. Finally, the relationship is terminated by the smaller partner who no longer needs the other party because she has discredited her to take her position.

The scenario differs from traditional dynamics that are discussed in economic and sociological literature. Schumpeterian cycles of innovation and imitation present entrepreneurs who are launching new products and gaining market shares, and imitators who follow their footsteps and gradually 'steal' their customers. Simmel's 'trickle-down' theory of fashions argues that fashion setters differentiate themselves by originality, but their differentiators are soon imitated by others and need to be replaced by something more original (Simmel, 1904/1957). The story of Eve Harrington extends this model. Innovator and imitator become close friends, and the more successful party does not expect the upcoming deception and substitution. The pattern has inspired numerous works of art such as the camp poetics of the 1980s that applied the symbol to the business world. This can be seen with 'Dynasty'-like movies teaching people how to betray friends in order to get rich or richer. No longer were organizations perceived as 'rat race' arenas because every rat found a mind of its own, and a portfolio of back-stabbing techniques.

Dilemmas of alliances

The Eve Harrington myth is re-enacted in modern corporations through individual careers, political games and intrigues. It can also inspire interorganizational strategies. These can include ways of working with partners, sharing knowledge and creating new value within partnership networks. The phenomenon calls for a more extensive discussion that is related to the origins of strategic management and culture-bound values. These are associated with the concepts of competition, partnership, loyalty and trust.

The notion of strategy is rooted within European military tradition. Probably the first analogy in management history was suggested by Colonel Maude, who translated the nineteenth-century Prussian military theoretician von Clausewitz and defined business as a 'form of human competition greatly resembling war' (Parks *et al.*, 1994, p. 68). One of McKinsey's directors supported this view by explaining the usefulness of ancient military approaches for corporate strategy with a focus on resources and plans instead of direct attack (Widmer, 1980). Michael Porter popularized the concepts by focusing on 'positions', 'advantage', 'defense', and 'offence' (Porter, 1985). In parallel, 'marketing warfare' became a widely discussed metaphor of relations with customers and competitors (Arndt, 1985, p. 16; Ries and Trout, 1986), and the notion of organizational leadership can also be traced back to traditional military studies that discuss the importance of a general's personality, courage and heroism (Windsor, 1995, p. 35). The military analogy emphasized needs for long-perspective planning and disadvantages of merely tactical actions. It is also inspiring because it 'romanticizes business as a heroic endeavor which unfolds a landscape of valiant and desperate combat, a setting in which a unique set of moral principles and values can easily be justified' (*ibid.*, p. 34).

The language of modern management relies, therefore, on terms such as 'battles', 'price wars', 'advertising campaigns', 'capturing, occupying and holding positions', or 'defending market shares'. It refers to conventional, institutionalized wars, and not to total wars or hatred.

Like wars in the eighteenth century that 'became ritualized with little bloodshed and inconclusive endings', modern business is interpreted as a 'ritualistic competition that allowed everyone to have "a piece of the pie"' (Parks *et al.*, 1994, p. 68). War can, however, be a very comprehensive term in modern language because it encompasses guerilla warfare and terror, which unlike classical battles, may not be regulated by codes of honour.

The European military tradition is radically different from its Asian counterpart. Sun Tzu's ancient Art of War teaches one how to win wars without escalation, and to use strategy to improve oneself and others (Sun Tzu, n.d.). The superior form of victory is based on strategy, not battles (Chen, 1993, p. 43), and creativity can help Davids win over Goliaths. Contrary to this perspective, von Clausewitz could not imagine wars without bloodshed and destruction (Friedman and Friedman, 1986, p. 12). Sun Tzu proposed specific ethics of war such as different norms and values applied to subordinates and to enemies. Intraorganizational ethics called for loyalty and obedience, but no compassion (Windsor, 1995, p. 40). In interorganizational relations, treachery of enemies was entirely justified (Windsor, 1995, p. 39). Not surprisingly, Sun Tzu's military perspective has inspired Japanese and Taiwanese managers, who regarded the market as a metaphorical battlefield long before their Western counterparts re-discovered the military metaphor (Chen, 1993, p. 42). More importantly, the parallel military metaphors in Western and Asian cultures were diverging, inspiring different strategic and ethical recommendations.

Facing the stunning success of Japanese firms in Western markets, management theorists decided to re-evaluate the concepts of war, enemies, supporters and loyalty. Hamel *et al.* (1989) analysed alliances formed by Western and Japanese partners, and identified two opposing approaches to the arrangement. Western companies were entering the alliances to reduce costs and to avoid investments in non-core business areas while their Japanese partners were focused on learning and gaining access to markets. A senior manager of a Western company described a joint-venture with its Japanese rival: as follows 'We complement each other very well – our distribution capability and their manufacturing skill. I see no reason to invest upstream if we can find a secure source of product. This is a comfortable relationship for us' (Hamel *et al.*, 1989, p. 134). These 'comfortable relationships' were bound, however, to turn into nightmares for Western players. Japanese partners had well-defined agendas for the cooperation by exploiting knowledge resources of partners.

Every time the European company requested a new feature on a product being sourced from its partner, the Japanese company asked for detailed customer and competitor analyses to justify the request. Over time, it developed a sophisticated picture of the European market that would assist its own entry strategy. (Hamel *et al.*, 1989, p. 136)

The most prominent example of this strategy was Japanese NEC, which has been reported to form numerous alliances to learn and to internalize skills of foreign partners in order to build its own capabilities in new technological areas. Hamel and Prahalad refer to it as 'borrowing resources' (Hamel and Prahalad, 1993, p. 80), although from the perspective of the company's partners, the word 'stealing' could be equally relevant.

Alliances are formed because of strategic needs that are not merely cost-related justifications (Eisenhardt and Schoonhoven, 1996). The most popular motivation, known as the complementarity of assets, means that large firms need small partners to innovate, while smaller organizations need support and capital. The fit seems perfect as long as there are no 'hidden agendas' creating strategic problems (Doz, 1988). But, these 'hidden agendas' may be exactly the key to strategy development (Hamel and Prahalad, 1993). The acquisition of the other party's knowledge and skills (also referred to as 'interorganizational learning') is regarded as a strategic dilemma. In fact, management literature offers both recommendations on how to be a 'good partner' (by deepening trust and exposing intangible resources), as well as how to participate in the 'race to learn' to make the partner's contributions redundant (Larsson *et al.*, 1998). The implicit need to acquire a partner's knowledge became a hidden assumption in strategic alliances literature (cf. Shenkar and Li, 1999). The methods for appropriating a partner's knowledge and becoming self-sufficient are euphemistically described as 'knowledge management processes' in alliances (Inkpen and Dinur, 1998). They should be managed by well-defined objectives (Hamel *et al.*, 1989; Inkpen, 1996) so that partners are treated strategically rather than emphatically. The notion of trust in relations becomes critical for corporate survival – 'the greater the trust between [Joint Venture] partners, the greater the openness in information sharing and the more likely alliance knowledge will be accessible' (Inkpen, 2000, p. 1028), so every partner has to reduce transparency and protect proprietary knowledge (Hamel *et al.*, 1989, p. 136), and exchange of intangible resources becomes the major challenge of alliances (Parise and Henderson, 2001).

In recent years, the abundance of 'learning races', fears of losing knowledge through close relations and the erosion of trust undermined the popularity of strategic arrangements. Transitory (non-strategic) alliances became a feasible substitute for long-term commitments. Thus, ad hoc cooperation, filling operational gaps and building flexible virtual organizations made trust and interorganizational learning less important (Duysters and de Man, 2003), so that informal aspects of alliances and direct communications are replaced by detailed, formalized contracts.

Playing the partnership game

A widely discussed *Harvard Business Review* article from 1968 questioned whether bluffing was admissible in business (Carr, 1968). It suggested that business is like a game of poker and is based on conventions where people do not expect to be told 'the whole truth'. More recent publications examine whether we are obliged to present all of our actual objectives in business relations (Dees and Cramton, 1991, pp. 154–6). The erosion of trust makes games a more appropriate metaphor of business rather than warfare, with its codes of honour and heroism. Games are governed by rules and conventions, but playing them does not require as much dedication as the pursuit of wars does. Rules of a game limit reciprocal trust, and then define social roles and expectations.

Exploring the game theoretical approach, Brandenburger and Nalebuff (1996) introduced the concept of coopetition, blending competition and cooperation, which suggests that a company could be one's friend and one's foe at the same time. The interpretation became widespread in business, inspiring both practitioners and researchers (Bengtsson and Kock, 2000). It emphasizes the need for strategic flexibility, self-awareness and limited attachment to other parties. Learning from their own mistakes, companies can then understand how to win friends and at the same time prevent them from turning into powerful competitors. They are often aware of the threats posed by their partners, which is a re-enactment of the Eve Harrington myth, so they avoid excessive reliance on smaller partners in numerous ways.

First, they preserve self-sufficiency by using knowledge as a source of power. Internal R&D and marketing research help understand what partners are doing, even when the company does not intend to engage in their area. Large companies often are reported to invest heavily in research activities not related to their core businesses, but with intentions to 'keep an eye' on partners and to gain a better market sensing.

Another partner management method involves maintaining multiple alternative partners or an extensive 'ecosystem' of partners. This conscious decision to have more than one partner in a certain area is described in organization theory as plural governance form (Bradach, 1997). As a Japanese company described its powerful partner, 'they would always remind us that they could go elsewhere if we didn't continuously improve' (Dyer and Ouchi, 1993, p. 57). Japanese mobile telecommunications leader, NTT DoCoMo, mastered the approach by working closely with a trusted 'inner circle' of partners, while remaining open to any other interested party. They did this by encouraging their innovativeness and even allowing some successful outsiders to join the 'inner circle' (Klincewicz, 2005, p. 77). The plural governance form is rooted in political history with the prominent example of the Medici family in Renaissance Florence: The Medicis maintained a network of intertwined ties, binding members of other families by marriages, loans, as well as political and economic support, thus restricting their free-riding opportunities and inducing commitment (Padgett and Ansell, 1993, pp. 1274–7).

Finally, corporate Margo Channings often have the courage to abandon partners, and are aware of their own strengths and of strategic alternatives. A dominant industry position (corresponding to Margo's status as a Broadway star) could make the substitution of unreliable partners relatively easy. This power is usually not abused since smaller partners are not exploited often by large high-tech companies (Klincewicz, 2005, pp. 160–1). At the same time an entire arsenal of retaliation techniques is always waiting for excessively ambitious partners that may endanger one's chosen territories.

Disarmed by the defence techniques of large companies, modern Eve Harringtons need to be wiser than their corporate patrons. They try to make the larger partners addicted in order to preserve control over unique knowledge and gradually to supplant the partners in the market. The most evident examples of this strategy are offered by offshore contractors, including Indian and Taiwanese companies. They started their development by carrying out relatively simple tasks before later moving towards knowledge-based activities. Western companies were traditionally outsourcing activities involving mature technologies (Roberts and Liu, 2001, pp. 28–30) and low added-value where the ability to reduce costs motivated shifts to external locations. By forming partnerships with trusted contractors, the largest American high-tech companies literally financed their strategic development by helping them later become serious competitors.

Indian IT services company, Infosys, was founded in the 1980s to develop software for American customers. India offered an attractive resource pool of low-cost, skilled programmers, attracting many large software and IT services companies, which decided to subcontract minor elements of the development process to Infosys and other firms. Infosys was actively learning from its foreign partners, and the knowledge acquisition was directly sponsored by these partners because specialist skills were essential for projects. Year by year, the company was becoming more self-sufficient. Instead of reacting to requests from Western companies, it proactively pursued technology alliances with leading software and hardware vendors and built its own portfolio of competencies and proprietary software products. Western partners were able to select Infosys' services from Infosys a la carte, and finally, the company decided to open its own sales offices abroad. This threatened large American companies with direct competition, while Infosys still conducted contracted development tasks for them. Eight years ago, Infosys was carrying out relatively cheap and low value-added subcontracted work for companies such as HP or Accenture, but later the power balance shifted. Nowadays Accenture and HP are not only using Infosys as a contractor, but also competing with the company in certain markets, and even selling its software products to customers in the banking sector.

This strategy is particularly attractive for project-based businesses, which can engage in trust building activities with foreign partners, learn from the joint projects, receive payments and at the same time, make the partners addicted. For cost reasons, large companies are inclined to reduce their own involvement in certain areas and to give up related knowledge so that they cannot function without their outsourcing partners. As soon as competencies and funds of the smaller companies allow, they might consider 'back-stabbing' partners by competing with them, while still remaining their essential contractors in some areas.

Telecommunications giant, Motorola, contracted the Taiwanese mobile phone manufacturer, BenQ, to make cheap, low-end mobile phones by offering a steady inflow of revenues, as well as transferring important technology know-how. BenQ gradually became independent, capable of not only manufacturing phones, but also of designing them. The company initiated cooperation with Motorola's competitors and later decided to start selling mobile phones under its own brand in Asia. Motorola realized this 'betrayal' too late just as Margo Channing did. Even though the company cancelled its contract with BenQ, several months later it decided to renew the agreement, failing to find another satisfactory contractor. In the meantime, BenQ became even more 'impertinent' and acquired Siemens' mobile phone division. It then turned into one of the top global phone manufacturers and aggressively marketed its own products in Western countries (Klincewicz, 2005, p. 194).

Conclusions

The myth of the insidious Eve Harrington is alive in today's business world, which has been re-enacted not only by personal careers and organizational games, but also by the hidden logic of interorganizational alliances. The career development of Eve Harrington matches the 'catching-up' scenarios of Asian companies. For instance, the Japanese initially forced their way into the American market, followed later by Indian and Taiwanese firms. All of them were learning from partners to supplant them with their own product and service offerings. In the course of time, strategic focus shifts from partner intimacy (similar to the phase, when Eve was gaining Margo's trust) through proven excellence (when Eve was charming other people) to standing out as an independent and powerful individual (when the actress became self-sufficient and no longer needed to imitate other more prestigious players).

The chapter does not discuss the ethical implications of this pattern, although the sophisticated use of deception and tricks represents vices rather than virtues. At the same time, the treacherous strategy is a promising catch-up scenario for smaller companies, particularly from developing countries. Thus, if a poor, provincial girl was capable of captivating and supplanting a Broadway star, then seemingly insignificant market players may also explore interesting strategic opportunities by following the example set by Eve Harrington.

Note

1. Quotations from Mankiewicz's movie script are retrieved from the website and thus no page numbers are available.

7
Representations of the Ideal as Symbols of Subversion

Christina Schwabenland

Introduction

This is a chapter about mythmaking and social change. My interest in this topic stems from a visit I made to India while carrying out research into the origins of voluntary organizations. The stories I heard were inspiring and humbling; stories of people who had been beaten up, had risked poverty, even death. These stories were not only inspiring to me but in many cases had become part of the organizations' folklore, their sacred texts (Schwabenland 2006a and b).

These stories recount the founders' visions of a more just society. In this sense they are utopian tales and while these visions are not always clearly worked through – in many examples they are very partial, and only present in an oblique sense – they retain their importance for the people who are associated with the organization.

However, these stories are not merely heroic tales; they are open to more ambiguous and paradoxical interpretations. First, they challenge the status quo. Founders create organizations in order to change an existing situation. Ricoeur comments that in 'the fantasy of an alternative society' utopian thinking 'work[s] as one of the most formidable contestations of what is' (Ricoeur, 1986, p. 16). The very act of imagining can, therefore, be subversive. These images offer organizations a heuristic for the interpretation of experience that is at one and the same time an appeal to the traditional and a 'contestation of what is'.

I have become very interested in this relationship between subversion and hopefulness and here I want to explore it through a discussion of three examples. The first is that of the founders' utopian tales. The second is a case study I carried out recently into an Indian voluntary organization that has created a goddess. Swachh Narayani, the goddess of good governance, is an appeal to a traditional value system but an appeal that serves to contest and reinterpret it. The third comes from examples from 'real life' that students have generated in order to establish a basis for constructing their own notions of the good in organizations. Throughout, I have employed a hermeneutic approach to suggest some potential readings of these representations of the ideal that highlight their subversive functions as well as their function in sustaining hope. In the final section I explore some of the possible implications for leadership.

Ludema *et al.* (2001, p. 191) suggest that 'human systems grow and construct their realities in the direction of what they most persistently, actively and collectively ask questions about'. Representations of the ideal give form to our visions, they structure our yearnings.

Founding stories as utopian tales

And he was, basically, appalled by the way some children were treated and was particularly concerned that there wasn't any effective legislation protecting children from cruelty at the hands of their parents or carers. (AB)

This is an excerpt from the story about an organization that was founded in the nineteenth century to protect children from abuse.[1] When founders take action against a situation that they see as undesirable, they are implicitly being critical of affairs in society as they currently are. In the story above there is passion (the founder's outrage at the way children were treated) but also his proposal about how to remedy the situation (through effective legislation). The stories that are told about the founding of voluntary organizations tell of people acting on their social (and sometimes physical and imaginative) environment because they want to change it and in their proposed remedies the founders are setting out a theoretical position about what they believe would be a more just society. They are the artefacts of utopian thinking, a 'comment on the existent, another means of making peace with, or challenging man-made suffering in the present' (Nandy, 1992, p. 20).

When I started researching these stories I was interested in exploring their ongoing relevance for the organizations. In their telling, the stories not only recount the way in which the organization was created but also contribute to its re-imaging and re-making. For example, the voluntary sector manager who told me the story cited above went on to say:

> Because if you created a culture which really revered children and loved its children and had it top of the agenda, I think it would transform what happened to children. And it's easy to say that child abuse is intolerable but it is a big step to go from a theoretical statement like that for people in this country to say 'we are not going to tolerate it'. (AB)

Ricoeur (1986) writes that utopian thinking stimulates us to create imaginative variations on things as they are. In this example the way in which the utopian ideal is imagined has changed from the founder's initial focus on legislation to what seems to be nothing less than a paradigm shift in thinking about children. The vision of 'a culture which really revered children' and 'had it top of its agenda' is still potent.

In the next example the chief executive is not only commenting about the founding of the organization but setting it within a larger context: 'So it was started . . . as a result of public outrage, something that's rare in this day and age' (BC). Here, too, the story contains these two elements of subversion and idealism: it demonstrates the potential productivity of 'public outrage' but also reproaches.

These stories can provide clarion calls for action:

> Well, you see there is a belief that that battle has been won, and it is true to say that many of the battles around that issue have been won, but the war itself is not won. And there are many other battles to be fought because there are still, in England alone, about 3,000 people with learning difficulties living in long stay hospitals, 4,000 in Scotland. (CD)

This organization was founded to campaign for alternatives to residential provision for people with learning difficulties. The use of battle imagery in this excerpt is striking; here the element of subversion lies in the reminder that the founder's vision has not yet been realized. Founders do not merely dream, they set about developing organizational structures to realize, or concretize their visions. However, although the founder's original intentions may have been radical, the need for survival can distort other organizational priorities. Here is one such example, in which the organization's current chief executive is looking back over a period of intense change:

> Moving from a very small, local provider, who can support people with disabilities and so on, to now a much bigger, regional organization, and the attempts that we have made to try to retain that local feel against the larger, infrastructure, the larger organization, the more bureaucratic organization, I think it's created a real tension. And I have heard from colleagues, who have worked for the organization in some cases for 12, 15 years, who remember it when it was very small, very personal, the focus was much more on the individual in that everybody knew everyone's name and their background and so on, to one that is much slicker, much more of a corporate machine, and along the way we have been challenged that have we actually lost sight of what we were set up to do. (DE)

In this example the reference to the founding story is anything but self-congratulatory. The CEO is not using the story to emphasize how successful the organization has become but to reflect on what has been lost. The story's subversive functioning is turned inward; what is being critiqued is the organization itself which is held up against its own image of the ideal.

These examples demonstrate that the founding stories are not only subversive in their recounting of the ways in which the founders came together to challenge something they thought was unjust. They continue to provide a mechanism for questioning the current state of affairs whether by demonstrating how much farther the organization has to go or if it is being led off course. The stories can also provide a powerful and inspiring call for action. In one interview the chief executive paid tribute to the courage of the founder:

> somebody who went about, quite courageously, to do something about that, in the teeth of quite a lot of opposition, and some of it quite personal, that's got quite a lot of resonance. And I still think that people nowadays, if you speak up on behalf of a cause, I mean my experience is that you'd better be prepared to take a few knocks. (DE)

In my next example the 'representation of the ideal' is somewhat different in that it is an artifice, specifically created by the organization.

Swachh Narayani, the goddess of good governance[2]

Manushi Sangathan[3] is a voluntary organization in India that has 'invented' a goddess as a symbolic representation of a campaign to combat government corruption and oppressive laws that obstruct the efforts of street vendors to earn their livelihood. Manushi Sangathan's work with street vendors originated from a research project that concluded that the vendors' continuing impoverishment came about largely as a result of systematic extortion – the confiscation of their goods and the enforced clearances of the land they occupy – which are regularly carried out by the municipal agencies, in collaboration with the police (Kishwar, 2002, 2003, 2005). Their effect is to ensure that the vendors are kept in a state of permanent insecurity and poverty regardless of the profitability of their goods (usually food such as vegetables, spices and fish or cheap and necessary household goods).

The municipal authorities maintain that the vendors create chaos and squalor (Kishwar, 2001) and this is not entirely unjustified; in many street markets the vendors and their goods spill out into the surrounding pavements and streets causing obstructions. However, according to Manushi Sangathan, the municipal corporation doesn't consistently provide even the most basic amenities of electricity and water. Kishwar suggests that the chaos created by the vendors and the chaos caused by the lack of good governance are mutually reinforcing. Kishwar notes that some of the very vendors who are in the pay of the police are among the ones who 'refuse to submit themselves to market discipline' (Kishwar, 2001, p. 4) and suggests that the prejudice that the vendors are dirty is sustained by the need to justify the regime of corruption. So, the issues of corruption and cleanliness, both physical and attitudinal, are interlinked:

> The chaos and the squalor one witnesses on most of our public streets is often used as an excuse for removing vendors. However, a closer look reveals that it is a deliberate creation of the municipal agencies and the police ... municipal and police officials encourage vendors to put up their stalls in a chaotic manner which in turn gives them justification for routine clearance operations that keep their terror alive ... those willing to pay big amounts [of bribes] are allowed to take prime spots – even if it means obstructing traffic and pedestrian movement. (Kishwar, 2006, p. 7)

Furthermore, for many Hindus the activity of cleaning is associated with low caste. 'Since the rest of society looks down upon the task of cleaning' writes Kishwar, 'the sweepers too do not respect their occupation' (Kishwar, 2001, p. 5). So, for the vendors, keeping their pitches in a clean and orderly condition is not necessarily seen as a means of achieving either self- or societal validation.

Manushi Sangathan's response is a multi-faceted programme of work including political lobbying to reform the regulations that cover the licensing of street trading. They have also initiated a demonstration project designed to promote the successful integration of the vendors into the local area. When this project was launched Kishwar ceremoniously drew the line in the ground around each vendor's stall with a broom to mark out the area that each vendor had agreed to keep clean and orderly. A pooja (worship) ritual was carried out to mark the importance of the event, incorporating the broom (jhadu).

The idea of the jhadu pooja was to drive home the message that ensuring:

> cleanliness and hygiene of their immediate, physical environment are sacred duties of every citizen, that this task should not be looked upon with disdain and handed over to lowly paid sweepers who are treated as untouchables for performing this vital service for society. (Kishwar, 2001, p. 5)

By 2004 the ceremony to sacralize the broom had evolved into the manifestation of Swachh Narayani, initially conceived of as the goddess of the broom (Kishwar, 2001), and then as the goddess of cleanliness (Kishwar, 2004a and b) before evolving into her present form as the goddess of good governance (Kishwar, 2005).

A description of Swachh Narayani's iconography provides insights into her symbolic functions. According to Kishwar the jhadu, or broom is her primary symbol. The broom represents the strength of individuals (the individual twigs) united for a common purpose, in this case that of creating order and cleanliness, not only in the immediate physical environment, but also in governance. In these tasks she is aided by her most recent acquisition, a video camera which she holds in one of her ten arms, symbolizing Manushi Sangathan's successes in lobbying and campaigning. Her other arms hold objects that demonstrate her affinity with three goddesses; Lakshmi (signifying wealth creation), Saraswati (the goddess of wisdom) and Durga (a powerful warrior goddess whose support was invoked to fight the corrupt officials).

While Hindu goddesses are highly individualistic, they can also been understood as facets of one Great Goddess (Sunder Rajan, 2004), representing particular aspects of a greater whole from which all things originated (including deities) and all will return (King, 1999). Pintchman (1994, p. 2) writes: 'the Great Goddess is identified with principles that are impersonal and cosmic, transcending all particularities ... represent[ing] both materiality ... prakrti and a principle of energy ... sakti'.

Therefore, the Goddess, (and Swachh Narayani, as one of her many representations), symbolizes the creation of the material world (the union of creative power, sakti, with undifferentiated matter, prakrti, from which all materiality derives). The Goddess is responsible for making order out of chaos; as the guardian of an ordered world she is order.

Swachh Narayani, as the goddess of the broom (creative energy) and of cleanliness (order) represents the power of the individual, as a member of a group, to create order and withstand chaos. However, while Swachh Narayani's role is, on one level to act as an inspiration for the vendors, as the representation of order she also exposes a paradox. The very institutions that are entrusted with the role of maintaining order and discipline on behalf of society as a whole, are actually sites of disorder and chaos.

Kishwar describes the complex systems of bribery and corruption in terms of an alternative, or anti-order:

> And from top to bottom everyone is getting their cut. So it's not even as if, if you complained to the higher-ups and said look, they are taking bribes from us, they are not going to be sympathetic ... every station house officer has to send a certain percentage of his extra legal income to the higher officials. (MK)

Swachh Narayani can be seen as exposing this paradox between the perception that the vendors are the originators of the chaos and disorder (although they are actually working to create an orderly and well-managed market) and the public institutions of order which create a shadow system of pseudo, corrupted order.

Furthermore, the role of maintaining the social order of caste belongs to women and to female deities.[4] Pintchman (1994, p. 207) writes that a woman 'must maintain purity of her offspring and, thus, purity of caste. Mixture of caste ... is matter out of place and thus represents disorder ... breakdown of caste is said to lead to breakdown of the social order'. However, Swachh Narayani represents the sacralizing of the task of cleaning which 'is associated with low caste activity' (Kishwar, 2001, p. 5). Here again Swachh Narayani is simultaneously guarding and subverting the social order.

Swachh Narayani's iconography creates an appeal to traditional symbolism but re-interpreted within the current context; both a representation of a traditional belief system and also a subversion of it. Swachh Narayani inspires the vendors to create order but challenges the public institutions of order. As a female deity she is a guardian of caste but overturns traditional notions of caste. She is a symbol of an ancient belief system but is invoked to create the possibility of reinterpreting that system in ways that are more relevant to contemporary aspirations about the good society.

Students' stories

My third example comes from my teaching practice in which I have asked students to generate their own representations of the ideal. Although Reedy writes that 'provid[ing] people with images of who they are or who they should be is to damage their ability to decide for themselves' (Reedy, citing May, 2002, p. 80), providing the opportunity for people to create their own images strengthens their ability to decide for themselves.

In the following quote an Indian community activist uses the metaphor of the mirror to describe the encounter between the actual and idealized self:

> The other thing is the mirror image we use, especially with our exchanges when communities talk to other communities. We say it is like a mirror ... because when you go, you can actually look at yourself, when other people are reacting and see how you look, so it's like a mirror when one community shares its experience with another community. And that in itself makes you grow because then you know what you look like, what you feel like. (EF)

I teach a course called Managing Diversity and Equality to postgraduates, mainly studying human resource management. Generally, at the start of a session, I ask them to work together in pairs, discussing some aspect of their own experience that relates to the subject of the lecture. During the session on the 1975 (UK) Sex Discrimination Act I ask them to think about women whom they find inspiring, whether these are women they know personally or more public figures. The majority of examples tend to be family members such as 'mum', 'my wife', 'aunty'

and 'grandma'. These are some of the qualities about these women that
they find inspiring:

> She goes all out for you. (FG)
>
> She didn't take any bullshit. (GH)
>
> She worked through hard times. (HI)
>
> She puts other people first. (IJ)
>
> She was always kind, sharing, even when we had very little. (JK)

And, in a slightly different vein:

> She came from a poor family, with no access to university, had seven
> children but still got a degree and PhD in fine art. (KL)

Examples of public figures include Mother Theresa: for 'her charity work
and her loving nature' (LM) and Oprah Winfrey who 'makes it OK to be
human and to talk about taboo issues, talking about rape, talking about
her life, her story' (MN).

We then go on to reflect on the contrast between the qualities that are
valorized at work and the qualities that the students themselves value.
This often leads to interesting discussions about the difficulties that both
men and women both face in bringing these qualities into the work
context, particularly in management positions.

Given the emphasis on valuing difference that is such a feature of
the literature on 'managing' diversity (see Kandola and Fullerton 1998
for a good example of this genre) I have also experimented with asking
the students to think about a time when they felt respected and valued
at work. What was going on at the time? What made it such a good
experience? Often the students find this quite difficult and I have to
prompt them before they identify an example. In one case a student said
that her boss had asked her advice about a particular problem. When she
came up with an idea to solve it she was put in charge of implementing
her proposal and her boss was impressed when there were improvements.

In another example a student who is an administrator in a human
resource department said that her manager, the HR director, asked her for
advice. The HR director had received a horrible email and had drafted an
angry reply. She showed it to my student who recommended that she 'sit
on it' for the night. Her manager took her advice and the next morning,
on re-reading her draft, decided not to send it. In telling this story my
student said she had deliberated for a few minutes before having the

courage to reply: 'does she really want to know what I think? Should I really tell her? Well, she did ask me ...' (NP).

Another student said that after reading the results of a staff satisfaction survey her manager asked her for her help in finding out why people said they were unhappy. One student received an e-mail from her manager thanking her for welcoming a new group of interns.

These anecdotes barely seem to even qualify as the 'small stories and tactical engagements' that Parker, in *Utopia and Organization* says are 'preferred to grand visions' (Parker, 2002, p. 217). To call them representations of the ideal possibly exaggerates their importance. However, they are, albeit small, examples drawn from lived experience that represent, to the students, the best of those experiences that came readily to mind. Telling these stories reinforces their confidence in their ability to know what is important for them, they know what it is to be valued and, by extension, how to make other people feel valued.

There is also a great deal of similarity across all of the stories in that they emphasize being respected, being trusted, being recognized and valued and allowed to use their own initiative. Reflecting on these similarities can demystify, but also, simultaneously, problematize students' acquisition of management skills.

Because, of course, the students said that these examples were very rare. The subversive element in these stories is their rarity. Why should the experience of working in organizations be so unrewarding, even for these employees who are sufficiently motivated to take on postgraduate study?

Concluding thoughts

In this chapter I have given three examples of encounters between the ideal and the actual. I have described these encounters as subversive because the ideal acts as a 'formidable contestation of what is' (Ricoeur, 1986, p. 16). In the first example this critique is of the circumstances that inspire the founders; in the second it is the corruption of oppressive government and in the third it is (implicitly) the scarcity of examples of a management practice that really values its workers. Ricoeur writes that 'it is only when [utopia] starts shattering order that it is a utopia. A utopia, then, is always being realized' (*ibid.*, p. 273).

From this 'shattering' comes the possibility of something new. 'Flights of the imagination may stimulate both counter knowledge and counter praxis' (Reedy, 2002, p. 185). These encounters are productive; productive of new organizations in the first example, of new ways of thinking about society and organizations in the others. They are also productive of hope which, as Freire writes, is 'indispensable in the struggle of oppressed men and women' (Freire, 2004, p. 23).

The examples given here bring together, in mythic form, the archetypes of nurturer and warrior; the women such as Oprah Winfrey who 'don't take any bullshit' (GH). The male characters also embody these qualities, for example the founder of the organization to protect children, whose chief executive spoke so passionately about his desire for a culture 'that really revered its children' (AB) (a metaphor of culture as nurturer). The founding stories combine these ideals of caring and courage through the use of battle imagery; 'public outrage' (BC), the 'war' to close long stay hospitals for people with learning disabilities (CD). These nurturers are not passive (although the story that harkens back to a past where people knew each other by name and were not caught in the 'slick corporate machine' is an elegy for times lost, a memory of childhood).

These archetypical representations of the warrior nurturer are angry – but they manage their anger. Swachh Narayani is single because 'spouse goddesses are benign... single goddesses are much more scary and can wreak vengeance... [they are] a space for female rage.' (MK). This is creative rage rather than destructive rage. She is connected to Durga rather than Kali because 'Kali is frightening... and people should never forget that at the heart of it is compassion... And it's not just rage... that does too much damage' (MK).

Swachh Narayani is 'a reminder that every woman has a Durga in her... if you are not afraid of [the goondas[5]] they will begin to be afraid of you' (MK). Oprah Winfrey and Mother Theresa use their anger to create organizations to nurture others – Mother Theresa's homes that care for the dying, Oprah's new school in South Africa. The manager who asks for advice about sending an angry e-mail accepts the advice and rewrites it. Rage is contained and channelled into creative action. This offers a model of leadership that reflects Huffington's study of women leaders who 'formulate an idea of the enterprise that people can work from ... mobilizing hope against feelings of despair...a containment that is about helping others to work through frustration' (Huffington, 2004, p. 66).

Abravanel (1983) proposed that one of the functions of myth is to mediate between the ideal and the actual. Therefore, one challenge for leadership is to create and maintain hope through an appeal to imaginative conceptualizations of the ideal. The paradoxical nature of these representations, their presentation of images that are incongruous with lived experience opens up new ways of seeing and constituting social reality. However, utopian thinking can lead to rigidity and inflexibility (Reedy, 2002; Ricoeur, 1986). Similarly the danger that these encounters will be productive of hopelessness and cynicism rather than hope is very real. Therefore, such mediation must be active and ongoing. But Ricoeur argues that more is required than just 'keeping the dialectic running', that we must be prepared to 'let ourselves be drawn into the circle and then try to make the circle a spiral' (Ricoeur, 1986, p. 312). In other words, while our visions provide a powerful heuristic we must always be prepared to move beyond them while never leaving them utterly behind.

Notes

1. I collected these 'founding stories' in interviews undertaken between 1994 and 2000. The methodology used is described in more detail in Schwabenland (2006a) In this chapter I have ascribed pseudonym initials to quotes taken from these interviews; however in the quotes from interviews with Madhu Kishwar she is referred to as MK.
2. A longer discussion of this case study can be found in Prasad, A. (ed) *Against the Grain: Advances in Postcolonial Organisation Studies,* Copenhagen: Liber/Copenhagen Business School Press, forthcoming.
3. Manushi Sangathan is the activist arm of the journal *Manushi,* established in 1978 by Madhu Purnima Kishwar.
4. Kishwar said that she was not aware of this interpretation of the role of the Goddess; that although there may be scholarly sources to support it, in her experience it is not part of day-to-day thinking about goddesses.
5. A colloquial expression for bullies, men in the employ of local elites, usually not afraid to resort to physical violence.

8

The Displaced World of Risk Management: Covert Enchantment in a Calculative World

Peter Pelzer and Peter Case

Introduction

The financial industry gets more and more attention for the risks inherent to its business. The crash of the dot.com bubble affected many non-professional investors and made them aware that profits are not guaranteed, leading to feelings of betrayal on the part of this public. When labelling hedge fund investors 'locusts', implying that they ravenously fall upon the country, Franz Müntefering, chairman of the Social Democrats in Germany in 2005, was simply giving expression to a widespread feeling of the public concerning globalized investment methods; after all, it was election time. It is, nonetheless, also a sign of a changing attitude to risk. The public no longer accepts the lack of transparency anymore. It feels threatened by the possible consequences of realized risks. Coining the term 'Casino Capitalism' to describe recent developments in financial markets, Strange (1986) highlights the fact that trading is increasingly moving away from deals linked directly to an underlying business toward deals where the original business becomes a distant referent, as in the case of derivatives. This trend leaves the public with the impression that something profoundly uncontrollable is happening. Since the publication of Strange's book, we have witnessed an intensification of this phenomenon in terms of: 'the sheer size of these markets, the volumes traded, the variety of possible deals to be done, the number of new financial centers, the men and women employed directly or indirectly in the business of international finance, including the victims, the involuntary gamblers in the casino' (Strange, 1998, p. 9). Of course this is subject to a highly rational regulatory process which tries to frame and standardize risk management in order to achieve stability of the markets. Despite this ostensive rationality, however, it is hard to resist the consideration of parallels between magic practices and risk management. This is particularly so when one reflects on Mauss' theory of magic (Mauss, 1902/1978) with its explanations of rituals, the description of the role of the magician and the social context and conditions that make magic effective. The danger of such comparison is that one could easily be seduced into thinking of risk management as a form of magic. This is not the conclusion we reach; rather we use Mauss' argument concerning magic casuistically to shed further light on the social relationships and processes entailed in modern risk management. Parallels do exist between magic and risk which support the impression that premodern dispositions and sensibilities, which Mauss and his contemporaries associated with 'earlier stages' of human development, have not been entirely superseded by the disenchanted rationalities of modernity. Judged from this perspective this chapter is a contribution to the thesis, most elegantly propounded by Latour (1993), that 'we have never been modern'.

A disenchanted world: figures represent risk

Weber (1948/1970) characterizes rationalization as a process that has as its ultimate end the disenchantment of the world, that is, the complete elimination of all wonder and mystery and its replacement by instrumental knowledge. Disenchantment is the outcome of rationalization and 'intellectualization which we have been undergoing for thousands of years' (Weber, 1948/1970, p. 138). The pursuit of formal rationality and its disenchanting project, Weber concludes, means that:

> [T]here are no mysterious incalculable forces that come into play, but rather that one can, in principle, master all things by calculation. This means that the world is disenchanted. One need no longer have recourse to magical means to master or implore the spirits, as did the savage [*sic*], for whom such mysterious powers existed. Technical means and calculations perform the service. (*ibid*, p. 139)

The banking industry seems to be a good example of the disenchantment Weber speaks of. An abstract world of figures, it can be seen as the industry where technical means and calculations perform the service, that is, the handling of risks. To illustrate our argument, we shall briefly introduce two examples of important figures used in risk management.

The decisive indicator for a financial institution, and for the regulatory authorities, concerning financial uncertainty in any situation is 'portfolio risk'. Given all the elements in the portfolio, what is the risk of loss for the whole portfolio? It is the intention of risk management to express this global market risk in one figure: Value at Risk (VaR). Denominated in units of a currency, it is a measure to determine the potential loss of the portfolio with a given level of confidence. It indicates that, under normal market conditions, there will be not more than a loss of $x€$ with a probability of y per cent during the next n days. If such a figure could be given reliably, this would greatly enhance the stability of the financial system. The entire bank's activities covered by one figure – Value at Risk (VaR) – sounds very operational and manageable and, to a certain extent, it is. However, although VaR is established as a market standard and acknowledged by international regulators, the discussion around potential drawbacks prevails. As mentioned, it is a forecast and as such it has to include not just the normal market changes but also the probability of unlikely, adverse events in an otherwise normal environment. Acknowledging VaR as a valuable development for risk management but at the same time clearly perceiving the drawbacks, Schachter (1977) offers the following rather sardonic description of this risk metric as: 'A number invented by purveyors of panaceas of pecuniary peril intended to mislead senior management and regulators into false confidence that market risk is adequately understood and controlled'. Furthermore, he wittily characterizes the underlying motivation to perfect the figure in quasi-soteriological terms as, 'the quest for the holy scale' (*ibid.*, 1997). While this may be taken as a somewhat arch association, it is perhaps worth reminding ourselves that number and numerology lay at the core of the forms of Renaissance magical arts out of which emerged the mathematics of Enlightenment science. In challenges to the orthodox historiography of science, writers such as Frances Yates and Stanley Tambiah have pointed to the part played by the likes of Marsilio Ficino, John Dee and Giordano Bruno to the development of knowledge that underpinned modern science (Tambiah, 1990/2004; Woolley, 2002; Yates, 1964/1971). While these Renaissance figures are often counted as influential with respect to the development of science, their links to the occult and their status as magicians in a 'golden age of magic' are often overlooked by the revisionist accounts of scholars eager to diminish associations that despoil the story of an inexorable march toward ever purer levels of rationality.

There is another example of a figure which contains memories of a distant past. The business of banks is to handle risks, or, to be more precise, the risk of not being able to fulfil a promise to pay (Baecker, 1991). Accepting that the realization of risks can never be prevented completely is the precondition of the business. A bank's risk management should, therefore, be able to deal with the consequences of the loss. This is the central concern of the international banking regulation of Basel II:[1] to limit the economic effects of realized risks. Very conscious of the potentially damaging effect of the collapse of a large international bank, the first Basel accord of 1988 was an attempt to strengthen the soundness and stability of the international financial markets. A bank must be able to survive the loss of its largest credit, or, in financial terminology, its largest exposure. To achieve this, the Basel Committee stipulates that banks should meet the 'capital adequacy of credits', that is, the total exposure of a bank has to be covered by 8 per cent of the risk weighted assets. In practical terms this means that the bank's business is restricted by its base capital. How to achieve 8 per cent and what is counted as capital in the bank's balance sheet is subject to complicated rules. The rate of 8 per cent was fixed, not arbitrarily, but in negotiations between regulators, banking associations and governments worldwide. It is a figure agreed, not proven as always sufficient to avoid bankruptcy.

Fixed and complicated rules to achieve a target which, we suggest, only gives the impression of precision invites speculation as to why the numeral '8' was chosen. The numeral 8 does, of course, carry deep significance for occultists. According to the *Encylopaedia Britannica* (2007, online):

> [T]he number 8 is generally considered to be an auspicious number by numerologists. The square of any odd number, less one, is always a multiple of 8 (for example, $9 - 1 = 8$, $25 - 1 = 8 \times 3$, $49 - 1 = 8 \times 6$), a fact that can be proved mathematically. In Babylonian myth there were seven spheres plus an eighth realm, the fixed stars, where the gods lived. As a result, 8 is often associated with paradise. Muslims believe that there are seven hells but eight paradises, signifying God's mercy. In Buddhism 8 is a lucky number [the number of factors in the Eightfold Path – PC/PP], possibly because of the eight petals of the lotus, a plant associated with luck in India and a favourite Buddhist symbol.

Eight is also the number of the octave which has an important part in both mediaeval numerology and the occultist notion of the 'music of the spheres'.

The numeral 8 has a long tradition of positive meaning, connected to images of paradise, a world without risk. Although it might be a bit too far-fetched to conjecture that its use in a banking context speaks of a desire based in a distant collective memory of some risk-less world, it at least suggests that there may be remnants of magic in a calculative modern world. It suggests, perhaps, that Weber's rationalization thesis and the marginalization of concrete magic under conditions of modernity (Weber, 1948/1970) is not as strictly realized as it first seems. While we acknowledge that this resemblance may be simply coincidental and judged by the reader to be an arbitrary comparison, the idea developed in the following section is a reversal of the claim that magic remnants exist covertly. We try to develop the hypothesis that the current move in risk management might be an unconscious move back to elements of the magical past.

The realm of the magic

In his 'sketch of a general theory of magic' Marcel Mauss (1902/1978) reads the rich ethnographic literature of that time – the turn of the twentieth century – to expose and theorize about the status of magic in societies. Mauss' enquiry embraces such questions as: what constitutes magic and its effects?; on what beliefs is it founded?; and what is its relationship to technology and science? By introducing the concept of 'mana' he also tried to coin a term for the opaque condition of possibility for magic. What makes Mauss so interesting is his insistence that magic played its part in the development of European societies and was not solely the provenance of distant, extinct or exotic cultures. He constitutes magic as a necessary step in the development of civilizations, possessing universal qualities that make it almost identical wherever in the world it is found. Without the authority granted by magic and the belief contained in it, many technologies would never have survived their initial failures (Mauss, 1902/1978, p. 173).

Magic includes actors, actions and ideas: magicians, magic rites and ideas and convictions on which magic is based. Mauss defines it in terms of its social function. To qualify as magic, as opposed to some other social practice, it has to be meaningful to the group and not restricted to individual idiosyncrasy. Physicians, blacksmiths or shepherds are separated from the community (in traditional societies) by practicing their profession. This separation already provides them with a magic authority, he suggests. The magician has a socially abnormal position. Her image is created by oral narratives and rumours to which the magician only has merely to correspond to gain credibility. Individuals become magicians by revelation, consecration or by tradition. Their lives are ruled by a corporative discipline which makes their profession visible to the public.

The conditions of magic rites include rules for one or several central operations and a defined amount of sub rules. The moment of executing the rite is as carefully chosen as the place of its performance. The magic rite is not an empty ritual. It is a language which translates an idea and corresponds to very rich imaginations:

> We are prepared to claim that all magical acts are represented as producing one of two effects: either the objects or beings involved are placed in a state so that certain movements, accidents or phenomena will inevitably occur, or they are brought out of a dangerous state. (Mauss, 1902/2001, pp. 75–6)[2]

For the individual it is not necessary to understand the details of the rite's structure to practice it. She doesn't care about the reasons why the techniques she uses work and is not interested in a rational justification of the choice and use of substances. It is possible to reconstruct the development of the ideas leading to the concrete practice, but usually the one who is performing is not able and not interested in doing so (Mauss, 1902/1978, p. 109).

Magic exploits the possibilities inherent in causal principles. This is self-evident considering the fact that it intends an effect. Each system of magic attempted a codification of abstract things like geometric figures, numbers, moral qualities, death and life. It is the place marker of emerging science because it observes and speculates about the concrete characteristics of things. Magic develops by research and experience and finally resembles science; or rather, from a historical viewpoint, science resembles magic. The relative role of collectivity in magic is reduced more and more as a result of the reduction of a priori knowledge and the irrational. Magic resembles science and technology once it maintains that the individual contributions by experiments and logical deduction are decisive. The step from the magical to the mundane is the shift from collective to individual use.

But why does magic work, or to put it in a less performative way, how does magic achieve credibility and importance in any given cultural milieu? And, to add to the provocation of this chapter, why do we find traces of magic surviving in unexpected places in the contemporary world?

Magic needs no proof. For it to 'work' a belief in magic is necessarily a priori; it precedes experience. Therefore the magician is not threatened by failure. The seriousness in all the actions proves the will to believe in magic's effectiveness. This casts the magician in a suspicious light. She is able to evaluate magic's effects. Performing magic against better knowledge could then be labelled deception and betrayal, but to do so would miss the point completely. The magician is not free. She is forced to play a traditional role or a role which satisfies an audience. She is not acting solely on her own account but as a kind of functionary who is provided with an authority by the community; an authority to which she herself is beholden to believe. Only in the context of the ritual setting, that is, the social milieu of shared ideas and sympathetic relationships, can such magic effects unfold. If the last trace of a secret is removed, the magic ritual changes into technology or science.

For Mauss all the identified elements and explanations so far cannot explain the effectiveness of magic completely. He looks for an additional element which is the source of magic power and names it 'mana'. First used by ethnographers to describe supernatural powers found in Melanesia, Mauss claims it as a universal background for magic. The mana is not part of everyday life. It is a milieu, or, it works in a milieu which is mana. It is the condition of its own possibility, a special world in which everything works as if only the mana is present (*ibid.*, p. 144). This sounds tautological and it has to be so. The idea of mana goes beyond animism, that is, the belief that all things, creatures and the world as a whole are filled with invisible powers. These powers are different from physical causality. They flow through the world and are responsible for all change. Magic is the use of these powers for the benefit of humans. The mana can be understood as the attempt to frame the powers to gain some kind of control by the use of magic. Magic, concludes Mauss, is a social phenomenon (*ibid.*, p. 172), as he states: 'We have now arrived at the conclusion that there are affective states, generators of illusions, to be found at the root of magic, and that these states are not individual, but derive from a mixture of sentiments appertaining to both individuals and society as a whole' (*ibid.*, p. 159).

The displaced world of risks

In order to take the next step in our argument we need to explain a crucial difference. Reflecting on risk with the help of Derrida's concept of différance makes us conscious of the derivative nature of risk management and how the gap between daily management and risk awareness might arise. The sign is already displaced presence (Derrida, 1990, p. 86). If we name something as 'a risk', the act of naming already imputes certain qualities to that which is so named. It is biased by the viewer; taken out of the situation. The act of naming is already a first step in the management of emotions connected with presence. There is no chance of grasping the whole. A situation is labelled risk in order to invoke the idea of 'threat' and to motivate action in response to it. Language is constitutive of a perceptual, affective and behavioural nexus (Burke, 1966). To state the seemingly obvious: without a concept of risk there would be no risk. The origin – the presence – is constructed and applied to a situation so as to open up new possibilities of action. A 'risk situation' is displaced by the labelling of it as 'risky'. This kind of différance is a more fundamental move than that which also takes place when we abstract from an individual case. To abstract we already need a notion from which to abstract to a level where a family of similar occurrences can be summarized. On each step of this progression, différance and supplements take place.

The initial presence of risk is always already absent in attempted acts of risk control. Risk 'management' needs to understand risk as something which can be controlled, that is, measured quantitatively and rendered predictable. The displaced presence of risk in the name 'risk' is thus further displaced and supplemented. This spiral goes on in risk reporting where the families of risks are again condensed and put together according to the logic of management and external regulation. On this level, the management of the actual risk and the external demonstration of this capability come together. But the risk meant here is a completely different one than the starting point of the risk of the individual business. On this level, risk is the possibility of not meeting the regulators' requirements and failing to achieve the magic number of 8 per cent. The 8 per cent of minimum capital underlying is itself a displaced and supplemented understanding of the economic risk of bankruptcy following the realization of individual business risks. Of course, this detached handling of risks involves the creation of a new kind of risk. It may well be the case that the requirements for risk management are met perfectly but the contact to the 'real' business and its risks is thereby lost. The risk reporting is so condensed that the multiple différances and supplements have the effect that a seemingly 'correct' reaction to the figures on paper may turn out to be a 'mistake' facing the business itself.

Risk has been displaced from first-order to second-order verification activities. With this move we arrive in a hyper-reality of organization and society regulated by report.

Reports, audit and governance

When risk is displaced into reports, the reports may start to lead a life of their own. The crucial question is what these reports are actually about.

Examining more closely the actual banking regulation Basel II, which is now implemented worldwide in banks, a very interesting move can be noticed. Besides the overwhelming amount of rules concerning quantitative measuring of individual risks, the regulation consists of two more topics: the regulatory review process and market discipline (BIS, 2004). The international regulators changed their focus from considering the appropriateness of mathematical models to auditing the process of risk management. Additionally, through rules of disclosure, market participants would be enabled to judge the appropriateness of a bank's risk management procedures. The point is not that risks are discovered and met with adequate action but that there are procedures which describe the necessary action. An audit will check if these procedures are in place and if they are documented in a way that externals can understand, but the audit will not judge the success or failure of the procedures, that is, whether or not the bank's judgements about the risk situation is correct. The auditing of risk management processes aims less at 'real' dangers – the original risks in the banking business – and more on procedural rigour and felicitous organization. The banks are obliged to show how they organize risk management, and it is this demonstration that is evaluated (Pelzer, 2005). Again, we see in this development a displacement of risk from a first-order to a second-order set of verification procedures. Michael Power understands such displacement as characteristic of the audit explosion (Power, 1994). Independent verification resulting in a formalized statement by external auditors for the balance sheet, a certificate for the ISO9000 norms of quality, or risk management in the Basel II process are examples of a worldwide fundamental shift in patterns of governance. Risk management has now become the basis to show how organizations govern themselves rather than what they do (Power, 2007).

While dealing with risks directly there is uncertainty but not anxiety per se; nothing uncanny – at least in a bank. Those responsible for credit usually know about the risk involved with a given client, with the industry concerned and with the effect it will have on cumulative risks. The same holds true for other businesses or for operational risks. The internal problem is to maintain responsibility for the business and steer the distribution of risks so that the bank never falls into danger of bankruptcy. The technical means by which this can be accomplished are well established. The problem is that both the business itself and the methods of controlling it are so complex that they are relatively incomprehensible to non-specialists, even including the senior management (Power, 2007).

The reaction to this situation is twofold. First, there is increasing public and regulatory concern regarding how to avoid possible adverse consequences. The world of derivatives and hedge funds has become so excessive and obscure that there is enormous pressure to control and regulate these activities on the part of both national and international regulators. One significant result of this pressure has been global regulation on the grandest scale, namely, Basel II, whose main task is to provide the image of security for a highly volatile worldwide financial system.

Second, there are processes and procedures within banks that seek to address the complexity and relative obscurity of risk reporting. Relevant personnel need to provide data to regulators and organize the disclosure of information to the market. A central unit responsible for the collection and delivery of data and the communication with the external world is required; with a concentration of all risk data collection in one unit under the direction of a Chief Risk Officer (CRO). Reporting replaces the handling of risks on the surface. The CRO has to represent the risk management process and declare its relative reliability. She acts as a master of ceremonies, so to speak, with the task of creating, orchestrating and maintaining an immaculate image (Power, 2007). The risks, of course, do not vanish. They are still there and it is the daily business task to deal with them. But the connection between the actual handling of risks and the reporting is lost to a large degree.

This is the point where matters start to take an interesting turn as far as governance is concerned, for the dawning of the audit society entails a significant shift in attitudes. The scope of governance is decreased under these new conditions. Becoming 'financialized' (Power, 2007) governance focuses its attention on the evaluation of 'good organization'. But this is a matter of surface rationality only. Risk management qua reporting and disclosure appeals to the rational sensibilities of those who inhabit the calculative world of banking. Yet displacing risks in this way reintroduces a distance between the actual handling and reporting of risks. With this distance, the knowledge and trust (or mistrust) that historically has been afforded to situated actors – people who actually know about risk – gets lost, together with the possibility of judging the effectiveness of actual risk handling. Risk management becomes a black box covered in expensive gift wrap. Stakeholders party to the process have to believe that the pretty exterior wrapping somehow reliably represents the contents. Believing instead of judging transfers risk management into a different realm.

Covert enchantment in a displaced calculative world

Writing at the turn of the twentieth century, Mauss gives a hint as to why magic had not completely vanished from societies of that time. His conjectures also help us think about how, and in what ways, it still endures. The magician is encouraged by the others, writes Mauss. The belief in magic which still survives in our societies and, as we have to emphasize, he includes the European societies, is the most real and vivid sign of a state of social unrest. It is indicative of a social sensibility in which vague ideas and empty hopes flow and get shaped by what remains of the old category of mana in our present age. In society there is an inexhaustible potential of diffuse magic on which the magician can rely (Mauss, 1902/1978, p. 170). Financial investors being characterized as locusts in an election campaign, we suggest, is a vivid sign of a state of social unrest and addresses a similar social sensibility.

If the step from magic to the mundane is the shift from collective to individual use and advantage, we are moved to ask, inferentially, if the move from the individual use and advantage of concrete risk management to public reporting and audits may be understood as a shift from the mundane back to magic. The direct handling of risks is technological, insofar as it involves the individual evaluating a concrete case with concrete criteria based on personal experience or informed by risk manuals. The mathematical models used in an individual bank to judge the portfolio are science – with all the reservations against the concrete models with which it is performed. These are known, at least they can be known, by an expert class of risk calculators separated from the business by their special knowledge, with the CRO as their head. The reports which they produce as one result already belong to another category. Risk is displaced into abstract, aggregated figures. The regulators acknowledge the different approaches of banks under the same label, for example, different models leading to VaR, and concentrate on controlling via the introduction of formal rules, audits and disclosure processes. We could interpret this development as the reintroduction of the secret. It is not clear how risk management works but there are rules followed and procedures performed. As such, these relatively obscure (to the outside observer) ritual processes entail a certain level of re-enchantment. Magic needs no proof, and the magician is not threatened by failure, or, as Power (1994, p. 6) put it, 'Audits have the remarkable capacity of being invulnerable to their own failure.'

A milieu emerged consisting of a worried public, concerned regulators, nervous politicians, a highly educated and separated group of risk specialists, CROs as symbols of successful containment, boards of direct-ors as responsible actors and, somewhat marginalized, those confronted with the actual risk. In this milieu the idea of risk management as a form of governance is configured and performed. 'Audit actually constructs the contexts in which it operates' writes Power (1994, p. 7), and with that he emphasizes the dependence on the social context. The world of risk and futurity, at once complex, difficult to fathom and hard to keep pace with, can be made understandable by telling comprehensible stories; or telling stories of how intensively, professionally and sophis-ticatedly the problems are dealt with: figures and formulas, statistics, reports and audits. The environment for this has to be created: 'Auditing is a peculiar form of alchemy which, in making auditees auditable, pro-duces regulatory comfort' (Power, 1994, p. 49). Risk is perceived as an independent force inherent in banking business – a threatening power – and magic is needed to tame it, as if its effect would be to take them out of a dangerous state (Mauss, 1902/1978, p. 94). Seen from this perspec-tive, Schachter's description of aspects of risk management as 'the quest for the holy scale' (Schachter, 1997) seems no longer to be far fetched. Or, to put it another way, the high priests perform their magic rites to allay public fears, clearly conscious of the fact that reports, audits and good governance do not provide the sufficient conditions for controlling risks. At the technical limits of calculation we find the re-emergence of magic to fill the vacuum of human need with respect to coping with risk and uncertainty.

Notes

1. Basel is the seat of the Bank for International Settlements (BIS), which hosts the central secretariat of the committee on banking supervisions called the Basel Committee. Basel II is the name of the framework for regulating risk management in banks: *International Convergence of Capital Measurement and Capital Standards* (BIS 2004) It is the continuation of the framework Basel I.
2. Direct quotes of Mauss are taken from the English translation in Mauss (1902/2001).

9

Divine Inspiration for Deities?

Frederic Bill and Anders Hytter

Idun spoke:

18. 'To Loki I speak not | with spiteful words
Here within Ægir's hall;
And Bragi I calm, | who is hot with beer,
For I wish not that fierce they should fight.'

Introduction

Drawn from the pre-Christian saga the *Poetic Edda*, Idun's words in the eighteenth verse places us in the centre of one its major poems. Thus, we enter into the *Lokasenna* (Loki's Quarrel), a part of the *Poetic Edda* that describes a final rupture in the Norse celestial world. The *Edda* contains a number of poetic narratives regarding dealings of the pre-Christian deities, villains and heroes of Scandinavia.[1] The actual age as well as the historical source value of the *Edda* texts is debated and seems hard to assess (Anderson, 2002; Frakes, 2002). Its mythical material has, however, undeniably influenced many Scandinavians' perception of their own past.

As a general outline, the giant semi-god ruling over the seas, Ægir has brewed beer in his gigantic kettle and is using the golden brew to throw an impressive feast. With the exception of Thor, the Norse god of thunder, the Æsir have all arrived at the reception. Also Loki, a very handsome but rather malign character, has been invited. Despite being the son of giants, he socializes with the Norse gods due to his status of blood brother with their ruler, Odin. During the festivities, Loki murders Fimafeng, one of Ægir's servants, and is driven from the feast. He returns, however, demanding to again be permitted to enter. By referring to his long-term relationship with Odin, he eventually succeeds in doing this.

His return initiates a quarrel, primarily since neither Loki nor the Norse gods demonstrate much humility or flexibility during the following verbal exchange. Especially upset is Bragi (the god of poetry) who, as we enter the developing story, has repeatedly been accused of cowardice by Loki. The temper of the gods is deteriorating rapidly, and the verbal combatants are slowly but surely edging closer to physical strikes. In the eighteenth verse (see above) we meet for the first time a more diplomatic statement, emanating from the goddess Idun, (Bragis wife and caretaker of the apples of youth) who apparently attempts to cool down sentiment in the hall.

We will treat the text as if it describes something that actually took place in the hall of Ægir at some indefinable point in time. The guiding proposition of this chapter is that the feast held by Ægir can be considered an instance of organizing, not least since the participants have interacted more or less closely before the *Lokasenna* begins, i.e. they can be expected to know one another in advance. Therefore, the actual behaviour of the characters in the story can be analysed from the point of view of organizational or interpersonal behaviour.

We therefore intend to explore how the deities, scoundrels and heroes of early Scandinavian mythology might have, in some specific instances, benefited from an understanding of and willingness to employ contemporary 'behaviour-style-analysis' tools and techniques. Applying this kind of analysis on four of the gods in the *Lokasenna* was done in order to pinpoint their behavioural characteristics, as well as to increase the understanding of the different conflicts described in the story. The analysis is carried out with an instrument called IDI, Interpersonal Dynamics Inventory.[2] Generally speaking, IDI is a so-called 360-degree sociometric instrument used to analyse how one's behaviour is perceived by others. Since this means that others do the input for the analysis of the focal person, it is more or less ideal for this kind of study.[3]

This chapter will however primarily challenge our taken-for-granted understanding of mythology by presenting an alternative perception. It will also, to some extent, lay bare the timelessness of a typology regarding inferior organizational behaviour.

What is an IDI-profile?

The interest for how we are perceived by others has manifested itself in, for example, a number of different tests and measurements. In general, psychometric instruments deal with personality traits (Hogan, *et al.*, 1994), while sociometric instruments deal with behaviour. IDI is a sociometric instrument and its roots are twofold. First there are the so called Ohio-studies (Halpin and Winer, 1957). Their two dimensions of initiation of structure and consideration can be found in a number of management development tools such as, for example, the Managerial Grid by Blake and Mouton (1985), the 3-D Theory of Managerial Effectiveness by Reddin (1970) and other instruments, (for an extended literature review, see Bass, 2008). Second, there are several instruments that derive their explanation from the archetypes of C.G. Jung (1971), for example the Myers-Briggs Type Indicator (see Gardner and Martinko, 1996 for a literature review) and Social Styles (Merrill and Reid, 1981).

Originally created to aid in selection of leaders, IDI combines these roots. It is an instrument which measures and evaluates the impression you make on others in your surroundings (Zackrison, 2006, p. 3).[4] Thus, IDI deals with behaviour since it was believed that good leaders/managers shared (or ought to share) some basic behavioural characteristics. No optimal behavioural style could however be identified. Instead, strengths and weaknesses can be found within each behaviour style (*ibid.*)

The basic idea is that human behaviour, as apart from feelings or processes of thought, is measurable. It is believed to remain rather constant over time. In an IDI-test, three different aspects of behaviour are measured; Directiveness, Affiliation and Adaptability. Directiveness deals with the influencing on others, and is defined in the following way: 'Directiveness measures how often a person is perceived as striving to impress, influence and control other persons and/or the environment' (*ibid.*, p. 5).

Affiliation deals with emotional contact and is defined in the following way: 'Affiliation is a measure of how often an individual is perceived as striving to establish emotional contact with many other humans' (*ibid.*, p. 6).

Adaptability measures flexibility in relation to the needs of others and is defined as: 'Adaptability measures the extent to which a person is perceived as being prepared to temporarily alter certain parts of his/her basic behavior style, based on the needs of others and/or various situations, while paying less attention to their own needs' (*ibid.*, p. 21)

Three aspects of the definitions are of particular importance; the measuring of 'how often', 'is perceived' and 'striving to'. First, 'how often' indicates that it is the frequency rather than the strength of the aspect that is being measured. Second, 'is perceived' indicates that it is how others experience the focal person's behaviour that decides the degree of directiveness a person is expressing, not his/her own perception of his/her own behaviour. Finally, 'striving to' indicates that IDI does not measure the degree of success or failure in someone's behaviour, that is whether the person actually manages to impress, influence, control, or establish emotional contact. It is only the behaviour, not the result, nor the consequences, which is being measured. (*ibid.*, p. 6)

Behavioural styles

Depending on the combined score for directiveness and affiliation, IDI makes it possible to distinguish between four major behavioural styles; Relator, Motivator, Processor and Producer. The Relator style scores medium to high on affiliation but low to medium on directiveness. The Motivator style scores medium to high in both respects, while the Processor style scores low to medium in both respects. The Producer style, finally, scores low to medium on affiliation and medium to high on directiveness.

Furthermore, each major style is divided into four sub-styles. The most typical style within each major style is found in the outer corner in the model (i.e. the coordinates A1, D1, D4, and A4, see Figure 9.1). Subsequently, A1 is called a friendly relator, D1 is called an expressive

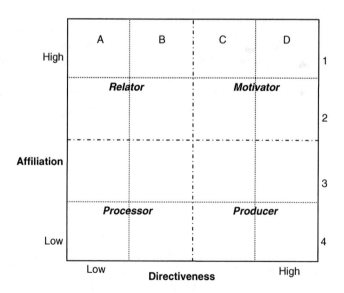

Figure 9.1 Directiveness and affiliation in the IDI frame work

motivator, D4 is called a driving producer, and A4 is called an analytical processor.

Following the same pattern, each major style is divided into four sub styles. Illustrating this by naming the four sub styles of the Motivator basic style renders that, C1 is influenced by the relation oriented behaviour of the Relator style, and thus is called a friendly motivator. D2 is influenced by the goal-oriented behaviour of the Producer style and is called a driving motivator. C2 is influenced by the analytical behaviour of the Processor style and is called an analytical motivator. This pattern is valid also for the three other major styles, Relator, Processor and Producer. On the sub-style level, the IDI-model thus consists in total of 16 quadrants in a four by four matrix.

The third dimension, adaptability, is measured on a scale from one to one hundred. The ability to adapt to the needs of others has been demonstrated to influence a person's effectiveness in leadership situations, and an average adaptability is about 50. When analysing adaptability, it can be said that the lower a person scores on this dimension, the more he/she gives priority to his/her own needs.

In the following part we will discuss the IDI profiles of the four gods Loki, Odin, Bragi and Idun, while elaborating on the strengths and weaknesses of their respective behavioural style.

The behaviour styles of the gods

Two of the gods, Loki and Bragi, score above medium on the affiliation scale, while the two others, Idun and Odin, score under medium. We should not be surprised by this since affiliation measures the extent to which an individual is trying to establish emotional contact, not the extent to which she or he is successful when doing this. It is hard to argue against the idea that Loki is trying to establish any kind of contact when stating:

> Loki spoke:
> 46. 'Be silent, Byggvir! | thou never couldst set
> Their shares of the meat for men;
> Hid in straw on the floor, | they found thee not
> When heroes were fain to fight.'

His success in creating constructive emotional bonds through statements such as this is however highly limited. Individuals like Loki, that behave in a way that is perceived as highly affiliative, could also be considered as having a lot of temper and a tendency to quickly become personal when involved in arguments and discussions. Now let's look at the behavioural styles of the four gods.

Idun – a Friendly Processor (A3)

The primary mediator of the story, the goddess Idun, scored low on directiveness and just under medium on affiliation. Thus, as can be seen in Figure 9.2, she ended up as a friendly processor. The exact position with regard to affiliation is however unsure, indicating that she is on the border between being a friendly processor (A3) and an analytical relator (A2). Her adaptability score is 24.

Being a friendly processor, it can be expected that Idun will not try to influence and impress others very often, but she is to some extent expected to strive for emotional contact with others. In one of the verses, she does indeed try to reach out to Loki, trying to get to him to calm down. This is actually somewhat unexpected, considering that he in the previous verse has accused her of being somewhat of a trollop:

17. 'Be silent, Ithun! [Idun]‖ thou art, I say,
    Of women most lustful in love,'

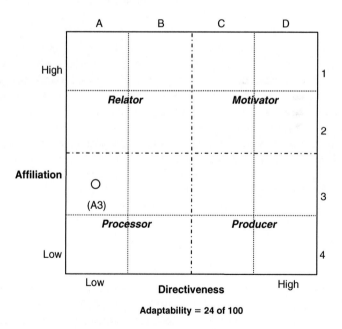

Adaptability = 24 of 100

Figure 9.2 Idun's IDI-profile

Thus, Idun's affiliation score is just under medium, which is likely taking into consideration her attempts to keep the combatants apart. In the subsequent verse, she answers Loki:

> 18. 'To Loki I speak not | with spiteful words
> Here within Ægir's hall;
> And Bragi I calm, | who is hot with beer,
> For I wish not that fierce they should fight.'

She claims Bragi to be speaking out of drunkenness and illuminates that Loki currently is in the hall of Ægir which, among the Nordic gods, was not considered an acceptable place to have a fight. Being a friendly processor, she wants to avoid the confrontation Bragi and Loki quickly seems to be heading for. Furthermore, she appears to be everything but comfortable with the high level of emotions in the situation, another characteristic of a friendly processor.

> 16. 'Well, prithee, Bragi, | his kinship weigh,
> Since chosen as wish-son he was;
> And speak not to Loki | such words of spite
> Here within Ægir's hall.'

So, she uses her diplomatic ability to avoid conflict. Strengths and weaknesses, as well as combinations of strengths and weaknesses, are expressed within all the behavioural styles. Hindering the solving of conflicts through avoiding or denying them is a common behaviour when friendly processors act in line with their weaknesses. (Zackrison, 2006). It seems as if Idun takes on this behaviour in the described situation. Furthermore, she is also demonstrating other behaviours that are typical for processors acting in line with their weaknesses. She is, for example, causing the group to remain stuck in details, rather than helping it focus on the important topics at hand. Thus, in the situation in the *Lokasenna*, she is demonstrating the stress-symptoms of both the relator (to flee responsibility) and the processor (to ask for time out). Both are behaviours that can be expected from a friendly processor under stress.

Loki – a Driving Motivator (D2)

The primary character in the *Lokasenna*, the half-giant Loki scored rather high on affiliation and very high on directiveness. Thus, he ends up as a driving motivator (Figure 9.3). Furthermore, with the score of one, he scores the lowest possible on adaptability.

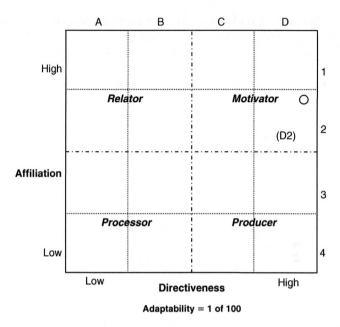

Figure 9.3 Loki's IDI-profile

Throughout the *Lokasenna*, he tries to establish (emotional) contact with people around him. He is also perceived as to a high degree trying to influence and control the behaviour of other individuals. As has been demonstrated in the verse regarding Bragi (no. 46, quoted above), Loki does not balk from using emotionally based arguments to achieve this when communicating with the characters around him. It cannot be said that he motivates anyone, at least not in the positive sense of the word. Thus, it appears that Loki acts in line with the weaknesses rather than the strengths of a motivator. When a motivator acts in line with his/her weaknesses, he/she tends to be competitive, to loose contact with reality, to let the baby out of the tub together with the water, to advance to fast for his/her surroundings and focus more or less solely on his/her own needs (Zackrison, 2006). Behaviours like these are demonstrated by Loki as soon as he returns to the feast:

> 6. 'Thirsty I come | into this thine hall,
> I, Lopt, from a journey long,
> To ask of the gods | that one should give
> Fair mead for a drink to me.'

He is not trying to find any ground for establishing a common understanding. He rather speaks of his own needs – to have a seat and
something to drink. This could be seen as Loki striving for being recognized or accepted, a very strong need for a driving motivator. Then
Bragi mouths his protest and tells Loki to leave Ægir's hall:

> 8. 'A place and a seat | will the gods prepare
> No more in their midst for thee;'

Loki refuses and invokes his old pact with Odin, the father of the gods.
The *Lokasenna* continues:

> 9. 'Remember, Othin (Odin), | in olden days
> That we both our blood have mixed;
> Then didst thou promise | no ale to pour,
> Unless it were brought for us both.'

Odin's positive answer becomes the psychological recognition Loki so
desperately is looking for. Equally important is that it also becomes the
acceptance needed to be allowed to join the party again. Loki is again
invited into the hall, but the conflicts and foulmouthedness continues.
Loki is not backing down, despite being offered gifts by Bragi.

It is quite clear that Loki is exposing the highly goal-oriented behaviour
of a driving motivator. He is also teasing and verbally provoking each and
everyone he is talking to throughout the whole *Lokasenna*, including
Odin. In some cases, especially with the goddesses, he is utilizing the
favourite weapon of a driving motivator – a verbal cross fire. This is
particularly evident when he accuses them of having lovers (i.e., more
than one), illegitimate children and even – in the case of Idun – to have
made love to the one who killed her brother.

Bragi – a Friendly Motivator (C1)

The first of the Æsir that confronts Loki in the story is Bragi, the god of
poetry. He scores rather high on directiveness and very high on affiliation. Thus, as can be seen in Figure 9.4, he ends up as a friendly motivator
(C1). The exact position with regard to affiliation is however unsure, indicating that there is a rather strong tendency towards the C2 quadrant,
i.e. being an analytic motivator.

Similar to the case of Idun, we can see how her husband, Bragi, tends
to act in line with the weaknesses in his behaviour style. Maintaining

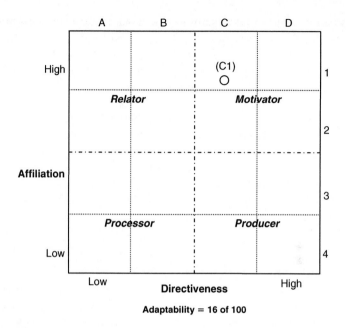

Figure 9.4 Bragi's IDI-profile

a good relation is important for a friendly motivator, and subsequently this is high on Bragi's agenda. From this perspective, it is interesting to note that, as the conflict between the two develops, he immediately tries to calm Loki down by offering him gifts.

> 12. 'A horse and a sword | from my hoard will I give,
> And a ring gives Bragi to boot.'

Loki, however, continues the string of insults, causing Bragi to loose his temper. This is also in line with the reaction of friendly motivators, who easily can take the rejection of an idea as a personal insult. Bragi then acts, without enough after-thought, from his own needs of respect rather than considering the needs of the group. Responding:

> 14. 'Now were I without | as I am within,
> And here in Ægir's hall,
> Thine head would I bear | in mine hands away,
> And pay thee the price of thy lies.'

This threat, however, does not intimidate Loki, who continues his verbal assault on Bragi unabated:

> 'Go out and fight | if angered thou feelest,
> No hero such forethought has.'

The two motivators, both acting in line with the weaknesses of their major behavioural style, thus enter into an ever more infected conflict. Neither of them is capable to transcend this antagonism as it quickly becomes personal for both parties, despite the initial attempts by the somewhat more adaptable Bragi. It should however be noted that although Bragi's adaptability of 16 is better than Loki's score of 1, it definitely has to be considered as low.

Odin – a Driving Processor (B4)

Odin, the somewhat forbidding father of the Norse gods, scored very low on affiliation and medium on directiveness. Thus, as can be seen in Figure 9.5, he ends up as a driving processor (B4), with an adaptability of 26.

Early in the *Lokasenna*, Odin manages to make the fatal mistake of inviting Loki back into the hall, thus allowing him to participate in the feast again. By being invited back, Loki is given an arena on which he can act out his needs. On his return, Loki invokes his old pact with Odin (as stated in verse 9 above), and Odin responds with an acceptance of their old understanding:

> 10. 'Stand forth then, Vithar, | and let the wolf's father
> Find a seat at our feast;
> Lest evil should Loki | speak aloud
> Here within Ægir's hall.'

In this example we could argue that Odin acts in line with the weaknesses of a driving processor, where the processor-part wants to reduce things to being logical, objective and within a structure that can be trusted, while the 'driving part' refuses to revoke a decision. He is not willing to accept that his pact with Loki might be problematic or untimely, insisting instead on it being respected. Despite Bragis objections (as stated in verse 8 above). Odin refuses to listen and acts more or less stubbornly in line with his own one-time decision.

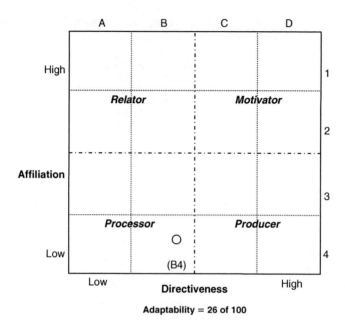

Figure 9.5 Odin's IDI-profile

As the *Lokasenna* continues, Odin also demonstrates behaviours that are typical for processors acting in line with the weaknesses of their behaviour style. Like most of the other Æsir he tries to solve the problem himself instead of facilitating the group in solving the problem. Thus, he does not help the group in finding a solution to its conflicts and problems. Instead, as he tries to solve them himself, the gods get stuck even more in details, and needed actions become delayed even further.

Conclusion

Despite the efforts of Idun and Thor, the quarrel ends with Loki leaving and the world starting to spiral towards Ragnarok.[5] Why this outcome? It could be argued that a motivator with low adaptability, like Loki, can be expected to be manipulating, irritable, over-competitive, shallow, impetuous, dominant and exaggerated. These labels fit Loki's behaviour in most of Norse mythology, and some of the labels definitely fit his behaviour in the *Lokasenna*. However, in this case he also seems arrogant, short sighted, presumptuous, single-minded and aggressive. When Siv, Thor's wife, offers him praise, he responds:

> 54. 'Alone thou wert | if truly thou wouldst
> All men so shyly shun;
> But one do I know | full well, methinks,
> Who had thee from Hlorrithi's arms,–
> (Loki the crafty in lies.)'

This latter set of behaviours is typical for producers demonstrating low adaptability. Thus it actually seems as if Loki, in this setting, tends to shift his behaviour towards that of a producer – allowing the 'driving' part in his style to become dominating. This is, furthermore, what basically causes most of the commotion among the gods. When Loki acts from his predominant behavioural style (i.e., motivator) with low adaptability, he is considered to be manipulative, rash and over-competitive. Even though these characteristics may not be all that good for the efficiency of a group, they neither proclaim a predetermined path towards open conflict. Why is Loki then suddenly expressing so much more producer behaviour? Reading the *Lokasenna*, you realize that Loki does not utter one nice word throughout the whole story. Maybe he just had a very bad day. Maybe there is a deeper psychological explanation to his behaviour. We can only guess.

Furthermore, the producer par excellence in Norse mythology is the mighty Thor, god of thunder and slayer of giants. His absence during the first part of the *Lokasenna* opens up an arena on which Loki takes a position. This position, however, will result in unsolvable conflicts with the other gods which becomes clear when we look at the development that takes place when Thor actually arrives at the feast towards the end of the *Lokasenna*. He immediately confronts Loki and threatens him with his famous hammer:

> 57. 'Unmanly one, cease, | or the mighty hammer,
> Mjollnir, shall close thy mouth;
> Thy shoulder-cliff | shall I cleave from thy neck,
> And so shall thy life be lost.'

Thor repeats the threat in several verses, thus expressing all the traits of a producer, most likely also a 'driving producer', with low adaptability. This causes Loki to shift his behaviour towards his basic style – motivator. The damage is, however, already beyond the point where the conflict can be solved in a friendly manner.

Judging from our analysis, there appears to be a timelessness in the organizational misbehaviour expressed in the *Lokasenna*, since modern(istic) tools for behavioural analysis seems to be capable of pinpointing this universal typology also in an ancient text. Whether this is due to the plasticity of the tool or the timeless nature of human behaviour is of course a valid question, even though the tool does make it possible to apply a useful typology on the story. Thus, our analysis demonstrates that the four gods offer a range of examples of how not to behave. The simplest way to understand this would be to actually consider it to be the intention with the text. Thus, we propose that the *Lokasenna* could in fact be considered to be a story ridiculing the all too well-known ways in which people misbehave in organizations. The familiar Norse Parthenon is used as a way of disarming the contemporary political dimension potentially inherent in the content of the *Poetic Edda*.

In the taken-for-granted manner of the early fathers of the Christian church, we [the authors] automatically believe that at some point in the past, the people listening to, or reading these narratives, believed them to represent actions of actual gods. In moving focus from the context to the actions of the poem, the strangeness of the narrative is to some extent bridged. The IDI-analyses illuminate that the gods and villains in the *Lokasenna* actually behaved in ways which, according to the scientific foundations of the IDI-frame, are utterly detrimental to cooperation and harmonious organizational life. Apparently, when looked upon as organization members, they were as bad during the Viking age as they would be in organizations of the twenty-first century.

As can be seen above, the gods tend to act out the weaknesses of their respective behaviour styles. This is however not surprising, considering their adaptability levels being as low as they are (between 26 and 1). So, in one sense, what do you expect if you bring together a group with such behaviour styles and offer them strong beer from a gigantic kettle?

Apparently, as this chapter suggests, ancient Scandinavians held the same expectations.

Acknowledgements

We would like to thank all those who kindly took upon themselves to fill out the questionnaires for the IDI-profiles and without whom this text could not have been written: So, Urban Ljungqvist, Hans Bååth, Göran Andersson, Anita Hall, Christina Enfors, Stig Johansson, Anna Alexandersson, Erik Rosell, Hans Lundberg, Susanna Holzer, Pernilla Nilsson, Ola Agevall, Ulf Larsson, Michaela Sandell, Lena Olaison,

Fredrik Pettersson, Susanna Björverud, Magnus Forslund, Andreas Janson, Rolf G. Larsson, Dan Halvarsson, Anna Lindahl, Patrik Persson and Lise-Lotte Jensen. Thank You.

Notes

1. Acker offers the following concise overview of the content in the *Poetic Edda*:

   > Taken together, the poems convey an outline of Old Norse mythic history, from the creation of the earth, heavens, giants, gods and humans; through the war of the Æsir and Vanir (two classes of gods) and the accidental killing of Óðinn's son Baldr; and ahead to the ultimate battle against evil beings at Ragnarok (the 'doom of the gods') Individually the poems present mythic episodes. (Acker, 2002, p. xiii)

2. Adapted from Zackrison (2006).
3. Literary characters can of course not fill out any questionnaires or offer any data themselves, so the method utilized cannot require any such. There is a self-evaluation questionnaire included in the IDI testframe, but it is only intended to make it possible to compare one's own perception with that of the people with whom you interact. Thus, we filled out the self-evaluation questionnaires ourselves.

   In order to analyse the gods' behaviour, we asked 24 persons to fill out the questionnaires. To complete an IDI-profile, requires the answering of six questionnaires for each focal person, making it possible for us to make the test on four gods (Bragi, Idun, Loki and Odin). Since we did not want the filling out of the questionnaires to be comparative, all persons were asked to respond to one questionnaire only, i.e. one person responded only for one of the four gods.
4. All quotes from Zackrison (2006) are our own translations into English.
5. The end of the world in Norse mythology.

10
Living Between Myths: Experiences at Wells Fargo Bank

David M. Boje and Anna Linda Musacchio Adorisio

Introduction

What are the myths that circulate in organizations? What is their role? How they connect to the experience of the people belonging to such organizations?

> They [Wells Fargo] have a videotape that gives you all the ... when we first converted to Wells Fargo I remember we had to watch this 20 minutes video with all the history, and all the things they did and where they have been. (A)

says one of the executives of a community bank integrated into the Wells Fargo system.

It is the history of its founding on 18 March 1852 by Henri Wells and William Fargo, who provided banking and express freight wagon service to the gold rush and as well as mail delivery to miners, merchants and farmers. In 1870 Wells Fargo gained control of the overland mail company leading to the operation of the Pony Express. Up until 1954 it was known as the Wells Fargo Bank and Union Trust Company, then it was shortened into Wells Fargo bank. This opening introduction is itself an abbreviation or abstract that does not do justice to the complexity of events that contributed to the emergence of Wells Fargo. The founding whirlpool of emergence did not cohere into this founding narrative for several decades.

Next we jump forward in time to Norwest's relationship to Wells Fargo. When in November 1998 Norwest acquired, in a $31.7 billion deal, Wells Fargo bank, in what was described by O'Reilly *et al.* (2004) as a 'merger of equals', it then changed its name into Wells Fargo & Company in order to 'capitalize on the 150 year history of Wells Fargo bank and on its trademark stagecoach' (Wells Fago, Wikipedia, 2007), logo; one of the ten most recognizable logos in the world and 'a staple of the mythology of the American West' (Stagecoach, Amazon.com, 2007). The headquarters were moved to the San Francisco base of Wells Fargo, while Richard Kovacevich, former head of Norwest became president and CEO of the newly formed bank. The integration between Norwest and Wells Fargo went rather smoothly as it took some three years to be completed, as opposed to the previous Wells Fargo hostile takeover of First Interstate.

There is a great simplification in assuming that the history of one bank in all its complexity can be superimposed onto another bank's history or by extension over 2,000 acquired banks. Norwest/Wells Fargo bank has absorbed more than 2,000 (Wells Fargo, Wikipedia, 2007) banking institutions and the consolidation seems still to be ongoing. Many smaller banks have been integrated into the Norwest/Wells Fargo culture and history. Will this integration into the Wells Fargo mythology and history be tenable in the long run?

'As of September 30, 2006, Wells Fargo has 6,165 branches, 23 million customers and 167,000 employees' (Wells Fargo, Wikipedia, 2007). Wells Fargo is well-known for its cross-selling focus – their goal is to be able to sell at least eight products to each customer. The cross-selling packages include checking and savings accounts, credit cards, home mortgages, home equity loans, personal loans and credit lines, asset-based lending, mutual funds, IRAs, life and health insurances. While the average cross-sell ratio of a financial institution is two, Wells Fargo shows a ratio of 4.6. The cross-selling comes to the Norwest superior sales culture and its dedication to customer service, Norwest branches were called stores, and banker salespeople and this still shows in the Wells Fargo organization. On the other hand Wells Fargo was known as the leader of online banking services and technology and for its dedication to efficiency. The passage from stagecoach and safe boxes to Internet and technology still needs to be investigated. Newly acquired banks are colonized with both the Wells Fargo logo and the Norwest culture. Richard Kovacevich, the former Norwest head, is the recognized figure of the bank by all interviewed Wells Fargo personnel.

Norwest history goes back to 1929 and the great depression as Northwester Bancorporation, simply known as Banco. When in 1983 the name was changed to Norwest Corporation 'bank' has been expurged from the name as 'the aim was that of creating a diversified financial service company' (Wells Fargo, Reference, 2007). Our key research proposition is whether this is the same bank, before and after the depression up to 1983 and to the 1998 merger.

In 1986 Dick Kovacevich was hired from Citicorp and held a variety of posts:

> until he became CEO in 1993. Kovacevich, president and CEO of Wells Fargo from 1998, was a recognized leader in the financial service industry and the one associated with the store, sales-people culture, along with cross-selling strategy. (Richard Kovacevich, Wikipedia, 2007)

The structure of this chapter is to present theories of mythmaking to apply implications to the Wells Fargo integration of 6,165 retail branches under a common mythological historical framework. Material in this chapter is based on document and history books of banking institutions and interviews with former Norwest and Wells Fargo personnel including those who had worked in other community banks before being acquired by Wells Fargo. We conclude by drawing implications of mythmaking for organization theory.

Theory of myth

> Myth making is an adaptive mechanism whereby groups in an organization maintain a logic framework within which to attribute meaning to activities and events (Boje *et al.*, 1982, p. 18).

In organizational development authors such as French and Bell (1973) view organization development (OD) as the demythification of organization using behavioural science principles while others such as Margulies (1972) view OD as more about helping clients find better myths. Jabri (1997, p. 21) argues that 'myths have been advocated as the basis for the conduct of interventions but mainly within the confines of the prevailing logic'. Table 10.1 gives a typology of organization myths.

In order to step out of a linear model we have to exploit interpretations of myth that accommodate for alternative interpretations. Demythologization using behavioural science overlooks the way rational exchange reverts to myths of legitimation. Rather than dualize myth and rationality one can look at them as dialogic. Different paradigms have been used in the study of myths. We propose a life cycle model following work by Boje *et al.* (1982) (see Table 10.2). And we make a number of further clarifications to the model, adapting it to dynamic and complex organization transitions.

Lévi-Strauss (1955, 1963) studied myths following a structuralist approach. While myths differ from one culture to another, their structure can be assimilated in a fashion that does not differ too much from the distinction from langue and parole made by Saussure.

Table 10.1   Typology of organization myths

Myths construct standards of desirability:
1. Myths that create, maintain, and legitimize past, present, or future actions and consequences.
2. Myths that maintain and conceal political interests and value systems.

Myths construct cause-and-effect relationships:
3. Myths that help explain and create cause-and-effect relationships under conditions of incomplete knowledge.
4. Myths that rationalize the complexity and turbulence of activities and events that allow for predictable action taking.

Source: Adapted from Boje *et al.* (1982).

Table 10.2   The mythmaking life cycle

Myth stage	Organization situation
I. Myth development	Rapid growth, high profitability, bright future outlook: no real competition
	Myth is successfully guiding decision making and organizational strategy – 'Developing myth'
II. Myth maturation	Company's growth slowing, but still recognized as solid leader. Some competition which is inconsequential.
	Myth and company identity completely intertwined. Myth strength is high. 'Solid myth'
III. Decline	Competition has become substantial. Profitability slipping. Mission is a hindrance to action.
	Most organizational units looking for ways to bolster myth, but some groups beginning to develop competing myths for renewal. 'Myth split'
IV. Reformulation	Company's situation has deteriorated to the point that precipitates a change in leadership.
	Myth redefined to include new quality range for products. 'Myth shift'

Structure is what makes it possible to understand myths, not their materials which are always changing.

> On the one hand it would seem that in the course of a myth anything is likely to happen. There is no logic, no continuity. Any characteristic can be attributed to any subject; every conceivable relation can be found ... but on the other hand this apparent arbitrariness is belied by the astounding similarity between myths collected in widely different regions. (Lévi-Strauss, 1963, p. 208)

Similarly, Fromm argues that 'the myth like the dream, offers a story occurring in space-time, a story which expresses, in symbolic language, religious and philosophical ideas, experiences of the soul in which the real significance of the myth lies' (1937/1951, p. 195). The structural interpretation of myth provided by Lévi-Strauss seeks for a logical system which can also be at the basis of every myth-making process, a common structure whose articulations are not unlimited. 'The characteristic feature of mythical thought is that it expresses itself by means of a heterogeneous repertoire which, even if extensive, is nevertheless limited' (Lévi-Strauss, 1966, p. 19).

Using a different approach Malinowski (1927, p. 21) argues the impossibility of understanding myth by 'mere examination of the texts' as the myths are 'living reality'. Similarly Dumézil criticizes the structuralist method by saying that we cannot understand the myths if we separate them from the life of the people that tell them, unless we want to interpret them using an a priori system (1968). Dumézil continues by saying that his work is not that of a philosopher, but rather that of a historian, as he does not seek to find results that are universally valid as he proceeds without any prejudice and without knowing before what he will find.

We are critical of Malinowski because elsewhere he affirms that myth 'supplies a retrospective narrative pattern of moral values, sociological order and magical belief' (1948, p. 122), contradicting the idea of 'living realities' that seemed so promising. It seems difficult to escape the tendency of understanding myth as a normative order, whether 'unconscious' (as in Fromm) or socially organized.

On yet another view than that of Lévi-Strauss or Malinowski, Adorno and Horkheimer argue that myth making is a process of rationalization of the irrational and of mastering of the unknown. Myth loses during history its opening to the irrational and the unpredictable which can overthrow the 'order' and becomes a tool of oppression of a totalitarian project. Bauer reads Adorno and Horkeimer as dialectic of enlightenment and its reversion to myth 'the dialect of enlightenment on myth cancels out any progression: enlightenment reverts to myth' (1999, p. 13):

> But this dialectic remains powerless as long as it emerges from the cry of terror, which is the doubling, the mere tautology of terror itself ... enlightenment is mythical fear radicalized. The pure immanence of positivism, its ultimate product, is nothing other than a form of universal taboo. (Adorno and Horkheimer, 2002, p. 11)

There is a conflict between the two aspects of myth: on one hand, the idea of myth as a model for human behaviour and on the other side the idea of myth as stories. Campbell expresses it in 'the story is the plot we assign to life and the universe, our basic assumption and fundamental beliefs about how things work ... we are in trouble now "because we live in between stories"' (Campbell with Moyers, 1988, p. 139).

Such a tension is inscribed in the definition itself of myth and in its historical changing notation. Myth is on the one hand the legitimate story of the creation, and thus seen as the paradigm for human conduct while on the other hand in the enlightenment pejorative notation they are nothing else than stories, false beliefs.

We believe that the postmodern and critical perspective can provide highlights on the matter.

As Marquard (1989, p. 90) puts it: 'the truth is one thing, but the way we can live with the truth is another. Knowledge serves the former, cognitively and stories serve the latter, vitally ... their tasks (stories) is not to find the truth, but to find a modus vivendi with truth.' Defining myths as stories, Marquard argues that polymythical thinking is healthy, while monomythical thinking is harmful. Dangerous is the destiny of the one who will leave monomythically one story as 'fascinated by the new myth of the sole history, one sticks to the path that is only supposedly the path to heaven on earth and is in reality the path to identity, on earth, of heaven and hell: to an integrated, all purpose identity' (*ibid.*, p. 103).

In the postmodern world there are multiple 'weakened truths' Vattimo (1989) and some very deceived consciousness. As Vattimo puts it, the myth cannot end with modernity, we are thrown in myth, although our experience is a postmodern experience of the myth, which is not the normative and unique foundation of modern thought. If we can't neglect the legitimating and foundative character of the myth for the communities in which it circulates, we can nevertheless accept it as a 'weakened truth' (Vattimo, 1989) for the postmodern subject.

In sum a postmodern approach to myth would have four facets:

1. Instead of one universally valid myth we look at a multiplicity of myths shaping memory and experience.
2. All mythmaking processes are not created equal some have more resources and commend more power while others are marginalized or even erased from being.
3. Myths interact in a given organization and although marginalized in the corporate visuality and textuality they nevertheless survive in the orality of the stories of people belonging to such organizations.
4. Myths are in the living of everyday life and are conflicting at every level of their cycle.

The results discussed in the following section have been achieved through research held in 2006 in Las Cruces, New Mexico. Funding was made available by a Swiss National Science Foundation Research Fellowship.

Executives were interviewed both in formal recorded interviews and ordinary conversations. More than one round of interviews was performed. Interviews took the unstructured form and lasted, on average, 2 hours. Transcripts for a total of 60 pages were produced during a total effort of about 70 hours of transcription and revision. Triangulation was achieved accessing as much as possible information regarding the decisions, the organization, the people involved in the organization, and the historical, cultural and economic context in which the organization operates. Data sources were books available on the bank's history, newsletters and publications from the bank, archival information, visits, and cassettes showing different moments of the life of the interviewed decision makers.

Experiences at Wells Fargo Bank

In their 1982 article Boje *et al.* posit a myth making life cycle and argue that 'myth evolution does not have to be a smooth process, but can be erratic, depending upon the support the organizational myth receives from divergent groups and the environment' (1982, pp. 23–4). In every stage of the model, negotiation is necessary between different antagonist forces. And this process in not always a democratic one.

If we read the Norwest/Wells Fargo organization in terms of mythmaking process, we can notice that the one integrated myth of selling culture plus the stagecoaches is not achieved without the systematic suppression of the fragments of different and alternative myths that cannot be incorporated. I am talking about the 2,000 banks that were incorporated into either Wells Fargo or Norwest.

They all have their own myths and symbols, but they are simply not part of the dominant mythology. When talking about stagecoaches and safe-boxes one of the executives of one of the acquired community banks says: 'we had all our own stuff . . . we had a big zia symbol . . . and we used to have pins with that symbol and we used to put diamonds every five years' (A). (A) then opens the cupboard with a big box full of newsletters and letter head sheets with his name under the symbol and a stack of photos of the bank and their buildings. 'See all these buildings, I took pictures of all the properties we had . . . and they didn't even know that they got all that property, they didn't . . . they just had no clue' (A).

He is talking about the buildings, but seeing his face and his voice trembling it's not hard to understand that he is referring to a much deeper understanding that they (the acquiring bank, which by the way was not Wells Fargo) lacked. What we want to show is that not all the myth-making processes have the same resources and in a case like this one, a whole system of mythology is completely erased from being in the new organization.

It is the myth of a bank called First National Bank of Dona Ana County and a man that was often referred to as Mr. First National who entered the bank in the 1950s and soon became a living legend, and example: Frank Papen. 'When the board decided, Frank ... well Frank was the board' says one of the interviewed executives (B). 'He was that kind of guy that he was always in charge' says another executive (C). Strong charisma, loyalty, and involvement in the community are just some of the traits of this leader: 'and he was always shaking everybody's hands' recalls one manager (A).

The mythology of this hero is very rich and often extravagant for a banker. In a book on the First National Bank Leon Metz (1991, pp. 154–5) writes:

> He had established himself as one of the SouthWest's most distinct individuals. Few have equaled him for energy, imagination and public service. He once considered becoming an actor. The *Las Cruces Sun* of October 10, 1940, noted his participation in the Coronado entrada reenactment. Papen had two parts: Viceroy Antonio de Mendoza (a principal character), and Father Padilla, a Franciscan priest. Newspapers gave both the play and Papen high marks. He was a diverse man too. Julie and he motored all over Mexico with no set course or schedule. They traveled across Europe and the Holy Land, receiving papal honors from Pope Paul and the Pilgrim Shell Medal from the Patriarch of Jerusalem. Frank hunted widely in his youth: mountain lions in Arizona's Tonto Basin, quail in the Carolinas. On one occasion he flew to Alaska, was lost at sea for a couple of hours but was returning to New Mexico when bad weather grounded him at Edmonton, Canada.

We have stated that not all the myths have the same resources, and the mythmaking process is often marginalizing if not erasing preexisting myths. But this can be true not only for delicate transitions such as those generated by merger or acquisition but also in a single and unique organization. The mythmaking process is a process of stabilization of a whirlpool of experiences often conflicting. And these conflicts arise in the everyday life of people involved. Here is the recollection of one executive of an assessment meeting to raise the salary of the employees of the bank:

> But I got a little bit more aggressive one year, I felt that if there was somebody that was not performing at the level ... with their salary

level they need to work somewhere else and I made that recommendation and when we were at meeting for a specific individual that has been working for the bank for some period of time and Frank Papen said 'no, that person has been with us for a long time,' we would keep that person . . . but the point was again that because of Frank's commitment to his employees we got overstaffed and one of the things that examiners began to look at in measuring the soundness of the bank was profitability it was not enough to have a solid asset portfolio if you were not generating a reasonable return on equity and on assets they viewed as an indication of poor management and poor management would of course be seen as a weakness in the bank and that forced us to look at some of the reasons for the lack of profitability and it wasn't that we were not profitable but we just weren't generating the rates of return that we should have been or could have been. (B)

The mythology offers some point of break down as a different logic insinuates, a logic that will allow for the emergence of another myth: that of selling the bank. 'We had no choice' says one of the executives (B). 'We could have gone in a different direction', argues another (C).

We provide these kinds of examples because we want to demonstrate that the process of mythmaking not only is emergent and dynamic but also never expurges fragments of emergent logics.

Another point of our thesis is that in the orality we can retrace elements that are erased in the textuality and visuality. If we walk on Main Street, in Las Cruces, New Mexico we will see a big building and on top of the building the name Wells Fargo. Not only has that building become Wells Fargo a few years ago, but also we can argue that that building is the exact expression of the First National Bank mythology. In the visuality there are no traces of this past. But if we talk with executives of Wells Fargo Bank we hear:

Frank wanted to build that building, which originally was going to be a seven storey, well he wanted a ten storey building but they couldn't justify the extra three stories so they finally had to settle for seven. But, the economy was in a trough in the late sixties and the guy that was building it had another job that fell through and he had a bunch of crew that he needed to keep busy so he went to Frank and said 'I'll put the other three stories on that building for $300,000'. I don't remember the number but it was significantly less than it would have been had we contracted before because he was trying to keep his crew busy, so that's how it ended up being a ten storey building. If you go downtown and you go though that building today you would see that the air conditioning and all the mechanical equipment is on the seventh floor and that's why because it was already been topped out when they came to it. (C)

Surprisingly also people that have never been with the First National Bank of Dona Ana can retrace elements of that mythology:

> when they built the building it was going to be seven stories and then Frank Papen was having a cocktail or two with the contractor and said what would it take to go up another three, so all the utilities, all that is on the seventh floor, where typically would be up on top, they had three more floors. (D)

Even though they refer to the building as the Wells Fargo tower, in the orality of the storytelling the myth still resists.

In a brochure called *Wells Fargo in New Mexico, the Legend Continues* which we found in one of the branches, it is shown how Wells Fargo has an established tradition in New Mexico that dates back to 1852 and pictures of the Albuquerque office of Wells Fargo and Coach are presented. In the last page of the brochure a history of banking in New Mexico is provided. Here is how the history is synthesized:

> In the 1990s, both Wells Fargo Bank and Norwest Corporation purchased many community banks in New Mexico. Among those community banks was the successor to the Bank of Roswell, and other pioneer New Mexico institutions, including First National Bank of Belen (1903), Sante Fe National Bank (1946), American Bank of Commerce (1962) and Republic Bank of Albuquerque (1972).
>
> In 1998, Wells Fargo and Norwest joined in a merger of equals. Then, at the beginning of this new century, Wells Fargo acquired First National Bank of Farmington (1902) and First Security (1928) offices in the greater metropolitan areas of Albuberque, Las Cruces, Roswell and Sante Fe. (Wells Fargo Brochure, p. 4)

First National Bank of Dona Ana County is not even mentioned in the brochure and completely expurged from history as the First Security acquisition had cancelled its traces.

There are other stories of the Papen mythology that still resists, such as that of the 'Anthony miracle':

> Thus a bank moved across a state line. Such an occurrence had not happened before and will not happen again because the law was amended to make such practices illegal. Only a guy like Frank Papen could have pulled it off. (Metz, 1991, p. 129)

Here is one account of the story provided by one of the executives:

> One of the most interesting stories that I like to tell, I grew up in the south valley and I worked in a bank in Anthony ... well, originally when Mr. Papen was putting his banks together the bank was on the other side of the street and it was called First State Bank of Anthony, Texas and he bought that bank and changed the name on it to the First National Bank and he was kind of detail orientated some times and he built a huge beautiful building but what he hadn't realized he got across the state line, so ... have heard of Mr. Haner ... he was one of our vice-presidents in charge and he had a lot of influence in Washington so Mr. Haner and Frank spent considerable time in Washington and then they had to change into First National Bank of Anthony, New Mexico and he changed to the First National Bank of Dona Ana county ... He was the only one to ever move a bank across the state line and change the name of the bank five times. (A)

Another executive recalls:

> In the nineteen sixties the bank got approval for a bank that they had bought in Anthony New Mexico, which was actually Anthony Texas, and they moved from the Texas side to the New Mexico side. (D)

Discussion and conclusion

In conclusion we can say the excerpts show how different mythmaking processes can interact at different levels of their cycles with living story fragments. Although dominant mythologies (or fossilized narratives) may be erased from being living memory, as alternative counter-stories and even counter-mythmaking processes, the living stories still survive in the orality of the community of the bankers we interviewed, as in the cases of the stories of the tower and the Anthony's miracle.

There appears to be a dialogic relationship between mythmaking (narratives), living stories, and antenarrative at Wells Fargo Bank. Antenarrative is a bridge of transformation between living story and narrative (Boje, 2001, 2008). Antenarrative has a double meaning: a bet and a pre-story. Antenarrative 'refers to both an approach, a way of dealing with research and to a different epistemological foundation of narrative research, which refuses every form of representationalism' (Musacchio Adorisio, 2008). We are developing the theory that antenarratives are of two sorts. First, it is a vampire-like antenarrative that accomplishes transformation to dead narrative by sucking the living diversity out until all that remains in organizational sensegiving currency is a more monologic narrative (or a myth that has certain stages). Second, it is a type of resurrection of living story from the fragments of a once mummified narrative order that is coming un-spun.

Norwest actually purchased the Wells Fargo Bank chain, then superimposed the stagecoach lore on to not only Norwest but also the subsequent community banks. The living stories co-constructed by each of the community banks, as well as Norwest own living stories, were erased from memory. This is an example of the vampire-like process of antenarrative transformations of embodied living story into a rather dead narrative, detached from lived human experience. This is countered by the second manner of antenarrative, where fragments of living story, such as those of Frank Papen, survive despite the corporate training, and quite definite hegemony of demanding that a community bank's living history be no longer told, its icons no longer shown. In sum, there is force and counter-force of the respective antenarrative processes, but the Vampire transformation of living story is stronger than Living Story transformation of the entrenched Wells Fargo myth.

It may well be that as the older employees, managers and partners of the community bank retire or leave, that the counter-force antenarrative will no longer challenge the Wells Fargo myth. The collective memory of the community bank stories will fade. New employees will not be told stories of their bank's history. New employees will only be taught to recite a Walls Fargo stagecoach myth that is not theirs, and never was part of their bank's history. In the case we examined, until they were acquired, Wells Fargo's past had nothing whatsoever to do with community bank storytelling. The Vampiric myth may be fiction, but it turned into a branded corporate narrative strategy and identity.

Rather than the stages of myth development, maturation, decline and reformulation, our case illustrates the abrupt branding of a corporate narrative on to a living story interplay with local myth (that evolved perhaps in stages) that was declared non-legitimate.

We conclude that Norwest purchased the Wells Fargo myth as corporate strategy narrative and as identity brand. Both are marketing devices that run roughshod on living story. There are processes in play beyond the local cases in the Southwest US. It appears that in each state Norwest (now branded Wells Fargo) crafts a stagecoach heritage into a strategy narrative that commands legitimacy on the part of employees and customers. Never mind that the constructed mythic narrative is a fabrication, a fiction. Perhaps the closest parallel example is how the US celebrates Columbus Day, even though Native residents and other explorers were there first. The fictive myth is dialogic among the living stories, but over the generations, the living native story has been erased from institutionalized memory.

11

Heinz Von Stem on the Myth of Myths: Confessions of a Master Mythmaker

Pierre Guillet de Monthoux

A year has gone by since the death of the Reverend Heinz von Stem. In keeping with his final wishes and through the generosity of the editors of this volume, I am now able to present excerpts of the confession he shared with me in a last interview. Before his death at a very old age, Vienna-born von Stem was nothing more or less than the von Braun of the corporate mind, a master mythmaker in his own right. Since it seemed most fitting that his confessions appear in this volume, I approached the editors and asked that they include von Stem's confession in their publication. As von Stem was largely unknown to the public – a status of which he was genuinely proud – it seems only fair that he be given the chance to unburden himself to the world through this medium. Following is the December 2005 conversation he had with me at The Olde-Time Religion Home where he was then living. The Reverend von Stem had summoned me to his room, and while the very old man got increasingly intoxicated and downright noisy on ice-cold schnapps, the following exchange took place.

Professor Pierre Guillet de Monthoux (PGM): Reverend von Stem, what brought you, a theologian from Berlin, to management?

Reverend Heinz von Stem (HS): Ach, management came to me. In Berlin I earned my living as scriptwriter to Josef Goebbels, who was pretty bad at spelling. I also studied rhetoric. With that background, when I arrived in the US, I immediately got hired, first by Madison Avenue and then by the Harmud Business School. There I became director of the Hellenist Institute of Capitalist Goodness. Aber, ach das ist sooooo long ago.

PGM: Hm, is that so? I thought you were only a parson in Germany.

HS: I shifted from Herr Professor Doctor to Reverend while I was in advertising. I quickly caught on to the fact that capitalism is more faith-based

Figure 11.1 Pierre Guillet de Monthoux during the last conversation with Heinz von Stem

than science-based, and two weeks after landing in New York, I founded my own Temple of Capitalist Classicism.

PGM: Never heard of that either...
HS: Well, it was a logical step. Clearly old consultants like Taylor, Drucker, and Peters were managerial evangelists, and I don't think it mere coincidence that Mormons and Jesuits have been elected presidents of the American Management Academy. Max Weber showed the links between Protestantism and capitalism, and others later demonstrated similar links to Catholicism. But I felt drawn to stoking the flame of capitalism with more than just the kindling of the Judeo-Christian tradition. I am a Hellenist at heart, you see.

PGM: So-o-o that is why you founded a temple and not a church?
HS: Genau, my Freund! And why not? They did it during the French revolution, so why not today? Classical Hellenism is just as cool, you see...

PGM: In advertising too, you think?
HS: Ah ... we must not forget that in the early twentieth century it was not called advertising but 'propaganda', and it was 'agitators' who delivered the stories then. At that time I even sold Greek stories to both Bert Brecht and Leni Riefenstahl ...

PGM: The communist playwright and the Nazi moviemaker who made the film about the Berlin Olympics?

HS: Genau, mein Lieber! It was that moviemaker's fascination with the Olympics that actually put me on track. She made a movie very much along the lines Martin Heidegger and I dreamed of while kicking a soccer ball around in Marburg. Ach dat was schööööön. Of course, Berlin backed this all up by financing the final excavation out of the original Olympic stadium in Greece.

PGM: But, Heinz, what does all this have to do with contemporary management?

HS: Glad you asked. I can actually see that the rebirth of classicism in totalitarian states spilled over in today's corporate capitalism. Stalin ordered new temples to be built, and Speer wanted to turn Berlin into a mega-classicist city. In the US, as I soon discovered, they built post offices and university libraries like Greek temples too. Power loves all that seems antique; that's why old movies like Ben Hur or bastions like Caesar's Palace became blockbusters.

PGM: So you saw the link between antique and modern design?

HS: Rather I saw the opportunity to opt for Greece instead of wobbling between other styles I fancied less. With Mandela they went for Zulu management in South Africa, and in Berlin the vulgar Nazis tapped Viking mythology. But me ... I was too much influenced by Friedrich Nietzsche to fancy those simple models.

PGM: Might it have been because Greece stood for the peaceful demo-cratic attitude?

HS: What? You must be joking! Greece was a place with ongoing violence that was only partly resolved by diplomatic efforts between cities and tribes. And its democracy was reality only for a few happy so-called free men. Labourers, foreigners, and women had to execute their orders. No, Greece – to me and Nietzsche – was a land where the elite managed but in a Dionysian way. Prost! (HS spills his schnapps and fumbles for the whole bottle.)

PGM: With drinking and dancing?

HS: Yes, with drinking and dancing, but only in order to reconnect to the almost unconscious energy generated by rituals and festivals.

PGM: So Greece became a model for reconnecting to hidden energies and making us consciously inspired?

HS: Ah, good you mentioned consciousness, for this connects to another of my favourites ...

PGM: You must mean Sigmund Freud?

HS: Yes, Freud and the many others inspired by his theories. I even developed a personal managerial version of his therapeutic methods. And I was not the only one; there were Reich, Grodech, and Dali as well.

PGM: Dali, the surrealist painter?

HS: The surrealists claimed they created art by tapping their unconsciousness.

PGM: Okay, but both Reich and Grodech were excommunicated by orthodox Freudians.

HS: And Dali scared the shit out of Siggi when the crazy Spaniard claimed he had transformed psychoanalysis into art. As for me, Freud objected to my taking the patients off the couch and turning the therapist from a patient listener into an active management consultant – from couch to coach, you might say.

PGM: Tell me more, Heinz.

HS: Well, when Nietzsche and Freud wrote their theories and philosophies, they were constantly hinting at antique knowledge. At that time, knowledge of Greek mythology meant schooling and education. The learned bourgeoisie read Homer at school, and that was the core of what we called Bildung.

PGM: Actually, Heinz, I do recall a visit to Freud's flat on Berggasse when I was a tourist in Vienna. I remember how the shelves of his study were filled – not with books, though, but with clay statuettes, as if he were an antiques collector . . .

HS: Freud lived in the antique; it was ever-present to him and to all of us in that cosmopolitan classicist culture. That is why he kept referring to Oedipus and to Narcissus; he knew everybody knew the stories.

PGM: Which is hardly the case today!

HS: No, today people might know of soap opera divas or computer game characters or rock stars. Or worse. Sometimes when I went with clients to golf courses or we had drinks, I was absolutely shocked over their lack of Bildung. On the other hand, they were so active and occupied that there was little or no time for learning. Managers live under constant time pressure. They struggle to survive and morph into switchboards or servers through which multitudes of people connect. I doubt they are individuals but rather biological clearing houses for scattered unsorted impressions and opinions. They hardly live under the conditions of the Greek philosophers although some managers end up pretty rich.

How would they have time to learn about ancient Greece, though, if they never picked it up, as schoolchildren from good families did in the days of Freud or of Nietzsche?

PGM: So let me get this clear, Heinz. What you say is that you use classicism for managers who do not have a clue.
HS: Ach, ja zis izz a problem indeed, although I was always careful not to offend my clients.

PGM: But how can you keep referring to myths and heroes in manage-ment? How can managers understand without a background?
HS: Ah yes, a little scepticism, I see! In one sense your scepticism is justified, but in another sense it is not. As scholars of antiquity would confirm, mythos was never a field of knowledge in ancient Greece. Mythos and logos overlapped, and only when the two were torn apart did the question of knowledge of myth occur. The separation meant those advocating logos were emphasizing clear arguments and logics. They cast suspicion on those who used myths and stories to convince, saying these contenders were appealing to the masses on the non-logical basis of emotion.

PGM: Ah yes, the battle of the Platonist against the Sophists!
HS: Jawohl and the Platonists claimed they themselves were serious sci-entific managers and charged the sophists with merely using emotions and illusions in the struggle for consent. No wonder those interested in myth had to defend themselves by creating links between myth and logic ...

PGM: ... which gave birth to mytho-logy?
HS: Genau! And there are a number of tricks to prove myth is serious and corresponds to reality ... like using poetry to account for actual historical events or by portraying heroes in terms of the guy next door or by treating myths as forms of literature open to investigation and scientific analysis.

PGM: And how about the creationists who feel urged to provide scientific proof of their religious faith?
HS: And how about that horrible example *Troy*, that Hollywood movie that intentionally sets out to market Homer's story sans all that divine and supernatural stuff? They turned a piece of narrative art into a banal pseudo-chronicle; it's no wonder the movie was an economic flop too.

PGM: Are you saying that reality minus myth loses its attraction? So we really have to overrule the separation between logos and mythos?

HS: Or at least forget the split for a moment. That's what Nietzsche argues when he wants to see the rebirth of the Dionysian Greek tragedy that was bumped off by logos and analysis. It's what he brands the Apollonian.

PGM: So that was why the Greeks liked, and even believed in, myths?
HS: Ach mein Lieber! You pose a very tricky question! As far as we know from the texts of Homer or Hesiod, myths were part and parcel of their accounts. They made distinctions we tend to overlook now, like the divide between the divine gods and less holy heroes. Sometimes it seems as if Greek texts assume a golden bygone time when gods directly interfered with humans. When you look at it that way, you see how close the Bible is to that tradition. Christianity was successfully marketed by adapting to, not confronting, antique mythmaking. But even though heroic stories are told and retold in many versions – as if they were necessary ingredients in art, performance, and rituals – did the Greeks believe in them?

PGM: Do we believe in the entrepreneur? Or have faith in brands?
HS: Here we have to make clear what we mean by the terms 'believing' and 'faith'. Our contemporary historians present people of antiquity as reasonably religious people, who treat myth with lots of common sense. Nevertheless Greek authors seldom, if ever, question myths, for they were not critical theorists. Rather they were just journalists accounting for the stories they were told. And furthermore, the myths people told were almost always set in a place where people lived. This or that hero had founded a specific city, had conquered this piece of land, or had drafted the constitution of a particular city-state. Myths never hovered in the thin abstract air as far as the Greeks were concerned; they were rooted in concrete places, like Troy, Athens, Corinth or Sparta.

PGM: But this does not seem to be how myths in management are used.
HS: No, and I think we are here discovering a big difference between new and old mythical thinking. As I said, I turned Freud from couch to coach. Now management scholars writing big books about management-myth inform practitioners that the whole field could be seen from a heroic perspective. It is like telling a patient, 'Hey, you behave like Narcissus,' something Freud would never conceive of. And superimposing characteristics of ancient heroes or myths over the official portrait of a person, as sometimes happens in the case of the manager and his edited HBR biography, is not something Greeks would do. To them myths basically had a place orientation, not a person orientation. It is a lot like Flemish master painters depicting rich merchants as biblical figures or suited up in royal guises.

PGM: You're right. I have never seen anything about myths connected to geographical place in management.

HS: Actually it would be difficult to find an age where concrete place has surrendered to abstract global space. Early industrialization became the wealth of nations, for it happened where there were forests or mines or waterpower. The geopolitical aspect was central to early firms and businesses. Today corporations are disconnected from territory, uprooted from nations or cities, and in consequence, the myths I successfully sold to managers were not intended as ways to understand the sense of place.

PGM: Hm . . . economic activity uprooted from the territories, and as you said earlier, corporate elites uprooted from Bildung.

HS: With the flattening of organizations, staffs that sometimes harboured experts with a classical education began and continue to shrink. Not only that, human-resource turnover leaves were little time to anchor experience locally in concrete settings.

PGM: Then does this uprooting of economic firms make us forget about concrete space?

HS: Well, it is time that rules our lives now. The shift from space to time is one of the most important separations between classical myth and contemporary mythmaking.

PGM: Do you mean that managers constantly worry about time, that managers want to make the distinction between what will become and what has been by overemphasizing actuality and their time-situated roles?

HS: Stimmt mein Freund! Time is everywhere – from Bloomberg's ticking stock prices to the idea of a CEO's being just in time and having the chronological competence of perfect timing. Modern myth is bound to be more about time while ancient myth made living place out of space.

PGM: But is the ancient idea of myth useful at all then?

HS: The more you learn about the Greek myth the less you see how it applies to actual mythmaking. While a myth today almost assumes to carry over some values, I do not think Greek mythology can teach us 'democracy' or any other general values. Myth is part of our timeless placeness and not a proxy for universal values.

PGM: But Heinz, you cannot just ignore the fact that myth is usually presented to us in a certain way. We are confronted with a hero who solves a problem or performs some action, and the whole story conveys a universally true value.

HS: Yes, you are right, you are right. And that is why I wanted you to come by and talk. I must confess how wrong it has all become. At the same time I admit that it is universalism that makes our clients pay the heavy fees mythmakers charge.

PGM: I don't follow you, Heinz. Who were your clients?
HS: At Harmud Business School we had managers come in to lecture now and then. And I can assure you that very few of these managers tipped their hats to the myths as they were practiced in antiquity. On the other hand, these lecturers were always on the hunt for principles of management. And the more globalization developed, the more they asked us researchers for globally universal rules. And that is where Greek heroes or gods may be useful.

PGM: So it was not the managers but the management researchers that started to apply classicism to management?
HS: Sure, and that is really how it is! When managers pose for their portraits, they pick pretty mainstream painters as they did in Amsterdam during Rembrandt's time. They are not looking for the avant-garde but want academic portraits, and the more learned-appearing it seems, the better. At the same time we, the faculty at Harmud Business School, were also pressed to appear really academic. We knew what scholars over at Harmud University really thought of us, their 'colleagues' at the business school. I, a scholar from the old world, got hired to improve the academic image of the Harmud Business School. Now follow me on this: the cradle of academia was Plato's Academy in Athens, right? So by founding the Hellenist Institute of Capitalist Goodness I took advantage of all that to make business, as well as the business school, into a classical advocate of eternal academic truth. And somehow they got it, for today you see a lot written about myth and management!

PGM: So was it all a humbug, Heinz?
HS: No, worse that that. It's a danger.

PGM: Aren't you being a bit dramatic and overestimating your role a smidgen? What is so bad about wrapping common people up in the toga of some old Greek heroes? It's just like any storytelling, isn't it?
HS: Hellenism of this sort is not only wrong because of everything I have talked about; it's also very dangerous. We have claimed that myths convey archetypes of eternal and universal value, and we have acted on that pretense, but there is no pure myth – no root myth – and if we allude to that, we are just practicing sloppy metaphysics that cannot be defended by any classical reference.

PGM: Then managerial mythmaking is based not on myth itself but on a sort of myth of myths. Is that what you mean, Heinz?

HS: Yes, precisely, mein Lieber. And that kind of metaphysics is not defensible from an intellectual position nor is it pragmatically good. To smuggle in ideals as the eternal value in myths can only reinforce the 'grand narrative' that postmodernists put under fire decades ago.

PGM: So this kind of metaphysical return by myth is a way to protect modernism in management education?

HS: It is, it is! And with the integration of Homer & Co., we might be turning business schools into bastions for grand narrative edutainment.

PGM: I am still a bit confused, Heinz. I understand you regret this, but why is it so bad?

HS: Because it is untrue. I know what work it takes to translate what goes on in business into a nice myth or story. Myths are so far from reality that no one can create even a mythical reality without employing a good deal of fantasy or having a real ignorance about managerial detail. As is the case with all grand narratives, myths are constructions, and this one is like a lofty classical temple that rises in the distance, light years from the temporal field camps of global corporations.

PGM: So you have been lying.

HS: Ach, I am so embarrassed when I think back on what I have done. After my death, you must promise me that you will tell everyone.

PGM: But, my poor Heinz, you have just been one of many storytellers.

HS: Ah yes, I don't deny that we are all storytellers, and I know the world is made up of stories, but my crime was to reduce it to market it in one classical form. There should be many stories, different stories, stories that grab at pieces of reality that float merrily on the stream of existence.

PGM: Isn't that what some researchers claim when they say we manage and make up our world by small talk, by nonsensical gossip, or by mere bull? It seems more like scattered short stories than grand novels.

HS: Yes, but then we are talking about storytelling as something different from grand moralistic mythmaking. Some say this was what Nietzsche really wanted by 'gay science'. And who is able to forget the catastrophe when Greek tragedy got reborn in the Third Reich.

PGM: But that was a long time ago, Heinz.

HS: Don't fool yourself, pass mal auf mein friend! That kind of tragedy is reborn in every battle for the 'good eternal values'. In today's world, each conflict or competition – and there are many – demands support from mythmakers. They want management professors and consultants preaching 'virtues' and 'morals' in a global scope and will not pay a cent to mythologists discovering everyday storytelling by gathering gossip and street-corner conversations in corporations.

PGM: But today many management scholars do go out there to listen to people in specific places. They take a fancy to 'cities' rather than 'corporations' and turn to anthropologists and ethnologists for their research models.

HS: And in doing so they actually take on the same attitude as the antique historians who revealed what myths people really lived by out there in Greece. While that kind of interest in myth may count as Nietzschean gay science, it will not contribute to a rebirth of grand tragedy in some Wagnerian or funky business ...

PGM: ... but rather, the re-appreciation or rebirth of a perspective on managerial life as human comedy. Or management as vaudeville and managers as music-hall artists with lots of slapstick acts.

HS: Yes. Wouldn't that be lovely? But as a moneymaking mythmaker I never dare to have such a perspective. Along with most of my teaching and consulting friends, I turned my back on real mythology and became a greedy mythomaniac. No, dear Freund, what you see here is a poor Hellenist bound for Hell.

Figure 11.2   Last-known picture of the Reverend Heinz von Stem

What a touching end to Heinz von Stem's confession! He was now extremely drunk and sobbing like a child. After the nurse came in and tended to him, I departed. On my way out I stumbled on a few books that the old man had recently been pondering. They may shed some light on Heinz von Stem's ethical predicament and clarify the reasons for his remorse, so I take the liberty of listing them here below.

References

Baecker, D. (1994) *Postheroisches Management*. Berlin: Merve Verlag.

Boltanski, L. and Chiapello, E. (2006) *The New Spirit of Capitalism*. London: Verso.

Czarniawska, B. (2002) *A Tale of Three Cities: Or the Glocalization of City Management*. Oxford: Oxford University Press.

d'Iribarne, P. (1989) *La logique de l'honneur. Gestion des entreprises et traditions nationales*. Paris: Editions du Seuil.

Hatch, M. J., Kostera, M. and Koźmiński, A. K. (2005) *The Three Faces of Leadership: Manager, Artist, Priest*. Malden–Oxford: Blackwell Publishing.

Liberman, J. (ed.) (2004) *Démythifier l'universalité des valeurs américaines*. Paris: Parangon.

Mbigi, L. (1997) *Ubuntu: The African Dream of Management*. Randburg: Knowledge Resources.

Ohlsson, Ö. and Rombach, B. (2006) *Metaforernas tyranni*. Stockholm: Svenska Förlaget.

Ranciere, J. (2000) *Le partage du sensible. Esthétique et politique*. Paris: La Fabrique éditions.

Vernant, J.-P. (2004) *Mythe et société en Grèce ancienne*. Paris: La Découverte.

Veyne, P. (1983) *Les Grecs ont-ils cru à leurs mythes?* Paris: Editions du Seuil.

von Stem, H. (1917) *Raum und Zeit im Mythologischen Griechentum*. Berlin (doktordiss; spurenlos weg).

von Stem, H. (1927) *Siggi Freud als Pfiffikus: Griechen, Götter und Gewinn*. Berlin: Edition Struwelpeter (leider nicht zugänglich; Gott sie Dank).

von Stem, H. (1938) *Zukunftshelden im Gengenwartsmythos: von Homer bis Hitler*. Berlin: Verlag Gernot Glückspilz (seit 1945 total verschwunden und vergessen).

von Stem, H. (?) *Handbook for Heroes: How to Turn Ordinary Guys to Greek Gods* (frequently refused typescript).

von Stem, H. (1989) *Empty Barrels: Myth and Meaning for Successful Managers*. New Claptown: Harmud Business School Press.

von Stem, H. (1998) *Narrating Nerds: Instant Storytelling for Business Bores*. New Claptown: Harmud Business School Press.

von Stem, H. (2004) *Lüge als Lebenskunst; autobiographische Bekenntnisse eines echten Managementscharlatanen* (unpublished manuscript).

12
Leading and Learning Through Myth and Metaphor

Lena Fritzén

Introduction

A group of about 20 city council directors takes a study trip to Toronto as part of a leadership-training course, in order to compare the Swedish and Canadian health care systems. The purpose of the course is to discover new organizational improvements that can contribute to improving the Swedish health care system. Even if everyone in the group has much experience with leadership, so far it has proven difficult to put into words the characteristics that leadership for change should embody in a complex organization. Theoretical models from various subject perspectives have been presented and discussed; yet the participants have still not been able to fully reflect on or question their own leadership. The group's discussions have taken place at the abstract level, which means that the group members' established ideas of the health care system and their own leadership have not changed at all. After a long trip over the Atlantic, the study trip to Toronto begins with a sightseeing trip to Niagara Falls. During the visit something happens that opens the group up for a different type of discussion. The power of the falls, their sheer height, human beings' insignificance in contrast to the enormous forces of nature, and a sense of wonder at the beauty of nature all meld together to form a new picture that summarizes the complexity of organizational change and what it means to find oneself on the brink of chaos.

Being the leader of a complex organization, with the responsibility to improve and renew, entails having the courage to put yourself 'on the edge'. Being on the leading edge requires acuity, constant presence and great sensitivity. However, it is not easy to get directly to the core of leadership; sometimes it is more effective to take a detour via metaphor. Theoretical models that had been presented earlier in the course could take on new meaning with the help of the Niagara Falls metaphor. For example, this is how Ralph Stacey's matrix, in which he identifies various types of 'management decisions' in terms of simple – complex – chaos, came to be seen in a new light (Zimmerman *et al.*, 2001). Niagara Falls allowed an idea to take shape about what it means for leaders to find themselves on the borderline between complexity and chaos.

The reality and understanding of this is constructed through language (Burr, 1995). Myth and metaphor can add energy to this process of linguistic construction. However, myth and metaphor should not be viewed as 'costume for thought', but rather, more as of a way of thinking and communicating. Metaphors create similarity rather than formulating an existing similarity (Black, 1962). The change in communication that takes place when the participants are challenged by myth,[1] or when their insight unites them around a metaphor, can be viewed as a learning process in which the taken-for-granted is questioned and new meaning is created.

What the instructors of the course witnessed was how the participants' newfound knowledge later formed the basis for organizational changes within the health care system. Niagara Falls as a metaphor for the complex organization thus took on meaning for both the ongoing course that the leaders were taking, as well as for the organizations that these leaders were part of.

What meaning, then, can be attributed to myth and metaphor in learning processes that aim to improve leadership? The purpose of this chapter is to discuss leadership from a pedagogical perspective in which learning is seen as an intersubjective process in which myth and metaphor can make it possible to create new contexts of meaning. The discussion follows mainly from the following starting points: (1) that learning and leadership are communicative processes that embody both sides of the same coin, and (2) that developing good leadership requires utilizing experiential knowledge.

Lead and learn – two sides of the same coin

A group of primary school headmasters gathers once a month to develop their pedagogical leadership. One evening they decide to go to the theatre instead of meeting the usual way in one of the school teachers' rooms. The classical drama *Antigone* is being shown at one of the city's theatres. *Antigone* depicts a struggle between King Creon and the young Antigone. While Antigone defends the idea family and blood ties (*oikos*), Creon is driven by external demands and a deep legal pathos (*polis*). For the headmasters, this Greek myth depicts the tension between the state (*polis*) and the lifeworld (*oikos*), tension that they constantly have to manage. Someone says that it is precisely this classic conflict that causes conflicts between teachers. While some of the teachers see themselves as an extension of the arm of the state, others say that their main objective is to accept the children as they are in order to understand their lifeworlds and build on them. Yet another headmaster claims that the conflict between *polis* and *oikos* permeates leaders' own leadership. The system's demands for order, such as bookkeeping, financing and scheduling, tend to steal time from pedagogical leadership, which is about creating conditions for both teachers and students to learn and develop. The discussion between the headmasters ends with a question to think about: How can we headmasters transcend the conflict between *polis* and *oikos*?

The headmasters aim to develop their leadership in a way that improves the conditions for learning and development for both teachers and students at their schools. Watching and discussing *Antigone* helps them put conflicts between teachers into words, conflicts that have serious consequences for how teaching is carried out. While some see it as their main task to transmit measurable knowledge, others maintain that teaching is about creating meaning for students by starting with the students' own experiences. The dividing line between the teachers is ultimately the different ways they view learning, a dividing line that also includes the headmasters' views on leadership.

Learning as a monologue or dialogue

The idea of learning is deeply rooted, primarily, in two tenacious metaphors that both reflect the idea that teachers are responsible for learning. One of these metaphors is 'house building', the other is 'radio transmitter'.

Viewing learning as 'house building' means that first the foundation must be correctly laid, after which the framework is erected, the roof built, and when the building is complete the house can be decorated in various ways. The teacher is the best judge of which construction methods suit each individual learner. In order to support teachers' classroom practice, educational research has long focused on how individual learners learn and remember (e.g., Skinner, 1968). As a consequence of this view, practically every academic discipline consists of a series of modules that build upon each other. The wealth of leadership courses that appeared in the 1980s and permeated both the private and the public sectors also took a similar approach. The consultants highest in demand have been those who provide the simplest 'recipes' for successful leadership development. Against this background, students/participants – regardless of their experience – are seen as blank slates (tabula rasa), ready to absorb the knowledge that teachers, consultants, or textbooks present. The teacher is an active 'subject' who transmits knowledge to a passive 'object', the learner. Oftentimes it is not until the post-graduate level that students are given the opportunity to 'decorate the house' based on an approach involving more problematization.

The 'radio transmitter' approach to learning also involves a subject (the teacher) transmitting knowledge to an object (the student) Seen from this perspective, the role of language is to transmit codes – information – to individuals who are disengaged from their contexts. In other words, the metaphor is learning as a monologue. I propose that both of these metaphors have, over time, been important for how we view the leader's role in an organization. The leader's task has been – and perhaps still is – to construct 'the house', whereas the employee's role has been to carry out the construction plan. It is the leader who gives orders in the organization, the leader who decides how the established plan shall be realized, while the employees are the receivers of that information.

The 'house construction' and 'radio transmitter' metaphors for learning can be traced to the view that learning is something that takes place inside the head of the individual learner. During the latter part of the twentieth century, language and communication became increasingly important for the way in which the world is perceived and, in turn, how we construct our knowledge of it. This change, which not least had consequences for pedagogical research, is usually called 'the Linguistic Turn'. It is through language that we construct reality and establish contextual knowledge (Burr, 1995). The Linguistic Turn has slowly shifted the focus in learning theory from a monological to a dialogical approach.

The Russian social psychologist Lev Vygotskij called transmitting knowledge through a monologue in 'predigested' form the most 'comfortable' form of teaching. Instead, learners must be confronted with complicated and unforeseen events so that their minds are entirely compelled to create new combinations of earlier experiences. The starting point must be that the human approach to learning is learning is diverse and complicated. Additionally, Vygotskij (1962) claimed that learning is a social process in which communication between teachers and students and between students and teachers is the supporting dimension.

Vygotskij is one of several pedagogues who, during the twentieth century, contributed to the shift in pedagogy from an individual perspective (monological) on learning to a relational approach (dialogical) that rests on a communicative foundation.[2] The dialogical takes its starting point in the intersubjective, that is, in the view that knowledge develops in the linguistic interplay between two or more subjects. The Canadian philosopher Charles Taylor (1971, p. 30) writes:

> Intersubjective meaning gives a people a common language to talk about social reality and a common understanding of certain norms, but only with common meaning does this common reference world contain significant common actions, celebrations and feelings. These are objects in the world that everybody shares. This is what makes community.

This tapestry of meaning making, intersubjectivity, which according to Taylor creates a community, is, I believe, the core of both learning and leadership. This means that learning and leadership are not an individual concern, but rather are something that that takes place in interaction with others. Thus, leadership can be seen as part of a pedagogical practice in which the participants – leaders and employees – develop socially as well as learn. Pedagogical practice is 'an intersubjectively manageable quantity' (Johannesson, 1994, p. 87) through which participants develop their understanding of themselves and the contexts they are a part of. Practice focuses on the idea that individuals' actions are context dependent, that context is important for learning, and that learning is relational (Fritzén, 1998).

The conflict between polis and oikos in pedagogical practice

Their encounter with *Antigone* caused the headmasters to notice that the conflict between polis and oikos is something that is constantly present in pedagogical practice. The tension between system-related demands and people's need for a sense of meaning and community is discussed by the German social philosopher Jürgen Habermas (1987) in terms of system and the lifeworld. While system-related communication is instrumental, effective and strategic, communication from the lifeworld perspective is characterized by reciprocity, mutual understanding, and the desire to exchange perspectives. The logic of the system and the lifeworld are in one sense incompatible, while at the same time, together they create an inescapable unity. The system is dependent on the lifeworld in terms of loyalty and legitimacy, while the lifeworld is dependent on the system in terms of efficiency. The way in which leaders shape their leadership cannot be independent of (rather, must be legitimized by) participants' ideas about how the organization should be run. At the same time that the leader needs to see that the available resources be utilized efficiently (system logic); the leader's striving for efficiency depends on the employees' loyalty towards the system.

Habermas (*ibid.*) cautions against the system's tendency to extend beyond its area of legitimacy. He believes that human beings' emancipation and independence, both as knowledge-constructing subjects and as free acting creatures, could be lost because of the system's 'colonization' of the lifeworld. The areas of life that are particularly sensitive to colonization should, according to Habermas's reasoning, be spared from one-sided, system-related actions. If learning and leadership are a relational process in which communication between participants creates the conditions for meaning making, then both of these domains should be protected from all too one-sided system-related action. What the headmasters in the example above testify to is that the discussion in schools is far too often driven by economical and financial issues instead of educational issues.

Learning from or through myth and metaphor

In a monological approach to learning and leadership, metaphor and myth become something to learn from, role models to consider. For a metaphor or myth to highlight a situation in practice, which would not otherwise be available to put into words, a dialogical approach to learning and leadership is required. In a dialogical approach, myth and metaphor instead become something to learn through. Myth and metaphor provide examples from which participants can develop their imaginations, deepen their ability to reflect, and expand their horizons of understanding:

> In everyday situations metaphors should not be seen as well-reasoned constructions; normally they are not planned in advance. Rather, they are something that appears suddenly in a flash of insight. Therefore there is no formula for how to effectively create powerful metaphors. In everyday contexts they are spontaneous and creative answers to a new and unexpected situation. (Göranzon, 2001, p. 134)[3]

The connections (analogies) that, in the example above, the headmasters create as a reaction to *Antigone* cannot be stipulated by anyone. Additionally, one particular analogy is not better than any other. Allan Janik (2003, p. 64) writes: 'Metaphors are not the kind of things that can be true or false … problems arise precisely when we take metaphors for truths.'

It is in the headmasters' discussion that the myth takes on its energy and its meaning. The myth confronts the headmasters' ideas about learning and leadership, which allows new meanings to emerge. Myth and metaphor can help set experiential knowledge in motion, and thus make it available for reflection.

Leadership and experiential knowledge

What can we learn from King Lear? is the title of one of many leadership seminars for the heads of one municipal administration. After watching a film of Shakespeare's *King Lear*, the participants begin a discussion. Things are sluggish. After a long silence the discussion finally takes off:

- The title of the seminar is too intimidating for me to be able to formulate my thoughts.
- I can't see a single similarity between my leadership and *King Lear*; it is all too far removed from my reality.
- We are just as silent as Cordelia. When King Lear asked his three daughters which of them loved him most, Cordelia was silent.
- Impossible questions make it meaningless to answer. They impede communication.
- I recognize something from my own days at school. When the teacher asked a question, she always knew the answer. It was like a 'guess what I'm thinking' game.
- How often do we as leaders ask questions that already have a given answer, or that are impossible for co-workers to answer? Perhaps we ask in a way that strangles communication rather than opening it up?

In his notebooks and manuscripts, Wittgenstein repeatedly referred to Shakespeare and theatre, including *King Lear*. He maintained that creating 'Gestaltung' and creative language must be an aspect of philosophy (Göranzon, 2001). The philosophy of praxis that the later Wittgenstein developed can aid us in understanding how myths as well as literature, film and theatre can help set experiential knowledge in motion, and therefore develop leadership.

Setting experiential knowledge in motion

Experience has been increasingly discussed and gained importance in both education and working life. There are no jobs for recently graduated engineers because they lack experience. Higher education is supposed to be based on science and reliable experience. Leaders are tasked with taking advantage of their co-workers' experiences in the same way that teachers are tasked with connecting their teaching to students' experiences. The concept of experience, however, has rarely been problematized. What does experience involve, and when can experience be said to be reliably tested? In academia the starting point is that knowledge should be able to be expressed verbally, defined and demonstrated empirically or with formal methods (Johannessen, 1992). Experience and values fall outside the domain of knowledge because they are seldom possible to measure or validate. Leaders' experiences encompass tacit dimensions that are also difficult to verbalize or describe. Leaders have developed patterns of behaviour that can be inaccessible to individual or group reflection. After watching *King Lear*, the directors were able to problematize each other's communicative patterns as well as their own. For behaviour patterns to develop, change and improve they need to be contrasted with the ideas of others. Cordelia's silence exemplifies this type of contrasting idea.

Wittgenstein's philosophy of praxis focuses on interpersonal language games (Johannessen, 1992; Wittgenstein, 1998). Learning to master a language, in a broad sense, entails mastering a vast repertoire of situations. At the same time there are concepts that cannot be fully expressed in words, but that show themselves in action only. Johannessen maintains that in everything that can be considered verbalized knowledge (explicit knowledge), we can also look for tacit knowledge. He also claims that tacit knowledge often plays a much more important role than knowledge that can be verbalized. The tacit dimensions of knowledge are particularly interesting to capture within areas related to professional expertise, in this case, the tacit knowledge of leadership. However, Johannessen cautions that there is no recipe for hunting down tacit knowledge. Each area must be examined separately.

Aided by the philosophy of praxis, Wittgenstein contributed to doing away with the distinction between subject and object, between 'sender' and 'receiver'. From the perspective of Wittgenstein's language games, all human concept formation can be understood as an intersubjective process. It is in conversations with each other, based on examples in our own practice, that we can set our tacit knowledge in motion. The exchange of experience cannot be solved by the calculated rationality of formalized processes, 'best practice' documents, or information technology. It is in the linguistic interplay between people, in deep situational involvement with each other, that crucial knowledge can be teased out. What myth, metaphor, literature, theatre, etc. can offer is a repertoire of examples that can help rebel against the rigid aspects of praxis, an impatient attack against the borders of our concept of reality. It is a rebellion against habitual views and, ultimately, against clichés (Hammarén, 1999).

Flexible thinking can be stimulated by these forms of expression because, in a different way to our own examples, they offer surprising material for comparison. Similarly, metaphors can create links between our own and others' experiences, and in this way break 'habitual views'. But developing good leadership requires more than setting one's experiential knowledge in motion and making it accessible for reflection. The next step is to put one's newly won knowledge into action.

Leadership and good judgement

> I should tell them, that the fruit of a surgeon's experience, is not the history of his practice, and his remembering that he has cured four people of the plague and three of the gout, unless he knows how thence to extract something whereon to form his judgment, and to make us sensible that he is thence become more skilful in his art. (Montaigne, 1588/1952, pp. 450–1)

The sixteenth-century French philosopher Michel Eyquem de Montaigne's essays take up the concept of judgement when he reflects on the importance of experiential learning for professional expertise. Experience that is not reflective and that does not influence how one acts in practice has very limited value, claims Montaigne. Developing the professional expertise of leadership entails, based on Montaigne's views, developing good judgement.

When Aristotle argues for scientific rationality, which was prevalent in the Greece of his time, he distinguishes between three forms of knowledge: *episteme, techne* and *phronesis*. It is a division that has been widely used within professional development courses and its related research. According to Aristotle, scientific knowledge, *episteme*, involves only that which is necessary, that is, that which is eternal and invariable.

The knowledge of craft, *techne,* and practical wisdom, *phronesis,* are characterized by knowledge that is variable. *Techne* can, according to Aristotle, be both learned and forgotten. Having *techne* means doing something based on a true understanding of the principles involved. But despite having sufficient knowledge, it is still not certain that it will be used in concrete situations. *Phronesis* entails a different relationship. Being practical in the same way as knowing which action is morally right in the concrete situation one finds oneself in. Forgetting one's practical knowledge involves ceasing to exist as a human being. Practical wisdom falls back on general moral principles than can be managed in a given situation. It does not only involve knowing which moral principle applies, but also knowing which moral principle a given situation demands. In other words, Aristotle's conceptions of knowledge encompass what could be called good judgement. It is important for leaders to know what should be done in a given situation, but it is just as important to know how to do it. However, it is most important of all to know when something should be done, that which is sometimes called 'timing' or 'intuition'.

Can good judgement be learned?

Dreyfus and Dreyfus (1986) have attempted to answer the question of whether or not good judgement can be learned. They describe professional expertise, in this case expertise in leadership, in five stages: novice, beginner, competent performer, proficient performer and expert. The three first stages – novice, beginner and competent performer – are characterized by adherence to rules. An inexperienced leader often looks for finished models to relate to, models built up of clear-cut rules. To learn these rules learners need good role models who can provide good examples. When faced with a given goal, learners at these stages look for the rules that will lead to the goal. In this phase, myth and metaphor can provide something to learn from, and to a lesser degree, something through which development is aided. In the fourth and fifth stages of the model – proficient performer and expert – there are no explicit rules to turn to. At these stages, it is more a question of picking out what does not work, experimenting, and transcending boundaries in order to develop good judgement. In other words, there are no explicit rules for transcendence; one must trust one's judgement or the knowledge that Aristotle calls *phronesis*. Practical knowledge is collective (intersubjective) knowledge that is developed through finding oneself in praxis. Good judgment cannot be formulated using precise language and precise definitions. Instead, one needs to find the connections between different situations, and from these situations (in Montaigne's words) gain something from one's experiences. In situations where it is impossible to be precise, metaphor has a given role. Metaphor can create similarities between situations that at first glance seem to lack connections.

Through *King Lear* the county council leaders in the example above developed a new way to talk about their practice. The way King Lear silenced his daughter became a metaphor for the way they silenced communication with their co-workers in their own organizations.

Myth and metaphor develop analogical reasoning

Using myth, classical drama, literature, etc. in education is not new. Being acquainted with classic literary works is part of traditional ideals in education. Education (Bildung) has partly been a question of each unique individual's development and self-education, and partly a question of learning certain things that educated people are expected to master. In academic programmes today, it is not entirely unusual to select a number of classical works that students are to read as supplementary material to their normal textbooks. These readings from the classical canon seldom have anything to do with the other content of the course; their purpose is merely to 'educate' the students. The risk with this approach is that the classical texts may fall into the theoretical framework of academic education in general, that is, a summative attitude toward learning and knowledge.

Wittgenstein's starting point, when he highlights the importance of creative language, does not build on a summative approach to learning and knowledge. In *Culture and Value* Wittgenstein (1998) expresses the following ideas about the characteristics of the learning process:

> I might say: if the place I want to reach could only be climbed up to by a ladder, I would give up trying to get there. For the place to which I really have to go is one that I must actually be at already.
>
> Anything that can be reached with a ladder does not interest me.
>
> One movement orders one thought to the other in a series, the other keeps *aiming* at the same *place*.
>
> One movement constructs & takes (in hand) one stone after another, the other keeps reaching for the same one. (p. 10e)

Wittgenstein compares summative knowledge to laying stone by stone. What Wittgenstein invites us to do, as I understand him, is to see knowledge as a formative process that involves constantly testing and re-testing the knowledge one has won. But 'aiming at the same place' is a much more difficult process that 'constructs & takes (in hand) one stone after another'. Perhaps Gadamer's hermeneutic spiral can illustrate a learning process characterized by 'reaching for the same one'. Gadamer (1989) claims that all understanding requires a pendular motion between whole and parts. Moving in the hermeneutic spiral entails moving from detail to whole, from the specific to the general. This type of movement demands analogical reasoning, that is, an approach in which people communicating with others see connections between specific situations, and from this knowledge tease out more generally applicable knowledge. Creating precisely these connections is what myth and metaphor can contribute to this learning process.

Conclusion

Leading an organization whose success depends on its members' ability to cooperate means being in a context of perpetual change, and therefore, perpetual learning. Through language, when people interact, discuss and reach agreements about new ways to perform and organize their work, they construct new meanings and contexts. Learning is ultimately about changing ideas and standpoints, about questioning habitual patterns, and examining concepts through new perspectives. Seen from this point of view, change (learning) requires dialogue and argumentation. Questioning habitual viewpoints and seeing new patterns is, however, a process that continually invites opposition. This type of learning process requires that both leaders and co-workers be prepared to reassess their prior experiences and to set their so-called tacit knowledge in motion so that it can be accessible for reflection. From this viewpoint, learning in public and private organizations cannot be achieved through calculated rationality in the form of formalized development processes, 'best practice' documents or IT applications.

Learning to master a language entails mastering an extremely vast repertoire of situations. At the same time, there are concepts that are not entirely possible for people to express verbally; these concepts show themselves in action only. In all areas where it is possible to talk about verbalized knowledge (explicit knowledge) it is possible to search for tacit knowledge. Additionally, tacit knowledge often plays a much more important role than the knowledge that is possible to verbalize. The tacit dimensions of knowledge are particularly interesting to capture within the areas of professional expertise, in this case, the professional expertise of leadership.

Flexibility of thought can be stimulated by the arts, because the arts invite us to stretch beyond our own experiences, and offer surprising material for making comparisons. Myths, legends, literature, theatre, films and other works of art can transport us to other points of view from which we can catch a glimpse of the time and the perspectives we are immersed in. Correspondingly, metaphor can create connections between our own experiences and the experiences of others, and thus break habitual ways of seeing things.

Notes

1. Myth (from the Greek *mythos*, meaning speech, word, story) is used here to denote stories that have fundamental meaning for humanity's existence. Therefore it does not concern religious stories exclusively, but encompasses literary works that, over time, have created meaning for humanity.
2. Other philosophers and pedagogues who have contributed to this shift within pedagogy include Dewey (1916/1966), Freire (1996) and, to a certain extent, Piaget (1997).
3. Author's own translation.

13
Open Sesame or Pandora's Box? Concluding Remarks on Organizing, Archetypes and the Power of Mythmaking

Monika Kostera

Myths about roles, organizations and metaphors

The three volumes, of which the current is the last one, contain texts lined up according to the main themes that emerged from the collected material:

1. *Organizational Olympians: Heroes and Heroines of Organizational Myths* focuses on individual actors and their roles.
2. *Organizational Epics and Sagas: Tales of Organizations* takes up stories of organizations and their mythical features.
3. *Mythical Inspirations for Organizational Realities* discusses the role of myth in general, as well as mythmaking in organizations and organizational discourse.

Archetypes and the collective unconscious

To summarize what I have said in the Introduction to Volume 1 (Kostera, 2007), the relevance of the study of organizational mythmaking is due, in part to the fact that work organizations try to replace churches and cults in providing for their employees' spiritual needs – more or less success-fully, albeit they are unable to quite take their place. Furthermore, some stories of and about organizations and organizational actors get mythol-ogized over time. However, as such, organizations and their actors have not acquired a truly mythical status. And yet there is, I believe, a good reason to explore the mythical dimension of these tales.[1] They are often populated by, and protagonists of, stories that resonate with something in us that is related to the mythical experience. Even if the chapters do not pertain to the supernatural or the spiritual as such, they touch the same strings in the reader and listener as do tales

> of matters fundamental to ourselves, enduring essential principles about which it would be good for us to know; about which, in fact, it will be necessary for us to know if our conscious minds are to be kept in touch with our own most secret, motivating depths. (Campbell, 1972/1988, p. 24)

The reason why this is so is, in my opinion, due to the presence of several fundamental ideas and characters in the narratives of and on organizations and their human actors – the archetypes. Mythical themes and experiences are invoked by these archetypes in ways that make narrative activities related to organizations possible ways to 'live by myths' (*ibid.*) in the contemporary society of organizations (Perrow, 1991). I will now briefly discuss archetypes and their uses in organization theory, and then conclude with a reflection on the mythical significance of archetypical roles and symbols in our theorizing on and practicing of organizing and organization.

In the literature of organization studies the term archetype is used in mainly two ways: as a structural pattern[2] (Greenwood and Hinings, 1988; Miller and Friesen, 1978, 1980)[3] and in the Jungian way, as a phenomenon located in the collective unconscious (Jung, 1968) It is in the latter sense that archetypes are understood in this chapter, that is, as a kind of hidden images of human motivations and inspirations concealed

> in the collective unconscious domain of reality and shared by all humans. They are the substance that myths and symbols are constructed of and because of their universality they have the capacity of turning individuals into a group. Thus they can be seen as the underpinning of culture and society. (Kostera, 2007)

Archetypes in the Jungian sense (Jung, 1968), remind one of riverbeds, ready to hold certain fundamental images or tales. They are deeply rooted in culture as well as in the psyche and constantly inspire new ways of expressing and reading them. They connect humanity throughout time and space, touching important strings in human consciousness, and turning individuals into communities. Myths use archetypes extensively and hence their fantastic ability to carry important cultural and psychological ideas through time.

According to Jung archetypes are located within the sphere of the collective unconscious and are universal. I share this conviction, but I am aware that this is controversial among social scientists nowadays, because it presumes an essentialist approach to social life. It is, however, not necessary to adopt an essentialist view in order to be able to use the concept – archetypes can also, with advantage, be thought of a construct deeply rooted in human culture, equipped with an extraordinary narrative and symbolic potential. Their ability to inspire constant reinterpretations make them a particularly open work[4] (Eco, 1973), especially useful for cultural analysis regardless of ontological assumptions.

For example, a well known archetype is the Shadow, holding denied and rejected aspects of the personality. It is usually a dark side of each one of us, the Mr Hyde part of our personality that surfaces as uncontrolled and uncontrollable impulses and sometimes takes over totally, making people behave 'strangely' or 'insanely'. There exist good aspects within the shadow, called the Golden Shadow, that are creative sides of the personality rejected together with its negative sides. In order to be able to use them, the person has to make conscious her or his darkest fears and face her or his dark side. It can is also beneficial if we want to have some control over our shadow side.

Other well known archetypes include mythical characters such as gods and goddesses. They can be used to express and communicate individuality, in a collective narrative process. It is possible to name them, but in order to activate them, they need to be linked with a character or storyline. For example, some key archetypes are: man, woman, warrior, lover, ruler, prophet. There are multiple images that can be linked to one archetype, for example aspects of the Greek god Zeus, the Norse Thor and Slavic Perun can be seen as characters corresponding to the same archetype: a supreme ruler.

To summarize what has been said above: the interest in mythical tales of and about organizations is of such vital importance to our knowledge of their spiritual side, because of the way that the archetypes that exist in them resonate with profound levels of the human soul. There exist, furthermore, studies that approach archetypes in organizations directly, not just by way of exploring myth. These studies aim at making visible the way myths and symbols work in the construction of culture and why they play such an important role in people's motivation and sensemaking. Archetypes can be used to understand organization or to propose a view on the place of organization in a broader context. Heather Höpfl (2002) presents management initiatives, such as benchmarking and continuous improvement, as a consequence of the quest of the lost feminine archetype (the Anima) of the organization. The constant preoccupation with the organization's masculine aspects leads to the lack of, and desire for, its femininity. The text adopts a Jungian perspective to depict managerial strategies as a quest for the Holy Grail, and, ultimately, a journey to find the primal mother archetype. However, organizations are busy constructing mere replacements, inadequate imitations of the female aspect, which is perceived as dangerous and unmanageable:

> Organizations, as collectivities, have understood the sense of loss of the feminine and have tried to construct it in symbolic and in representational terms. This is a profound conceit as is evidenced by the contradictions of contemporary organizational life and the pervasive melancholy that arises from the knowledge of an ill-defined loss. (Höpfl, 2002, p. 20)

Kaaren Hedblom Jacobson (1993) believes that the mother archetype can be overwhelming for organizations. She defines archetypes as 'images that are transformed into typical emotional attitudes or action patterns' (p. 63). She points out that an unreflective approach to organization makes the participants blind to its limiting manifestations, such as becoming a place where immaturity is cultivated and the capacity for individual moral action is lost. This can be seen and understood through the use of the mother archetype: a too intensive identification with this archetype inhibits growth and maturation. The organization man loses his or her individuality and gives up his or her responsibility, letting the ego melt into the broader context. As a consequence, the organization becomes a kind of captivity and fails to pursue its mission. Elisabeth Ryland (2000) explores environmental consciousness through the archetype of Gaia. She points to the need of individuation, the healing of the mind, as a way of connecting human and organizational consciousness to deep environmental awareness. The author understands archetype in the Jungian way, as 'pre-existing forms in the collective unconscious' (p. 384) The notion serves her to depict the gap between individual, organizational and environmental consciousness and to propose a way of integrating them with help of the symbol of Gaia rising. Gaia – the collective mother needs to become healed, and can, in turn, help to heal the humans who are connected to her. The sustainable organization can be one of such links, a holistic human system, not just concerned with financial aims but also dedicated to environmental issues and to helping people to feel whole and to develop as human beings.

Other uses of archetypes include the depiction and interpretation of the human side of organizing. For example, Burkard Sievers (1994) explores several archetypes such as connected to immortality, life and death, expressed through Greek gods and goddesses, in order to depict the paucity of contemporary management, its spiritual shallowness and lack of anchoring in important things such as meaning and wisdom. Sandra King and Dave Nicol (1999) reflect on the possibilities of spiritual development within organized contexts. In order for management to recognize the necessity and the benefits of opening up the workplace for the spiritual experience, individual spiritual growth can be perceived and understood with the help of archetypes such as self, individuation, shadow and others. Together with Jacques' systems theory these archetypes may help to build a learning environment that would develop and make use of the employees' individual talents. In a book about the quest for the self-actualizing organization (Kostera, 2005), I use several archetypes, such as enlightenment and spiritual quest to look for possible forms of and uses for a type of organization that would be equally concerned about the individual and the collective dimension. Martin Bowles (1993) portrays social life in the organization with the use of archetypes expressed as gods and goddesses. These gods and goddesses reflect the values that are held in the contemporary work organization, and in the realization of the present and the absent divinities, one can learn about the organization's capacity for cooperation, change, development and many other important potentials.

Archetypes can also serve to understand organizational change, as a planned procedure as well as a spontaneous dynamics. Adrian Carr (2002) discusses how archetypes are related to the management of change. Organizations steer behaviours in certain ways, thus encouraging the development of a shadow-side of undesired behaviours that accumulate and influence attempts at the introduction of planned change. Martin Bowles (1991) addressed the shadow of the organization, which is its unconscious dark side, and showed how it can have a serious impact on its culture and potential for advancement. A suppressed shadow can erupt with reckless violence, and thus lead to dramatic uncontrolled and often dangerous developments. Strong control and little personal autonomy foster the growth of a strong collective shadow. In order to be able to deal effectively with the challenges it poses, it is important consciously to integrate it.

Archetypes can also be used for throwing light on specific organization phenomena, such as competition (Matthews, 2002) and leadership (Hatch *et al.*, 2005) Many important figures are present in the competition archetype (Matthews, 2002), which is often seen as one of the fundaments of capitalism. Strategic management can make use of the potential for development and motivation that archetypes provide, if they are made conscious and utilized for imagination. Inspiration for business leaders is another interesting use of archetypes. Hatch *et al.* (2005) have shown how archetypical ideas can be used for an inspired and successful leadership in organizations. The book uses the term archetype in the Jungian sense, as deep unconscious meanings surfacing as images and ideas. Archetypes connected to leadership turned out in the analysed material to be in active use by successful managers who engaged in mythologizing of their companies and their own role as their managers.

Whereas there is definitely much to gain in insight and understanding in the study of archetypes, I would like to emphasize that they are not managerial tools and cannot be 'used' in an instrumental way to gain certain planned benefits. Archetypes are larger than the human being, larger than even the most powerful organization and cannot be controlled by any single 'strategic intent'. Furthermore, as such they can be good and evil, beautiful and ugly, they can awake empathy and hatred. King Arthur as well as Hitler, Ghandi and Charlie Manson are all connected to archetypes of leadership. Hitler and Stalin were, furthermore, with some probability both consciously seeking to connect with powerful symbols of power that we recognize as archetypes. The effects were sinister and almost universally destructive. The power of archetypes is great, but not necessarily benevolent. To consider using archetypes as one more managerial fad, a suave tool for enhancing productivity or another buzzword is as insane as playing with an atomic bomb.

So, is it worth it? Is the threat overwhelming or are the benefits greater? Is the study of organizational archetypes like the opening up of Pandora's Box, or something akin to the unlocking of Sesame? It's probably both, I believe, but it is still worth the effort. Even Pandora's box, apart from all its sinister contents, also held hope. As Vaclav Havel put it, '[p]erhaps hopelessness is the very soil that nourishes human hope; perhaps one could never find sense in life without first experiencing its absurdity' (Havel, 2006).

Notes

1. I agree with Yiannis Gabriel (2000) that not any narrative should be called myth, even if it contains an abundance of symbols.

2. According to Pinnington and Morris (2003, p. 86) an archetype is 'a set of structures and systems that reflect and are underpinned by a single interpretive scheme or set of values and ideas as to what ought to be' (with reference to Greenwood and Hinings, 1988, p. 298) The term archetype is also sometimes used in the sense: *broad type*, taxonomic ideal type (e.g. Lemon and Sahota, 2004; Rutenberg, 1970).

3. For examples of use of his notion of archetype, see, e.g., Pinnington and Morris (2003); Tranfield and Smith (2002); Tyrrall and Parker (2005).

4. 'The poetics of an "open" text aims ... to inspire the interpreter to "acts of conscious freedom," to make him an active *center* for an unlimited net of relationships, whom he is to give an own shape, not being limited by a *compulsion* implied by the given rules of organization of a given text' (Eco, 1973, pp. 27–8).

Bibliography

Abravanel, H. (1983) Mediatory Myths in the Service of Organisational Ideology. In Pondy, L. R., Frost, P. J. and Morgan, G. (eds), *Organisational Symbolism*. Greenwich, CT: JAI Press.

Acker, P. (2002) Introduction. In Acker, P. and Larrington, C. (eds), *The Poetic Edda – Essays on Old Norse Mythology*. New York–London: Routledge, pp: xi–xv.

Adorno, T. W. and Horkheimer, M. (2002) *Dialectic of Enlightenment: Philosophical Fragments* (ed. Schmid Noerr, G.; trans. Jephcott, E.). Stanford, CA: Stanford University Press.

Alighieri, Dante (2003) *Inferno* (trans. Esolen, A.). New York: The Modern Library.

Anderson, Ph. N. (2002) Form and Content in Lokasenna: A Re-evaluation. In Acker, P. and Larrington. L. (eds), *The Poetic Edda – Essays on Old Norse Mythology*. New York–London: Routledge, pp: 142–57.

Armstrong, K. (2005/2006) *A Short History of Myth*. Edinburgh: Canongate.

Arndt, J. (1985) On Making Marketing Science More Scientific: Role of Orientations, Paradigms, Metaphors, and Puzzle Solving. *Journal of Marketing*, 49, pp. 11–23.

Arnett, J. J. (1996) *Metalheads: Heavy Metal Music and Adolescent Alienation*. Boulder, CO: Westview Press.

Augustine, Saint (1873) On Christian Doctrine. In Dods, M. (ed.), *The Works of Aurelius Augustine, Bishop of Hippo. Vol. IX*. Edinburgh: T. & T. Clark, pp. 1–172.

Baecker, D. (1991) *Womit handeln Banken?* Frankfurt: Suhrkamp.

Barolini, T. (1992) *The Undivine Comedy: Detheologizing Dante*. Princeton: Princeton University Press.

Barthes, R. (1957/1973) *Mythologies*. London: Paladin.

Bass, B. M. (2008) *Bass and Stodgill's Handbook of Leadership: Theory, Research and Managerial Applications*. New York: The Free Press.

Baudrillard, J. (1990) *Seduction*. London: Macmillan.

Bauer, K. (1999) *Adorno's Nietzchean Narratives*. New York: State University of New York Press.

Bauman, Z. (1990) *Att tänka sociologiskt*. Göteborg: Korpen.

Bauman, Z. (1999) *Vi vantrivs i det postmoderna*. Göteborg: Daidalos.

Bengtsson, M. and Kock, S. (2000) Coopetition in Business Networks: To Cooperate and Compete Simultaneously. *Industrial Marketing Management*, 29, pp. 411–26.

Bettelheim, B. (1976) *The Uses of Enchantment: The Meaning and Importance of Fairy Tales*. New York: Knopf.

Biberman, J. and Whitty, M. (1997) A Postmodern Spiritual Future for Work. *Journal of Organizational Change Management*, 10(2), pp. 130–8.

BIS (2004) *Basel Committee on Banking Supervision: International Convergence of Capital Measurement and Capital Standards*. Basel: Bank for International Settlements.

Black, M. (1962) *Models and Metaphors: Studies in Language and Philosophy*. Ithaca, NY: Cornell University Press.

Blake, R. R. and Mouton, J. S. (1985) *The Managerial Grid III*. Houston, TX: Gulf Publishing House.

Boitani, P. (1981) Inferno XXXIII. In Boyde, P. and Foster, K. (eds), *Cambridge Readings in Dante's Comedy*. Cambridge: Cambridge University Press, pp. 70–89.

Boje, D. M. (2001) *Narrative Methods for Organizational and Communication Research*. London: Sage.

Boje, D. M. (2008) *The Storytelling Organization*. London: Sage.

Boje, D. M., Fedor, D. B. and Rowland, K. M. (1982) Myth Making: A Qualitative Step in OD Interventions. *Journal of Applied Behavioral Science*, 18(1), pp. 17–28.

Bonaventure, Saint (1978) *The Soul's Journey to God – The Tree of Life – The Life of St. Francis*. Mahwah, NJ: Paulist Press.

Bowles, M. (1989) Myth, Meaning and Work Organization. *Organization Studies*, 10(3), pp. 405–21.

Bowles, M. (1991) The Organization Shadow. *Organization Studies*, 12(3), pp. 387–404.

Bowles, M. (1993) The Gods and Goddesses: Personifying Social Life in the Age of Organization. *Organization Studies*, 14(3), pp. 395–419.

Bowles, M. (1997) The Myth of Management: Direction and Failure in Contemporary Organizations. *Human Relations*, 50(7), pp. 770–803.

Boyd, B. (2001) The Origin of Stories: Horton Hears a Who. *Philosophy and Literature*, 25, Baltimore: Johns Hopkins University Press, pp. 197–214.

Bradach, J. L. (1997) Using the Plural Form in the Management of Restaurant Chains. *Administrative Science Quarterly*, 42, pp. 276–303.

Brandenburger, A. M. and Nalebuff, B. J. (1996) *Co-opetition: A Revolution Mindset that Combines Competition and Cooperation*. Doubleday: New York.

Brunel, P. (1996) *Companion to Literary Myths, Heroes, and Archetypes*. London: Routledge.

Burke, K. (1945) *A Grammar of Motives*. Berkeley: University of California Press.

Burke, K. (1966) *Language as Symbolic Action: Essays on Life, Literature and Method*. London: University of California Press.

Burr, V. (1995) *An Introduction to Social Constructionism*. London: Sage.

Cacioppe, R. (2000) Creating Spirit at Work: Re-visioning Organization Development and Leadership, Part I. *The Leadership and Organization Development Journal*, 21(1), pp. 48–54.

Campbell, J. (1949/1993) *The Hero with a Thousand Faces*. New Jersey: Princeton University Press.

Campbell, J. (1972/1988) *Myths to Live by: How We Recreate Ancient Legends in our Daily Lives to Release Human Potential*. New York: Bantam Books.

Campbell, J. (1976) *Primitive Mythology*. Harmondsworth: Penguin.

Campbell, J. (1988) *The Inner Reaches of Outer Space: Metaphor as Myth and as Religion*. New York: Harper & Row.

Campbell, J. (2004) *Pathways to Bliss: Mythology and Personal Transformation*. Novato: New World Library.

Campbell, J. with Moyers, B. (1988) *The Power of Myth*. In Flowers, B. S. (ed.), *The power of myth*. New York: Doubleday.

Carr, A. (2002) Jung, Archetypes and Mirroring in Organizational Change Management: Lessons from a Longitudinal Case Study. *Journal of Organizational Change Management*, 15(5), pp. 477–89.

Carr, A. Z. (1968) Is Business Bluffing Ethical? *Harvard Business Review*, January–February, pp. 143–53.

Cassirer, E. (1946) *Language and Myth* (trans. Langer, S.). New York: Dover.

Catechism of the Catholic Church (1995) London: Geoffrey Chapman.

Chen, M. (1993) Sun Tzu's Strategic Thinking and Contemporary Management. *Business Horizons*, March-April, pp. 42–8.

Christe, I. (2003) *Sound of the Beast: The Complete Headbanging History of Heavy Metal*. New York: HarperCollins.

Churchill, W. (1940) *We Shall Fight On The Beaches*. Retrieved 2 October 2007 from http://www.winstonchurchill.org/i4a/pages/index.cfm?pageid=393

Coates, P. (1991) *The Gorgon's Gaze: German Cinema, Expressionism, and the Image of Horror*. Cambridge: Cambridge University Press.

Coelho, P. (2003) *Manual of the Warrior of Light*. London: HarperCollins.

Cooke, G. (2005) The Disabling Shadow of Leadership. *British Journal of Administrative Management*, 46, pp. 16–17.

Czarniawska-Joerges, B. (1988) *To Coin a Phrase*. Stockholm: Stockholm School of Economics.

Dees, J. G. and Cramton, P. C. (1991) Shrewd Bargaining on the Moral Frontier: Toward a Theory of Morality in Practice. *Business Ethics Quarterly*, 1(2), pp. 135–67.

Derrida, J. (1987) *The Truth in Painting* (trans. Bennington, G. and McLeod, I.). Chicago: University of Chicago Press.

Derrida, J. (1990) Die Différance. In Engelmann, P. (ed.), *Postmoderne und Dekonstruktion*. Stuttgart: Reclam, pp. 76–113.

Dewey, J. (1916/1966) *Democracy and Education: An Introduction to the Philosophy of Education*. New York: The Free Press.

Docherty, T. (1996) *Alterities*. Oxford: Clarendon Press.

Dourley, J. P. (1990) *The Goddess, Mother of the Trinity*. Lewiston: The Edwin Mellen Press.

Doz, Y. L. (1988) Technology Partnerships between Larger and Smaller Firms: Some Critical issues. *International Studies of Management and Organization*, 17(4), pp. 31–57.

Dreyfus, H. L. and Dreyfus, S. E. (1986) *Mind over Machine: The Power of Human Intuition and Expertise in the Era of the Computer*. New York: The Free Press.

Dumézil, G. (1968) *Mythe et Epopée*. Paris: Gallimard.

Duysters, G. and de Man, A.-P. (2003) Transitory Alliances: An Instrument for Surviving Turbulent Industries? *R&D Management*, 33(1), pp. 49–58.

Dyer, J. H. and Ouchi, W. G. (1993) Japanese-Style Partnerships: Giving Companies a Competitive Edge. *Sloan Management Review*, 35(1), pp. 51–63.

Eco, Umberto (1973) *Dzieło otwarte: Forma i nieokreśloność w poetykach współczesnych*. (*Opera aperta: Forma e indeterminazione nelle poetiche contemporanee*). Warszawa: Czytelnik.

Eisenhardt, K. M. and Schoonhoven, C. B. (1996) Resource-based View of Strategic Alliance Formation: Strategic and Social Effects in Entrepreneurial Firms. *Organization Science*, 7(2), pp. 136–50.

Eliade, M. (1961) *The Sacred and the Profane: The Nature of Religion*. New York: Harper & Row.

Eliade, M. (1963/1998) *Aspekty mitu*. (*Myth and Reality*) (trans. Mrówczynski, P.). Warsawa; KR.

Encylopaedia Britannica (2007) Retrieved on 23 January 2007 from http://www. britannica.com/eb/article-248165?hook=849778

Esolen, A. (2003) Introduction. In Alighieri, D., *Inferno*. New York: The Modern Library, pp. xi–xxv.

Ferrante, J. (1984) *The Political Vision of the Divine Comedy*. Princeton, NJ: Princeton University Press.

Fineman, S. (1996) Emotion and Organizing. In Clegg, S. R. Hardy, C. and Nord, W. R. (eds), *Handbook of Organization Studies*. London: Sage, pp. 543–64.

Ford, J. and Harding, N. (2003) Invoking Satan or the Ethics of the Employment Contract. *Journal of Management Studies*, 40(5), pp. 1131–50.

Frakes, J. C. (2002) Loki's Mythological Function in the Tripartite System. In Acker, P. and Larrington, C. (eds), *The Poetic Edda – Essays on Old Norse Mythology*. New York: Routledge, pp: 159–75.

Freccero, J. (1986) *Dante: The Poetics of Conversion*. London: Harvard University Press.

Freccero, J. (1993) Introduction to *Inferno*. In Jacoff, R. (ed.), *The Cambridge Companion to Dante*. Cambridge: Cambridge University Press, pp. 172–91.

Freire, P. (1996) *Pedagogy of the Oppressed*. Harmondsworth: Penguin Books.

Freire, P. (2004) *Pedagogy of Hope*. London: Continuum.

French, W. L. and Bell, C. H. (1973) *Organizational Development: Behavioral Science Interventions for Organization Improvement*. Englewood Cliffs: NJ: Prentice-Hall.

Fresh (2007) Retrieved on 10 February 2007 from http://www.fresh.se

Friedman, H. H. and Friedman, L. W. (1986) Applying Warfare to Business Competition. *Business Forum*, Winter, pp. 8–12.

Fritzén, L. (1998) *Den pedagogiska praktikens janusansikte: Om det kommunikativa handlandets didaktiska villkor och konsekvenser*. Lund: Lund University Press.

Frölich, D. and Pekruhl, U. (1996) *Direct Participation and Organisational Change. Fashionable but Misunderstood? An Analysis of Recent Research in Europe, Japan and the USA*. Dublin: European Foundation for the Improvement of Living and Working Conditions.

Fromm, Erich. (1937/1951) *The Forgotten Language*. New York: Grove

Furusten, S. (1992) *Management Books: Guardians of the Myth of Leadership*. Uppsala: Uppsala University.

Furusten, S. (1995) *The Managerial Discourse: A Study of the Creation and Diffusion of Popular Management Knowledge*. Uppsala: Uppsala University.

Gabriel, Y. (2000) *Storytelling in Organizations: Facts, Fictions, and Fantasies*. Oxford: Oxford University Press.

Gabriel, Y. (ed.) (2004a) *Myths, Stories and Organizations: Premodern Narratives for Our Times*. Oxford: Oxford University Press.

Gabriel, Y. (2004b) Introduction. In Gabriel Y. (ed.), *Myths, Stories and Organizations: Premodern Narratives for Our Times*. Oxford: Oxford University Press, pp. 1–10.

Gadamer, H.-G. (1989) *Truth and Method* (2nd rev. edn.), London: Sheed and Ward.

Galea, Ch. (2006) All You Really Need is Love, *Sales and Marketing Management*, 158(2), pp. 24–8.

Gardner. W. M. and Martinko, M. J. (1996) Using the Myers-Briggs Type Indicator to Study Managers: A Literature Review and Research Agenda. *Journal of Management*, 22(2), pp. 45–83.

Gherardi, S. (1995) *Gender, Symbolism and Organizational Cultures*. London: Sage.

Göranzon, G. (2001) *Spelregler – om gränsöverskridande.* Stockholm: Dialoger.
Greenleaf, R. (1998) Servant Leadership in Business. In Hickman, G. R. (ed.), *Leading Organizations: Perspectives for a New Era.* Thousand Oaks, CA: Sage, pp. 115–29.
Greenwood, R. and Hinings, C. R. (1988) Organizational Design Types, Tracks and the Dynamics of Strategic Change. *Organization Studies,* 9(3), pp. 293–316.
Habermas, J. (1987) *The Theory of Communicative Action: The Critique of Functionalist Reason* (vol. 2). Boston: Beacon Press, pp. 1–457.
Halpin, A. W. and Winer, B. J. (1957) A Factoral Study of the Leader Behaviour Descriptions. In Stodgill, R. M. and Coons, A. E. (eds), *Leader Behaviour: Its Description and Measurement.* Colombus: Bureau of Business Research, pp. 39–51.
Hamel, G. and Prahalad, C. K. (1993) Strategy as Stretch and Leverage. *Harvard Business Review,* March-April, pp. 75–84.
Hamel, G., Doz, Y. L. and Prahalad, C. K. (1989) Collaborate with Your Competitors – and Win. *Harvard Business Review,* January-February, pp. 133–9.
Hammarén, M. (1999) *Ledtråd i förvandling.* Stockholm: Dialoger.
Harvey, D. (1990) *The Condition of Postmodernity.* Oxford: Blackwell.
Hastings, W. (1998) *Dr. Seuss* (Theodor S. Geisel 1904–1991) Retrieved on 21 August 2006 from www.northern.edu/hastingw/seuss.html
Hatch, M. J., Kostera, M. and Koźmiński, A. K. (2005) *The Three Faces of Leadership: Manager, Artist, Priest.* Malden–Oxford: Blackwell Publishing.
Havel. V. (2006) *Vaclav Havel Quotes.* Retrieved on 15 November 2006 from www.brainyquote.com/quotes/authors/v/vaclav_havel.html
Hedblom Jacobson, K. (1993) Organization and the Mother Archetype: A Jungian Analysis of Adult Development and Self-identity within the Organization. *Administration and Society,* 25(1), pp. 60–84.
Hillman, J. (ed.) (1980) *Facing the God.* Dallas: Spring Publications.
Hoad, T. F. (1986) *The Concise Oxford Dictionary of English Etymology,* Oxford: Oxford University Press.
Hogan, R., Curphy, G. J. and Hogan, J. (1994) What We Know About Leadership: Effectiveness and Personality. *American Psychologist,* 49(6), pp. 493–504.
Höpfl, H. (2000a) The Suffering Mother and the Miserable Son, Organising Women and Organising Women's Writing. *Gender Work and Organization,* 7(2), pp. 98–106.
Höpfl, H. (2000b) On Being Moved. *Studies in Cultures, Organisations and Societies,* 6(1), pp. 15–25.
Höpfl, H. (2002) Corporate Strategy and the Quest for the Primal Mother. *Human Resource Development International,* 5(1) [January], pp. 11–22.
Höpfl, H. (2003) The Body of the Text and the Ordinary Narratives of Organisation. In Czarniawska, B. and Gagliardi, P. (eds), *Narratives We Organize By.* London: Routledge, pp. 75–92.
Höpfl, H. (2005) The Organization and the Mouth of Hell. *Culture and Organization,* 11(3), pp. 167–79.
Höpfl. H. (2006) Frame. *Culture and Organization,* 12(1), pp. 11–24.
Huffington, C. (2004) What Women Leaders Can Tell Us. In Huffington, C., Armstrong, D., Halton, W., Hoyle, L. and Pooley, J. (eds), *Working Below*

the Surface: The Emotional Life of Contemporary Organisations. London: Karnac, pp. 49–66.

Hughes, R. L., Ginnett, R. C. and Curphy, G. J. (1998) Contingency Theories of Leadership. In Hickman, G. R. (ed.) *Leading Organizations: Perspectives for A New Era*. Thousand Oaks, CA: Sage, pp. 141–57.

Hunter, S. (2005) *Hell Bent For Leather: Confessions of a Heavy Metal Addict*. New York: Harper Perennial.

Iacocca, L. (1984) *Iacocca: An Autobiography*. New York: Bantam.

Inkpen, A. C. (1996) Learning and Knowledge Acquisition through International Alliances. *Academy of Management Executive*, 12(4), pp. 69–80.

Inkpen, A. C. (2000) Learning through Joint-Ventures: A Framework of Knowledge Acquisition. *Journal of Management Studies*, 37(7), pp. 1019–43.

Inkpen, A. C. and Dinur, A. (1998) Knowledge Management Processes and International Joint Ventures. *Organization Science*, 9(4), pp. 454–68.

Inskeep, S. (2004) *Philip Nel Discusses The Literary and Political Legacy of Dr Seuss and His Books: NPR Interview on Talk of the Nation*. Retrieved on 21 August 2006 from http://nl.newsbank.com/nl-search/we/Archives?p_action=doc&p_theme=nr& p_topdoc=1&

Irigaray, L. (1985) *Speculum of the Other Woman* (trans. Gill, G.). Ithaca: Cornell University Press.

Iron Maiden (1981) Prodigal Son (From album *Killers*). EMI. [sound recording: Vinyl].

Jabri, M. (1997) Pairing Myth with Type Change: Implications for Change Communication. *Journal of Organizational Change*, 10(1), pp. 21–9.

Jackall, R. (1988) *Moral Mazes: The World of Corporate Managers*. Oxford: Oxford University Press.

Janik, A. (2003) The Use and Abuse of Metaphor. *Dialoger*, 65–6(3), pp. 3–88.

Johannessen, K. S. (1992) Rule-Following, Intransitive Understanding and Tacit Knowledge: An Investigation of the Wittgensteinian Concept of Practice as Regards Tacit Knowing. In B. Göranzon and M. Florin (eds), *Skill and Education: Reflection and Experience*. Berlin: Springer-Verlag, pp. 41–61.

Johannessen, K. S. (1994) *Tradisjoner og skoler i moderene vitenskapsfilosofi*. Bergen: Sigma.

Johansson, R., Holsanova, J. and Holmqvist, K. (2007) *Hur vi tänker i bilder*. Lund: Humanistlaboratoriet, Lunds Universitet.

Jung, C. G. (1968) The Archetypes and the Collective Unconscious. In Read, H. (ed.), *The Collected Works of C. G. Jung* (vol. 9). London: Routledge and Kegan Paul.

Jung, C. G. (1971) *Psychological Types*. Princeton, NJ: Princeton University Press.

Jung, E. and von Franz, M. L. (1998) *The Grail Legend*. Princeton: Princeton University Press.

Kandola, R. S. and Fullerton, J. (1988) *Diversity in Action: Managing the Mosaic*. London: CIPD.

Kelley, R. E. (1998) Leadership Secrets from Exemplary Followers. In Hickman, G. R. (ed.), *Leading Organizations: Perspectives for a New Era*. Thousand Oaks: Sage, pp. 193–201.

Kilmeister, L. and Garza, J. (2003) *White Line Fever: The Autobiography*. London: Simon and Schuster.

King, R. (1999) *Indian Philosophy*. Edinburgh: Edinburgh University Press.

King, S. and Nicol, D. M. (1999) Organizational Enhancement through Recognition of Individual Spirituality: Reflections of Jaques and Jung. *Journal of Organizational Change Management*, 13(3), pp. 234–42.

Kishwar, M. (2001) Jhadu Pooja at Sewa Nagar: Manushi's Campaign for Cleansing Governance. *Manushi*, 127, pp. 3–11.

Kishwar, M. (2002) Working Under Constant Threat: Some Setbacks and Some Steps Forward in Seva Nagar. *Manushi*, retrieved on 26 January 2005 from www.highbeam.com/library

Kishwar, M. (2003) *A Rare Gesture by the Government: Salient Extracts from the MCD Petition to the Supreme Court: Municipal Authorities Admit Flaws in Government Policy for Street Vendors*. Retrieved on 26/01/05 from: www.highbeam.com/library

Kishwar, M. (2004a) *Lecture at the Spalding Symposium*. (April) University of Oxford.

Kishwar, M. (2004b) *Lecture at the School of Oriental and African Studies (SOAS)*. (May) University of London.

Kishwar, M. (2005) Emergency Avatar of a Secular Goddess. *Manushi*, 147, pp. 4–16.

Kishwar, M. (2006) Destroying Swadeshi Retail Sector to Make Way for Videshi Retailers? *Manushi*, 153, pp. 4–11.

KISS (1976) God of Thunder. (From album *Destroyer*) Casablanca. [sound recording: Vinyl].

Klincewicz, K. (2005) *Strategic Alliances in the High-Tech Industry*. Berlin: Logos Verlag.

Klosterman, C. (2001) *Fargo Rock City: A Heavy Metal Odyssey in Rural North Dakota*. New York: Scribner.

Konow, D. (2002) *Bang Your Head: The Rise and Fall of Heavy Metal*. New York: Three Rivers Press.

Kostera, M. (1995) The Modern Crusade: Missionaries of Management Come to Eastern Europe. *Management Learning*, 26(3), pp. 331–52.

Kostera, M. (2005) *The Quest for the Self-Actualizing Organization*. Malmö: Liber.

Kostera, M. (2006) The Narrative Collage as Research Method. *Storytelling, Self, Society*, 2(2), pp. 5–27.

Kostera, M. (2007) Archetypes. In Clegg, S. and Bailey, J. R. (eds), *International Encyclopedia of Organization Studies*, London: Sage.

Kovacevich, Richard (2007) Wikipedia. Retrieved on 27 January 2007 from http://en.wikipedia.org/wiki/Richard_Kovacevich

Kristeva, J. (1982) *Powers of Horror* (trans. Roudiez, L.). New York: Columbia University Press.

Kristeva, J. (1984) *Desire in Language: A Semiotic Approach to Literature and Art* (trans. Gora, T.S., Jardine, A. and Roudiez, L.). Oxford: Basil Blackwell.

Kristeva, J. (1987) *Tales of Love* (trans. Roudiez, L.). New York: Columbia University Press.

Lacoue-Labarthe, Ph. (1989) *Typography*. Stanford: Stanford University Press.

Lakoff, G. and Johnson, M. (1980/1983) *Metaphors We Live By*. Chicago: Chicago University Press.

Larsson, R., Bengtsson, L., Henriksson, K. and Sparks, J. (1998) The Interorganizational Learning Dilemma: Collective Knowledge Development in Strategic Alliances. *Organization Science*, 9(3), pp. 285–305.

Latour, B. (1993) *We Have Never Been Modern*. London: Prentice Hall.

Lee, T., Mars, M., Neil, V., Sixx, N. and Strauss, N. (2002) *Mötley Crüe: The Dirt*. New York: HarperCollins.

Lemon, M. and Sahota, P. S. (2004) Organizational Culture as a Knowledge Repository for Increased Innovative Capacity. *Technovation*, 24, pp. 483–98.

Lemprière, J. (1788/1963) *Classical Dictionary of Proper Names Mentioned in Ancient Authors, with a Chronological Table* (commentary from Wright, F. A.). London: Routledge and Kegan Paul.

Lévi-Strauss, C. (1955) The Structural Study of Myths. *Journal of American Folklore*, 68(270), pp. 428–44.

Lévi-Strauss, C. (1963) *Structural Anthropology*. New York: Basic Books.

Lévi-Strauss, C. (1966) *The Savage Mind*. Chicago, IL: The University of Chicago Press.

Lokasenna. Retrieved on 14 February 2007, from http://www.sacred-texts.com/neu/poe/poe10.htm

Lonergan, C. S. (1977) The Context of Inferno XXXIII: Bocca, Ugolino, Fra Alberigo. In Nolan, D. (ed.), *Dante Commentaries*. Dublin: Irish Academic Press, pp. 63–84.

Ludema, J. D., Cooperrier, D. L. and Barrett, F. J. (2001) Appreciative Inquiry: The Power of the Unconditional Positive Question. In P. and Bradbury, H. (eds) Handbook of Action Research Reason, London: Sage.

Luhr, E. (2005) Metal Missionaries to the Nation: Christian Heavy Metal Music, 'Family Values', and Youth Culture, 1984–1994. *American Quarterly*, 57(1), pp. 103–28.

MacIntyre, A. (1984) *After Virtue: A Study in Moral Theory*. Chicago: University of Notre Dame Press.

Malinowski, B. (1927) *The Father in Primitive Psychology: The Myth in Primitive Psychology*. London: Kegan Paul.

Malinowski, B. (1925/1948) *Magic, Science and Religion and Other Essays*. Garden City, NY: Doubleday Anchor Books.

Mankiewicz, J. (1950) *All About Eve: Movie Script*. Retrieved on 24 November 2006 from http://www.dailyscript.com/scripts/all_about_eve.html

Margulies, N. (1972) The Myth and the Magic in OD: Powerful and Neglected Forces. *Business Horizons*, 15(2), pp. 77–82.

Marquard, O. (1989) *Farewell to Matter of Principles*. Oxford: Oxford University Press.

Matthews, R. (2002) Competition Archetypes and Creative Imagination. *Journal of Organizational Change Management*, 15(5), pp. 461–76.

Mauss, M. (1902/1978) Theorie der Magie. In Mauss, M. (ed.), *Soziologie und Anthropologie* (vol. 1), Frankfurt am Main: Ullstein, pp. 43–179.

Mauss, M. (1902/2001) *A General Theory of Magic* (trans. Brain, R.). London: Routledge.

McClelland, D. C. (1967) *The Achieving Society*. New York: Free Press.

Menand, L. (2002) Cat People: What Dr. Seuss Really Taught Us. *The New Yorker*. 23 and 30 December 2002. Retrieved on 1 June 2007 from http://www.newyorker.com/printables/critic/021223crat_atlarge

Merrill, D. W. and Reid, R. H. (1981) *Personal Styles and Effective Performance*, Radnor: Chilton Book Co.

Metz, L. C. (1991) *Southern New Mexico Empire: The First National Bank of Dona Ana County*. El Paso, TX: Mangan Books.

Mezirow, J. (1991) *Transformative Dimensions of Adult Learning*. San Francisco: Jossey-Bass Inc. Publishers.

Miller, D. and Friesen, P. (1978) Archetypes of Strategy Formulation. *Management Science*, 24(9), pp. 921–33.

Miller, D. and Friesen, P. (1980) Archetypes of Organizational Transition. *Administrative Science Quarterly*, 25, pp. 268–99.

Miller, D. L. (1974) *The New Polytheism: Rebirth of Gods and Goddesses*. New York–Evanson–San Francisco–London: Harper and Row.

Monbiot, G. (2003) America is a Religion. *The Guardian*, 29 July, Retrieved on 11 July 2007 from http://www.guardian.co.uk/comment/story/0,3604,1007741,00.html

Montaigne, M. E. (1588/1952) The Essays of Michel Eyquem de Montaigne In Hutchins, R. M. (ed.), *Great Books of the Western World*. Chicago: Encyclopaedia Britannica, pp. 1–543.

Morgan, G. (1983/1987) Research Strategies: Modes of Engagement. In Morgan, G. (ed.) *Beyond Method: Strategies for Social Research*. Beverly Hills: Sage, pp. 2–42.

Morgan, G. (1986) *Images of Organization*. Newbury Park, CA: Sage.

Mukherjee, S. (2007) Non-conventional Entrepreneurial Learning: Spiritual Insights from India. *Journal of Human Values*, 13(1), pp. 23–34.

Musacchio Adorisio, A. L. (2008) Living Among Stories: Rough and Organized Accounts from an American Banking Institution. Unpublished doctoral dissertation. Universita della Svizzera Italiana, Lugano, Switzerland.

Nandy, A. (1992) *Traditions, Tyranny and Utopias: Essays in the Politics of Awareness*. New Delhi: Oxford India Paperbacks.

Nel, P. (2002) *The Avant-Garde and American Post-modernism: Small Incisive Shocks*. Mississippi: University Press of Mississippi.

Nel, P. (2005) *Dr. Seuss: American Icon*. New York: Continuum International Publishing Group.

Normann, R. (2001) *När kartan förändrar affärslandskapet*. Malmö: Liber.

O'Reilly, C. A., Pfeffer, J. and Chang, V. (2004) Wells Fargo and Norwest: 'Merger of Equals', *Harvard Business Online*, case HR26B.

Pace, E. (1991) Dr. Seuss, Modern Mother Goose, Dies at 87. *New York Times, Obituary*. Retrieved on 21 August 2006, from http://www.nytimes.com/learning/general/onthisday/0000302onthisday_bday.html

Padgett, J. F. and Ansell, Ch. K. (1993) Robust Action and the Rise of the Medici, 1400–1434. *American Journal of Sociology*, 98(6), pp. 1259–319.

Parise, S. and Henderson, J. C. (2001) Knowledge Resource Exchange in Strategic Alliances. *IBM Systems Journal*, 40(4), pp. 908–24.

Parker, M. (2002) Utopia and the Organisational Imagination. In Parker, M. (ed.), *Utopia and Organisation*. Oxford: Blackwell, pp. 1–8.

Parks, B., Pharr, S. W. and Lockeman, B. D. (1994) A Marketer's Guide to Clausewitz: Lessons for Winning Market Share. *Business Horizons*, July-August, pp. 68–73.

Pelzer, P. (2005) The Futility of Excess, or: Where's the One to Understand the Data? In Gustafsson, C., Rehn, A. and Sköld, D. (eds), *Excess and Organization*, Stockholm: The Royal Institute of Technology, pp. 162–79.

Perrow, Ch. (1991) A Society of Organizations. *Theory and Society*, 20(6), pp. 725–62.

Peters, T. (1989) *Thriving on Chaos*. Basingstoke: Palgrave Macmillan.

Peters, T. and Waterman, R. (1982) *In Search of Excellence*. New York: Harper and Row.

Piaget, J. (1997) *The Moral Judgement of the Child*. New York: Free Press Paperbacks.

Pinnington, A. and Morris, T. (2003) Archetype Change in Professional Organizations: Survey Evidence from Large Law Firms. *British Journal of Management*, 14, pp. 18–99.

Pintchman, T. (1994) *The Rise of the Goddess in the Hindu Tradition*. New York: State University of New York Press.

Porter, M. E. (1985) *Competitive Advantage: Creating and Sustaining Superior Performance*. New York: The Free Press.

Power, M. (1994) *The Audit Explosion*. London: Demos.

Power, M. (2007) *Organized Uncertainty: Designing a World of Risk Management*. Oxford: Oxford University Press.

Ratzinger, J. (2004) *Introduction to Christianity*. San Francisco: Ignatius Press.

Reddin, W. J. (1970) *Managerial Effectiveness*. New York: McGraw-Hill.

Reedy, P. (2002) Keeping the Black Flag Flying: Anarchy, Utopia and the Politics of Nostalgia. In Parker, M. (ed.), *Utopia and Organization*. Oxford: Blackwell, pp. 169–88.

Ricoeur, P. (1986) *Lectures on Ideology and Utopia*. New York: Columbia University Press.

Ricoeur, P. (1991) *A Ricoeur Reader* (ed. Valdez, M.). Hemel Hempstead: Harvester Wheatsheaf, pp. 463–81.

Ries, A. and Trout, J. (1986) Marketing Warfare. *The Journal of Consumer Marketing*, 3(4), pp. 77–82.

Roberts, E. B. and Liu, W. K. (2001) Ally or Acquire? How Technology Leaders Decide. *Sloan Management Review*, 43(1), pp. 26–34.

Rodrigues, S. B. and Collinson, D. L. (1995) Having Fun? Humour as Resistance in Brazil. *Organization Studies*, 16(5), pp. 739–68.

Rohrer, F. (2007) *The Devil's Music*. Retrieved on 21 February 2007 from http://news.bbc.co.uk/2/hi/uk_news/magazine/4952646.stm

Rutenberg, D. (1970) Organizational Archetypes of a Multi-National Company. *Management Science*, 16(6), pp. 337–49.

Ryan, C. (1993) The Theology of Dante. In Jacoff, R. (ed.), *The Cambridge Companion to Dante*. Cambridge: Cambridge University Press, pp. 136–52.

Ryland, E. (2000) Gaia Rising: A Jungian View of Environmental Consciousness and Sustainable Organization. *Organization and Environment*, 13(4), pp. 381–402.

Saxon (1980) Stand Up and Be Counted. (from album *Wheels of Steel*) Carrere/EMI. [sound recording: Vinyl].

Schachter, B. (1997) An Irreverent Guide to Value at Risk. *Financial Engineering News*, 1(1), Retrieved on 25 May 2006 from http://www.gloriamundi.org/introduction.asp

Schumpeter, J. A. (1983) *The Theory of Economic Development*. London: Transaction.

Schwabenland, C. M. (2006a) *Stories, Visions and Values in Voluntary Organisations*. Aldershot: Ashgate.

Schwabenland, C. M. (2006b) Founders' Stories as Creation Mythology. In Brewis, J., Boje, D., Linstead, S. and O'Shea. A. (eds.) *The Passion of Organizing*. Copenhagen: Liber-Copenhagen Business School Press, pp. 205–28.

Scott, O. (2000) Sense and Nonsense. *The New York Times Magazine*. (November 26) New York: *New York Times*. Retrieved on 21 August 2006 from http://www.nytimes.com/library/magazine/home/20001126mag-seuss.html

Seuss, Dr (1940) *Horton Hatches the Egg*. New York: Random House.

Seuss, Dr (1949) *Bartholemew and the Oobleck*. New York: Random House.

Seuss, Dr (1950) *Yertle the Turtle*. New York: Random House.

Seuss, Dr (1954) *Horton Hears a Who*. New York: Random House.

Seuss, Dr (1957) *The Cat in the Hat*. New York: Random House.

Seuss, Dr (1957) *How the Grinch Stole Christmas*. New York: Random House.

Seuss, Dr (1958) *The Cat in the Hat Comes Back!* New York: Random House.

Seuss, Dr (1991) *Six by Seuss*. New York: Random House.

Seuss, Dr (1996) *A Hatful of Seuss*. New York: Random House.

Shenkar, O. and Li, J. (1999) Knowledge Search in International Cooperative Ventures. *Organization Science*, 10(2), pp. 134–43.

Sievers, B. (1994) *Work, Death and Life Itself: Essays on Management and Organization*. Berlin–New York: Walter de Gruyter.

Simmel, G. (1904/1957) Fashion. *American Journal of Sociology*, 62(6), pp. 541–58.

Singleton, C. (1950) Dante's Allegory. *Speculum*, 25(1), pp. 78–86.

Skinner, B. F. (1968) *The Technology of Teaching*. New York: Appleton-Century-Crofts.

Spiegel, G. M. (1990) History, Historicism, and the Social Logic of the Text in the Middle Ages. *Speculum*, 65(1), pp. 59–86.

Spitzer, R. J. (2000) *The Spirit of Leadership: Optimizing Creativity and Change in Organizations*. South Provo: Executive Excellence Publishing.

Stagecoach (2007) Amazon. Retrieved on 25 January 2007 from http://www.amazon.com/Stagecoach-Wells-Fargo-American-West/dp/product-description/0743234367

Strange, S. (1986) *Casino Capitalism*. Oxford: Blackwell.

Strange, S. (1998) *Mad Money*. Manchester: Manchester University Press.

Sun Tzu (1910/2006) *The Art of War* (trans. Giles, L.). Retrieved on 24 November 2006 from http://www.online-literature.com/suntzu/artofwar/

Sunder Rajan, R. (2004) Is the Hindu Goddess a Feminist? In Chaudhuri, M. (ed.), *Feminism in India*. London: Kali for Women, pp. 318–33.

Swiercz, P. M. and Lydon, S. R. (2002) Entrepreneurial Leadership in High-Tech Firms: A Field Study. *Leadership and Organization Development Journal*, 23(7), ABI/INFORM Global, pp. 380–9.

Tambiah, S. J. (1990/2004) *Magic, Science, Religion and the Scope of Rationality*. Cambridge: Cambridge University Press.

Taylor, C. (1971) Interpretation and the Sciences of Man. *Review of Metaphysics*, 1, pp. 3–51.

Toynbee, P. (1968) *A Dictionary of Proper Names and Notable Matters in the Works of Dante*. Oxford: The Clarendon Press.

Tranfield, D. and Smith, S. (2002) Organizational Designs for Teamworking. *International Journal of Operations and Productions Management*, 22(5), pp. 471–91.

Trzciński, Ł. (2006) *Mit bohaterski w perspektywie antropologii filozoficznej I kulturowej*. (*The Myth of the Hero from the Philosophical and Anthropological Perspective*). Kraków: Wydawnictwo Uniwersytetu Jagiellońskiego.

Tyrrall, D. and Parker, D. (2005) The Fragmentation of a Railway: A Study of Organizational Change. *Journal of Management Studies*, 42(3), pp. 507–37.

Vattimo, G. (1989) *La società trasparente*. Milano: Garzanti.

Vygotskij, L. (1962) *Thought and Language*. Cambridge, MA: MIT University Press.

Wall, M. (2006) *Mick Wall's Commentary*. Retrieved on 12 October 2006 from http://www.maidenfans.com/imc/?url=album03_notb/mickwall03_notb&lang=eng&link=albums

Walser, R. (1993) *Running With The Devil: Power, Gender, and Madness in Heavy Metal Music*. London: Wesleyan University Press.

Weber, M. (1948/1970) *Essays in Sociology* (trans. Gerth, H. and Mills, C. Wright). London: Routledge and Kegan Paul.

Weinstein, D. (2000) *Heavy Metal: The Music and its Culture*. New York: Da Capo Press.

Wells Fargo (2007) Wikipedia. Retrieved on 25 January 2007 from http://en.wikipedia.org/wiki/Wells_Fargo

Widmer, H. (1980) Business Lessons from Military Strategy. *McKinsey Quarterly*, Spring, pp. 50–67.

Windsor, R. D. (1995) Military Perspectives on Organizations. *Journal of Organizational Change Management*, 9(4), pp. 34–41.

Wittgenstein, L. J. J. (1998) *Culture and Value: A Selection from the Posthumous Remains*. Oxford: Blackwell Publishing.

Woolley, B. (2002) *The Queen's Conjuror*. London: HarperCollins.

Yates, F. (1964/1971) *Giordano Bruno and the Hermetic Tradition*. London: Routledge and Kegan Paul.

Zackrison, R. E. (2006) *IDI: Interpersonal Dynamics Inventory*. Täby: Effectiveness Consultants.

Zimmerman, B., Lindberg, C. and Plsek, P. (2001) *Edgeware: Insights in Complexity Science for Health Care Leaders*. Irving Texas: VHA.

Index